Moroccan Female Religious Agents

# Women and Gender

THE MIDDLE EAST AND THE ISLAMIC WORLD



VOLUME 17


The titles published in this series are listed at *brill.com/wg*

# Moroccan Female Religious Agents

*Old Practices and New Perspectives*

*By*

Aziza Ouguir

BRILL

LEIDEN | BOSTON

Cover illustration: ʾal-Qarrawiyyīn Mosque in Fez, Morocco. The first mosque and university in the world, founded by a Sufi Moroccan woman. Photo: istockphoto.com/ugurhan.

The Library of Congress Cataloging-in-Publication Data is available online at http://catalog.loc.gov
LC record available at http://lccn.loc.gov/2020009920

Typeface for the Latin, Greek, and Cyrillic scripts: "Brill". See and download: brill.com/brill-typeface.

ISSN 1570-7628
ISBN 978-90-04-42988-8 (hardback)
ISBN 978-90-04-42989-5 (e-book)



This book is printed on acid-free paper and produced in a sustainable manner.

*This book is dedicated to my parents and my husband who believed in me and never stopped to encourage and support me.*

# Contents

# Preface

My encounter with my first interviewee whom I met at the shrine of *Lalla* ʿĀʾisha ʾal-Baḥriya, a shrine on the outskirts of Azmour, and her words about women's abilities to achieve a particular self left an enduring impression on me. Her advanced age rendered her wise and knowledgeable, but her knowledge emanated not from any kind of formal education, as she is illiterate, but from her extensive experience with the practicalities of life. "Look!" she said to me, pointing to the grave of ʿĀʾisha ʾal-Baḥriya. "These are the lovers of God … and the lovers of people." She chose these words because she felt my strong desire for knowledge about the woman saint. My assumptions about approaching the study of women saints were changed by this old woman's words of wisdom. Our conversation in the shrine inspired me to rethink my research questions. It helped clarify the issues I would examine in this book, issues regarding the paths undertaken by women Sufis to cultivate saintly personalities and the challenges that these paths posed to the conventional gender norms. It became clear to me that I would have to consider the way women saints undergo formation of the self and what made them different from conventional women. Furthermore, it aroused my curiosity about the reception of their legacy, particularly among contemporary Moroccan women in general and among today's Moroccan women activists. This book examines the way women's agency in the religious sphere transgressed conventional cultural norms and the way their agency is portrayed in the discourses of Moroccan women. My analysis of archival material and fieldwork data suggests that women saints as moral exemplars impacted and continue to impact society. I invite the reader to reflect on women Sufi saints and on the undefinable historical importance of their development of counter-cultural social and religious personalities. The stories of these historical female exemplars impel me to rethink the relationship between women and Islam.

# Acknowledgements

This book has been made possible thanks to a grant of the Netherlands Organization for Scientific Research. First and foremost, my thanks and gratitude go to my supervisors, Professor Fāţima Sadiqi and Professor Ruud Peters, for their invaluable advice and scholarly supervision. My thanks are also due to Dr. Karen Vintges for her pertinent supervision, advice, help and support. I deeply thank her for her friendship as well as her generous hospitality over the years. Many thanks also to the Universiteit van Amsterdam, especially to the staff members of the Faculty of Humanities and the Department of Philosophy; and to the Faculty of Letters and Human Sciences Dhar Mehraz Fes for help during the years of my research. I am thankful to Dr. Jan Hoogland, who is the director of the Dutch Institute in Morocco, and to its coordinator Cynthia Plette for their assistance and encouragement. I am also thankful to many family members and friends (Rachid Touhtouh, Hanane Dahour, Yachoulty Mohamed) for their help and support throughout my work in this research. I would as well like to thank my parents who taught me how to read and write and for whose souls I ask God for mercy and blessings. I am indebted to my husband, for many fruitful discussions on the various issues and themes of this book and for accompanying me during my fieldwork in the mountains of Morocco. His love and support have nourished this research. I would also like to thank my daughters, sisters, brothers for their encouragements, love and their continuous prayers to God to help me to successfully complete my research.

# Notes on Transliteration

The system of transliteration I use in this book is IJMES (International Journal for Middle Eastern Studies).

## Consonants

| | |
|---|---|
| ʾ | (hamza) |
| ب | b |
| ت | t |
| ث | ð |
| ج | j |
| ح | ḥ |
| خ | kh |
| د | d |
| ذ | dh |
| ر | r |
| ز | z |
| س | s |
| ش | sh |
| ص | ṣ |
| ض | ḍ |
| ط | ţ |
| ظ | ẓ |
| ع | ʿ |
| غ | gh |
| ف | f |
| ق | q |
| ك | k |
| ل | l |
| م | m |
| ن | n |
| ه | h |
| و | w |
| ي | y |

## Vowels

### *Long Vowels*

| | |
|---|---|
| ا or ʾ | ā |
| و | ū |
| ي | ī |

### *Doubled*

| | |
|---|---|
| يّ | iyy (final form ī) |
| وّ | uww (final form ū) |

### *Diphthongs*

| | |
|---|---|
| وَ | au or aw |

### *Short*

| | |
|---|---|
| - - - | a |
| | u |
| | i |

CHAPTER 1

# Introduction: Theories and Concepts

This book explores Moroccan female religious agents. In particular, it studies historical women saints and their reception by modern women and feminist activists. Women saints have been present throughout much of the history in several regions of North Africa and the Middle East since the advent of Islam. The shrines dedicated to them still stand erect and are visible in various urban and rural locations throughout Morocco as proof of their existence and importance to the surrounding communities.

In spite of their existence in Moroccan history, little is known about these women saints. Their lives, practices, and contributions to their local communities are rarely studied by scholars. This book examines these women constructions of sainthood within the context of Islam as a religion, and of Sufism as the mystical dimension of that religion. It discusses the role of these female religious agents in Morocco's past and present in the context of the current broader discourses on Moroccan women and feminism. Within that context, it specifically addresses the questions: how did these historical female saints develop themselves and how are they received by contemporary Moroccan women. The broader argument I make in this book is that Moroccan women saints gained access to authority and leadership and therefore deserve to be integrated in feminist scholarship and discourse. To present and document this argument I explore a number of questions.

The first set of questions, which focus on the historical women saints' access to and construction of sainthood, includes the following. How did women who were active in the historical-religious realm become saints? What techniques did the women saints employ to reach the highest levels of piety and sainthood? Did their piety and sainthood enable them to gain access to power and authority? Did their achievement of sainthood emanate from personal decisions and individual choices or from conventional norms? Did their religious personalities impose challenges on the Dominant order?

To explore the legacy of the historical women saints, I pose the following questions. How do the women who venerate them interpret these historical women saints? Do they consider historical women saints to be role models? On what level do the women venerators appreciate them? Do they follow their techniques to acquire access to, and exercise, religious agency? If so, does this agency enable them to pursue religious self-formation in ways that

 | DOI:10.1163/9789004429895_002

are unrestricted by conventional norms? Finally, how do Moroccan women feminist activists today, and *murshidāt* (religious guides), integrate/interpret/present receive/ these historical women saints in their discourses?

The remainder of this chapter is divided into four sections. In section two, I discuss the scholarly literature on my topic of research. In section three, I describe the sources and fieldwork on which I base my research and in the fourth section, I elucidate the conceptual background for the book. In the fifth and final section, I present the organization of the book.

## 1 A Review

Scholarly research on Muslim saints is still rare. Most researchers have focused primarily on whether or not the women saints' modes of behavior and the rituals concerning their veneration either contradict or conform to the dominant order. This approach was instigated by a number of scholars and researchers who studied Muslim women's religious agents, in particular the women saints and Sufis, and their venerators, to restore feminist voices that had been ignored in past narratives; feminist scholarship on Muslim women's agency did positive work and highlighted Muslim women's voices.

This feminist scholarship offers an alternative discourse to the Muslim women's agency that has been described for decades in the West in terms of submission to patriarchal norms. One of these scholars is Fatima Mernissi (1977, 112). She interpreted male and female saints as ideal models who refused to submit to local traditional norms. Instead, they constructed saintly personalities that contradicted conventional understandings of masculinity and femininity. Moroccan women's important roles in history urged Mernissi to study Islamic and Moroccan history to learn more about these heroic female figures. In her book *Forgotten Queens*, Mernissi uncovered Moroccan historical women who impacted their communities and marked history with their legacy. Her pertinent analysis of Moroccan sainthood throughout the Maghreb has developed awareness about Sufism and its relation to gender. She paved the way for me to take her study of historical women as a basis for analyzing historical Moroccan women and their power at great depth. Mernissi's belief in historical women, saints and Sufi Islam inspired me to explore the saints and their construction of sainthood in detail and to contribute other materials to her scholarly findings and highlight the feminist messages that both saints and Sufis encompass. Daisy Dwyer (1978, 583) also studied Moroccan saints in Taroudant and focused on the way women venerators' religious rituals reveal the women's ability to make their own decisions, independently of their husbands. Likewise, Willy Jansen (1978), in her book *Women Without Men*, discussed Algerian women's religious actions in relation to the societal order, and drew attention to signal their marginalization in the dominant society. She argued that women's exclusion from orthodox public religion pushed them into popular religion. Algerian women, Jansen argued, in fact failed to affect the dominant stratified society (Jansen 1987, 9). Edien Bartels studied the phenomenon of saints' veneration in Tunisia, investigating the significance of saints for Tunisian women and whether their veneration revealed a protest against patriarchy. Bartels concluded that Tunisian women's veneration of saints had a double face, enabling both their submission to, and transgression of, local norms (Bartels 1993, 114). Margaret Rausch (2004, 221) is one of the modern researchers who studied Ishelḥīn Moroccan women's religious gatherings in shrines in Tiznīt in the Southwest of Morocco. She demonstrated that these Amazigh women created their own forms of religious expressions, which incorporated their ethnolinguistic identity and spirituality Rausch (2004, 221). These scholars form a solid base for my critical analysis of Moroccan female sainthood and their veneration, and their reception by women today.

Another group of researchers focus on the study of historical documents and use these to guide their approaches to historical women's religious practices. Moroccan historians (Ferḥat and Triki 1986; Hamam 1998; Maḥmah 1978; Qaṭṭān 1998) studied hagiographic and historical records to highlight female religious personalities of the past. Most of these historians attested that women's absence from recorded history is mainly due to male writers' and historians' desires to document male saints and Sufis Chodkiewicz (1993, 103). Women, as Andezian Sossie (1995, 2) puts it, who were marginalized in written history found in oral tradition a refuge for the survival of their religious life stories. These historians inspired me to do more research on historical and hagiographic records and re-read history from a gender perspective to rediscover historical female saints and their feminist voices. Before I discuss this issue, I would like to discuss the way this scholarship addresses historical religious women.

The literature reviewed above interprets the relationship between women and Islam from different but simultaneously approaches. On the one hand, the analyses are couched in a historical framework that relies on an available written primary historical context, as is the case with Ferḥat and Triki (1986), Hamām (1998), Mahmāh (1978), Qattān (1998) and Zouanat (2009). On the other hand, the anthropologists discussed earlier draw on data from fieldwork interviews and observation, approaching the phenomenon of women's religious actions from an anthropological point of view and relying on oral primary sources and fieldwork methodologies, as is the case with Andezian (1995), Bartels (1993), Mernissi (1977), Rausch (2004) and Torab (1996). Obviously, the latter approach dominates, given the spectacular emergence of social sciences in the second half of the last century. It advocates for the use of fieldwork in an extensive way and emphasizes the importance of reconsidering Moroccan women's spirituality and piety from the perspective of local participants.

An important point I would like to raise is that the researchers referred to above understand women's religious actions in different ways. The earlier feminist researchers (Bartels 1993; Dwyer 1978; Mernissi 1977) played an important role in re-defining debate on gender in Muslim countries taking it far beyond the structure of submission and subordination. They focused on Muslim women's religious actions and interpreted them as resisters. Their studies of women's agency are understood in terms of the achievement of an individual desire against the constraints of cultural norms. Their aim is to present Muslim women as resisters and not as passive and oppressed beings. Thus, earlier feminist scholarship seeks to restore the absent voices of Muslim women.

More recently, however, feminist scholars such as Abu-Lughod (1990), Buitelaar (1993), Moors (2004), Rausch (2004) and Sadiqi (2008) have, on the basis of the fieldwork, developed a more nuanced approach to women's participation in the religious sphere, namely one that explores the ways in which Muslim women perform their religion and construct a particular personhood. They focused on women's agency and its meaning and used these concepts to interpret power relations. Saba Mahmood (2005), an important writer on Muslim women's agency, has criticized Western feminists' definition of Muslim women's agency and introduced another type of agency. Later, in the next section, I will discuss Mahmood's definition of agency and my alternative ways of thinking about Moroccan women's religious agency. Following the approach of the researchers I discussed earlier, I will examine Moroccan historical women saints' construction of sainthood in detail. It is true that the literature I examined earlier did not problematize Muslim women's agency and overlooked the envisioning of Muslim women in terms of their ability to perform religion and to construct religious personalities. Despite this, this literature remains an important basis upon which to develop Moroccan women's religious agency further, in particular the techniques that women employed to become pious and to explore the impacts of their religious performances on their surroundings. Both the historians and anthropologists whom I discussed earlier have, therefore, paved the way for me to study other historical records and explore other cases of historical Moroccan women saints and the way they lived their piety and constructed sainthood that impacted positively on their communities. I also analyze these women saints' legacies and the contributions they made within the context of contemporary discussions on women and religion. More specifically, my study focuses on the way contemporary women venerators of women saints, as well as Islamist and secularist feminist activists, /see earlier suggestions/receive/ these women saints and their legacies and contributions, and the way they understand the religious agency of these historical women saints. Finally, this book explores whether or not one can speak of the continuity of female religious agency in Moroccan history. The section below discusses the methodology of my research.

## 2 Research Design

The present study draws its data from a variety of sources and is based on both written and oral material. Besides the *Qur'ān, Hadīth,* and stories of the Prophet, I consulted manuscripts belonging to a variety of genres, including genealogy (*sulalāt*), hagiography (*manāqib*), biography and autobiography (*tarājim*). All of these genres are categorized under the general heading of *kutub tarājim wa manāqib* (hagiographic and genealogical books).

Hagiographic texts are important sources of historical information on saints and Islamic religion in pre-modern Moroccan society. The word "hagiography" has a Greek origin. It is derived from the word "hàgios," which means "holy person" or "saint", and the word "gràphein," which means "writings". Thus, hagiography signifies writings about holy people and saints. Hagiography constitutes a historical genre, consisting of pious religious scholars' and saints' biographies and accounts of their contributions to the religious life. It was often written by scholarly saints, who themselves were venerated.

My research on Moroccan women saints' life stories started with an examination of hagiographic records, most of which are original, unedited manuscripts, without a table of contents or index. They are recorded in a traditional Arabic style, which is hard to read nowadays. In some manuscripts, the names of women saints were mentioned in passing within the life stories of men saints. Individual detailed life stories focusing exclusively on women saints were rare.

I consulted not only the life stories of women saints but also those of male saints in order to compare and discuss the differences and similarities between male and female saints. I specifically focused on women saints who undertook a life dedicated to piety and spiritual advancement. I include *majdhūbāt* (female *majdhūb*) whose mental capacities were consumed by an attraction to God as well as *faqīhāt* (legal scholars) and *'ālimāt* (religious scholars), who transformed themselves spiritually and intellectually, achieving a high religious status that resulted in their access to, and exercise of, authority and power.

The number of women saints whose names are mentioned in hagiographic records is impressive. I selected three for an extensive analysis, namely *Lalla* 'Azīza 'al-Saksāwiyya (14th Century), *Lalla* 'Ā'isha 'al-'Idrīsiya (16th Century), and *Lalla* Fāṭima Muhdūz (19th Century). These three women saints belonged to different social classes and ethnic groups, and they acquired diverse religious statuses and roles. 'Azīza and Fāṭima originated from Southwestern Moroccan Berber tribes, whereas 'Ā'isha is a Northern Arab woman saint. From my fieldwork on these three saintly women, I noticed that they are all very well known. Many people in Shafshāwun and Qaṣr l-Kabīr still speak about 'Ā'isha, and many people in Imintanūt and Tiznit still admire 'Azīza and Fāṭima.

My selection of these women saints is based on interesting and unusual details in their life stories, the historical spectrum that their lives represent, and on the fact that their entries are more detailed than those of other women saints. The relative abundance of detail enabled me to undertake a more in-depth study of their lives and, in particular, to examine the different self-techniques that they used to transform themselves and reinvent themselves as saintly personalities.

I supplemented the data that I extracted from the narratives I found in written hagiographies by collecting the narratives of the lives of women saints that are still transmitted orally today. The most effective way to collect these oral stories is to visit the shrines of the saints, where the pilgrims exchange them among themselves. Some hagiographers' entries on saints mention the location of their tombs. Finding the exact location of the women saints' shrines was sometimes not without difficulty. When I was in Qaṣr l-Kabīr, a city in the Northwest of Morocco, I asked the taxi driver to take me to 'Ā'isha's shrine in the *medina*. He told me that there were many women saints called 'Ā'isha in *bāb* Sebta (Port Ceuta), which obliged me to visit them all. The shrines of some of these women saints were destroyed and their oral life stories lost, which means that only their names are known by the people in their regions of origin. Those whose shrines still exist enjoy great popularity, thanks in particular to their descendants, who take care of their shrines.

An advantage that I had in conducting this research was my childhood experience of visiting shrines. I still remember my mother taking me with her to visit her favorite saint, *Mawlay* Driss, in Zarhun Meknes. As a child, I was more interested in playing with the other children in the courtyard of the shrine than in visiting the saint and attending the women's rituals. During my fieldwork on Moroccan saintly women and the rituals around their lives in their sanctuaries, I attempted to recall my childhood experiences. I found that I had not forgotten all the rituals that my mother had taught me. Some of them were still engrained in my mind. For example, she always advised me to tie a rag to objects belonging to the shrine. My research prompted me to ask my family, friends, and acquaintances for stories about women saints, the rituals surrounding them, and their significance.

The fieldwork for this study was carried out between June 2009 and September 2011. The first period, in June and July 2009, encompassed a preliminary study of the saints and their cults in *Sīdī* ʿAllāl ʾal-Baḥrāoui, a village near Rabat. Next, I went to the *medina* of Salé, which is referred to in the historical sources as the city of saints. Salé has several important shrines. I visited the shrines of the male saints *Sīdī* bin ʿAshīr and *Sīdī* bin Ḥassūn in search of female saints. According to the venerators I met, there were a few women saints, but their shrines had been destroyed.

My second period of fieldwork took place in January 2010 in ʿAzīza's village in the High Atlas Mountains which is situated about 30 kms to the East of Imintanūt (south of Marrakech). After spending one week with my host family, I returned home to review and assess my findings. My first visit was very fruitful, as it helped me to prepare for additional visits to ʿAzīza's shrine. I returned to the High Atlas in March 2010 and spent the entire week of the *musim*[1] there. The *musim* gave me the opportunity to meet a lot of pilgrims and to observe and discuss their rituals.

My third fieldwork phase, from June 2010 until September 2010, in the South and North of Morocco, involved research on two other women saints I had selected to study. At the end of June, I went to the Sūs region of Southwestern Morocco to visit the women saints' shrines in that region. I went to many towns, namely Imintanūt, Tiznīt, and Shtuka Ait Baha and visited several shrines, but especially the shrines of Fāṭima ʾal-Hilāliyya in Shtuka Ait Baha, and Fāṭima Muhdūz in Tiznīt. In each location, I spent one-week studying women venerators' rituals. I returned to the Sūs in July 2010 to visit other women saints' shrines. Subsequently, I changed my focus to the city of Qaṣr l-Kabīr. There, I spent the last week of August and the last two weeks of September 2010.

1 *Musim* is the French spelling of the Arabic word. The English spelling is *musim*. *Musim* actually means 'season' in modern standard Arabic, but Moroccans use it to refer to the annual festival, the annual meeting that venerators and saints' descendants organize to celebrate either their saint's birth or death. *Musim* is not used for similar annual festivals in other Arab countries. For more details on Moroccan *musim* see Feneke Reysoo 1988.

In the same period, I also visited another city in that region, Shafshāwun, to study ʿĀʾisha's life story. I was able to acquire access to the people who venerate these women saints as I have relatives who live close to their shrines and who were willing to put me in touch with the people who visit them.

One subsequent fieldwork phase entailed conducting interviews with *murshidāt* who held lessons in mosques, in Rabat and Salé, and some of the women who regularly attended their mosque lessons. During my conversations with some of the venerators in the ʿĀʾisha shrine, I learned that they also attended the mosque lessons held by *murshidāt*. It was their recommendation and encouragement to attend the mosque lessons that awakened my interest in *murshidāt* and prompted my decision to contact and eventually interview some of them and some of their women attendees.

During the month of Ramaḍān, July/August 2010, I contacted the mosques *masjid ʾal-ʾaʿḍam* and *masjid Sunna* in Rabat and *masjid ʾal-Quds* in Salé. I spoke to the *murshidāt* of these mosques and attended the Friday afternoon religious courses and sermons held at all three locations. My intention was to employ the same research methods as I had previously used, but I found the research situation to be very different. Unlike the venerators and pilgrims, the *murshidāt* understood my academic interest; they appreciated my research and were willing to cooperate and assist me.

Some of the *waʿiḍat* I interviewed turned out to be activists in Islamist feminist associations. They paved the way for me to contact their associations and conduct my fieldwork there. Thus, during the final phase of my research, I was able to interview some Islamist and secular feminist women activists to study the way these feminist activists receive historical women saints in their discourses.

The secularist and Islamist women feminists I interviewed are as follows. The secularists included (ADFM) Association Democratique des Femmes Marocaine (the Democratic Association of Moroccan Women) and (UAF) Association Action Feminine (the Association of Feminine Action). The Islamists I studied were the Justice and Development Party (*ʿAdāla wa Tanmiyya*), Justice and Spirituality (*ʿAdl wa l-Iḥsān*) Association and *Zahrā* Forum (*Muntadā Zahrā*). I worked with the feminist associations between September and December of 2011, both in Rabat and Salé. From 2011 until 2017, I was in contact with feminist Islamist activists so I could learn more about the development of their religious agency and feminist discourses.

Before discussing the results of my research, some research tools and concepts used in this book need to be highlighted. In the section that follows, I will outline some of the concepts to provide insight into the theoretical backgrounds to my research.

## 3 The Conceptual Background

The first concept that needs clarification is Sufism (*ʾal-Taṣawwuf*). Sufism emerged in the Middle East in the 8th Century in Arabia. It is a path in Islam that traveled to North Africa and other parts of the global world. Prophets brought Islam, but saints and Sufis propagated it in different parts of the world. The adherents of Sufism were found around the world teaching people Sufi ethics and norms. I have chosen to study Sufism and its properties in detail for the following reasons. Sufism is the spirit of all religions (*rūḥ ʾal-ʾaddyān*). It is a discourse which encompasses universal values that are shared with other religions and cultural discourses. It addresses universal values in a way that attracts respect, dignity and admiration from people who are members of different religious, ethnic and cultural backgrounds. Finally, Sufism constitutes the ideal space for the study of women's religious agency. In chapter 2, I will examine the basic principles of Moroccan Sufism in more depth. Here I will only discuss some main characteristics of Sufism in brief.

### 3.1 *Sufism and Sainthood*

Although Sufism is often defined simply as Islamic mysticism, its accurate definition is multi-faceted. It is derived from the Arabic root *ṣūf* meaning wool, and it is related to the woolen cloaks worn by the early ascetics and dervishes as a sign of their renunciation of the material world. Another definition suggests that Sufism originated from the word *ṣafāʾ* (purity) or *ṣafw* (best), thus related to the purity of the Sufis and dervishes, and the spiritual advancement that accompanies it. Others define Sufism in terms of the annihilation (*fanāʾ*) of ego that Sufis undergo in order to become a knower of God (*ʿārif bi Allāh*), to achieve ever more intimate proximity to God, and, ultimately, to attain divine union (ʾal-Tādilī 1997, 34). These different definitions show that Sufism has been understood and experienced in different ways in different locations and historical moments.

Different levels of Sufism can also by distinguished: orthodox and popular. The former is associated with the "official" or "formal" dimension of Islam and is based on the foundational sources of Islam: the *Qurʾān* and the *Sunna*. Popular Sufism is also based on the *Qurʾān* and *Sunna*, but includes additional cultural beliefs and practices that orthodox *ʿulamaʾ* consider non Islamic. Orthodox Sufism conforms strictly to the tenets of Islam and stresses Islamic law and the social relations and practices of religion. It is also articulated by *ʾulamāʾ*. Philosophical Sufism constitutes the third face of Sufism. Its major idea and central belief is surrounded by the concept of "*wḥadat ʾal-wujūd*", meaning "unity of being", which focuses on the idea that the only truth within the universe is God's. Ibn ʿArabī (d. 638/1240), ʾal-Halaj (9th Century) and ʾal-Ghazlī (d. 505/1111) were pioneers of Sufi philosophy.

Moreover, Sufism is the spirit of Islam and is focused on one's inner spirituality and faith. Jurisprudence and jurists focused on the external practice of religion. Their worship of God followed the regulations of the Islamic law very closely, in the hope that the Muslim's external physical activities would compel the inner soul to be regulated and that his/her practice of the religion would be ameliorated. Sufis go directly to the inner soul, which they consider to be independent of the mind, the body and their external practices. Sufism, as Ibn Khaldūn (1960) states, is a personal relationship between God and the individual soul, and each human soul, as mentioned earlier, is free to choose her or his own way to worship God and establish a direct relationship with Him. The jurists, however, look at God with the gaze of reason, while Sufis look with the gaze of love. People looked at Islam therefore through very different lenses.

The various definitions of Sufism mentioned above offer a variety of designations for a saint. The central figure of Sufism is the friend of God (*walī Allāh*) which I use here interchangeably with the term "saint". *Walī* emanates from the root *w-l-y*, meaning to be near and the one who is near is a friend; *walī Allāh* is therefore translated as a friend of God. A friend of God, or saint, is recognized by a number of characteristics. First and foremost a saint is a reminder of the divine. Saints are channels through which virtue and sacredness are revealed. They propagate Islamic virtues, moral conduct, and good social relations. They are known by their mystical choice to follow the Sufi path to spiritual advancement, and their engagement and intense exertion at the different stages along that path to reach divine proximity and ultimately union with God. Thus, saints are persons to whom people with different social statuses, show respect and admiration, and who are thought of as holders of sacredness.

As a path in Islam, Sufism traveled in different parts of the World and a number of methods for spiritual advancement towards God emerged. There are many larger or smaller methods for pursuing spirit advancement, which are commonly referred to in English as Sufi orders, whose suborders and branches have expanded over the centuries throughout the world, including the US and Europe. One example is the Mevlevi Sufi order, which was inspired by and founded in honor of Jalāl Dīn Muḥammad Rūmī (13th Century) after his death in Konya, Turkey. It was Rumī's technique for composing his world-renowned poetry that the central whirling ritual is believed to be based on. Originating in Bukhara in Central Asia, the Naqshbandi Sufi order, which is named after its founder Bahāʾ Dīn Naqshaband (14th Century) is widespread in South Asia, Turkey, London, and Chicago. The Qadiri Sufi order, founded by Abd l-Qādir Jīlānī (12th Century), a native of the Iranian province of Mazandaran, has many branches, sub-branches, and off shoots worldwide, including the Qādiriyya-Būtshīshiyya in Morocco.

The Sufi path has different bases, as formulated by 'al-Ghazālī, the renowned 11th Century Persian scholar of religion, philosophy, and Sufism and author of *'Iḥyā' 'Ulūm 'al-Dīn* (Reviving the Religious Sciences).[2] In his chapter on mysticism, 'al-Ghazālī explains the meaning of Sufism, its principles and rules. According to him, there are different views and guidelines that were agreed upon by many Sufi scholars, but which were criticized by others in the quest for spirituality. 'Al-Ghazālī emphasized the importance of the human heart as a source of one's spiritual illumination. The heart plays the role of its possessor's guide. This role, however, emanates from *ma'rifa* (knowledge). The type of *ma'rifa* 'al-Ghazālī stresses is knowledge of *'al-'anbiyā' wa l-'awliyā'* (the Prophets and saints) and *ma'rifa-t 'ulamā'* and *ḥukamā'* (the knowledge of religious scholars and jurists). These two types of knowledge are important in the fulfillment of spiritual illumination because jurisprudence is acquired through one's senses; Sufism emanates from one's inner heart and prevails in the universal world. If a Sufi, in 'al-Ghazālī's view, wants to be a gnostic (*'ārif bi-Allāh*) and see God with a love, she/he must combine the outer and inner knowledge of *sharī'a*.[3] Thus, the purification of the heart and its tranquility emanates first from Islamic law, and then flourishes and gains spiritual illumination from the inner knowledge of Islam.

From 'al-Ghazāli's approaches to mysticism, one understands that a Muslim mystic is required to undertake a "way" to reach God, in other words to become a wayfarer (*sālik*). The wayfarer engages in journeying toward God. On her/his way to God, she/he is exposed to different stages that could be summarized in the following points: *sharī'a*, *ṭarīqa* and *ḥaqīqa*. The *sharī'a* refers to Islamic law and the guidelines that a mystic must learn and follow faithfully. The *ṭarīqa* (the path) on which the Sufi walks emanates from *sharī'a*. The wayfarer proceeds from one stage to another by performing strict regimens of behavior and maintains challenging daily schedules until she/he reaches *ḥaqīqa* (truth), the stage where the Sufi achieves God's closeness. Therefore,

2 After many years of employment at a famous college in Baghdad, 'al-Ghazālī abandoned teaching the religious and legal sciences and dedicated the rest of his life to Sufism. Most Sufi scholars of the Islamic world include 'al-Ghazālī's work in their teachings and religious courses. His book, *'Iḥyā' 'Ulūm 'al-Dīn*, deals with *mu'āmalāt* (social acts that regulate relations among humans) and *'ibādāt* (spirituals acts that regulate relations between God and the believer). In other words, this book provides detailed teachings and instructions on spiritual acts and social interactions.

3 *Sharī'a* means Islamic law.

FIGURE 1 ʾal-Qarrawiyyīn bāb ʾal-khalwa
PHOTOGRAPH BY AZIZA OUGUIR

*sharīʿa*, *ṭarīqa* and *ḥaqīqa* are interdependent and essential to the achievement of God's proximity.

On the path to God the wayfarer, who is also referred to as disciple or adept (*murīd*), needs a guide, known as a *shaykh* or *murshid* (spiritual master) to guide her/him through the different stages of the Sufi path. The disciple must diligently follow the guide's instructions in order to reach proximity to, and union with, the divine. The spiritual master offers the necessary advice to train the *murīd* and enable her/him to undertake the required exercises and perform the requisite practices on the path to God and become able to look at God with the gaze of love.

On the path, the Sufi is exposed to several types of embodiment. Before the Sufi engages in the endeavor, she/he has a sensual and procreative body. It is a body that is totally submissive to *ʾal-nafs ʾal-ʾammāra bi sūʾ* (the evil soul) that guides the body to worldliness. At this stage the sexual function of the body is highly stressed. To free the body from material orientation, it chooses to practice some religious rituals. But the body needs to go further and listen to the blames of *ʾal-nafs ʾal-lawwāma* (the blaming soul) to achieve *ʾal-nafs ʾal-muṭmaʾinna* (the peaceful soul). The latter implore the Muslim body to renounce worldliness, to reconsider her/his inner spiritual desires and to ensure the success of the soul control over the body. At this point, the body ignores its sexual identity and comes to be known by a new identity, namely divine love. As documented earlier, the Sufi here looks at God with a gaze of love. The renowned saint Rabīʿa ʾal-ʿAdawiyya (8th Century)[4] remains the greatest female spiritual master and the first female founder of divine love. As I will show in the next chapter, Rabīʿa stressed that God has to be loved for God's sake and not for a reward. She reflected her strong love of the divine in her poetic texts that Sufis still chant today at their gatherings. Ibn Arabī is also another advocate of spiritual love. His *Futuḥāt ʾal-Makiyya* includes several poems about his strong love for God. Through poetry, the great spiritual masters wanted to transmit their message, namely the love of God, to the world. Rabīʿa's and Ibn ʿArabī's spiritual approach, divine love, is highly approved of by their followers such as Bahaʾ Dīn Naqshaband, Jalla Dīn Rumī and others, who transmitted Rabīʿa's and Ibn ʿArabī's views of divine love to their disciples and followers. Therefore, God's love and closeness endow the Sufi with a divine grace.

---

4 Rabīʿa ʾal-ʿAdawiyya was a mystic woman from Basra, Iraq, where she lived from 714 to 801. She is seen as one of the founders of Sufism. She originated the idea of unconditional love for God ʿĀṭṭār 1905; ʾal-Sulāmī 1993; Smith 1984.

### 3.2 *Baraka*

The concept *baraka* is usually understood as a divine gift or blessing that God bestows on those among his people who pursue advancement on the path, i.e., the journey to God. It is often equated with a beneficent force of divine origin, which brings superabundance in the physical sphere and prosperity and happiness in the psychic order. In this book, *baraka* is considered a symbol of power. A saint achieves sainthood and develops a saintly personality, not only to gain *baraka* from the divine as a gift for her or his *mujāhada* (spiritual hard work), but also to prove their ability to construct a religious personality. Therefore, a saint is in a position to activate her or his spiritual capital through specific actions and social interactions, which enables her or him to impose her or his dominance. *Baraka* is an independent force that endows its possessor with the power and competence to serve people.

Saint veneration is an aspect of popular Sufism that centers on the saints' *baraka*. Moroccans believe in the divine blessing that a Sufi saint possesses. They perform *ziyāra* (visitation rituals) to the shrines of holy men and women to acquire some of their *baraka*, and to invoke her/him as a paradigmatic intercessor who can ask God to fulfill the venerators' desires and requests. Chapter 4 will demonstrate how pilgrims acquire some of the saint's *baraka* through the performance of different rituals such as the sacrifice of an animal or the recitation of devotional prayers. *Baraka* and the performance of wonders are the most important criteria for a holy man or woman to be considered a saint in Morocco. The data I gathered show that Moroccan pilgrims considered only people who have *baraka* and the ability to perform wonders to be saints. This means that saints have to display *baraka* and wonders to prove their sainthood.

A saint's sainthood is believed to enable her or him to play the role of mediator between the divine and the people. The saint's achievement of sainthood also gives her or him the power to become an intercessor among people. The latter also seek out the saints to serve as intercessors with God on their behalf, to answer their prayers, fulfill their wishes, and alleviate the hardships in their lives. For this, people forge strong relationships with saints (whether alive or dead). Thus, a saint's tomb remains a sacred place for people and houses the daily rituals that are performed by pilgrims to express their strong loyalty attachment to their favorite saint.

### 3.3 *Rituals*

Another concept that is important to my research is that of ritual, which in itself constitutes another topic of debate among researchers. Sadiqi (2004, 54) stresses that rituals are the sum of actions and utterances that characterize meaningful cultural events. Rituals here are understood as the remnants of past actions and moral performances. They are performed through the repetition of utterances and actions that have different meanings, messages, and ideologies. They convey moral messages that are transmitted from one generation to another, underscoring their continuity and stability. They combine the historical and current meaning of practices. Rituals are thus to be understood as a way of expressing one's relationship to a particular entity who is a saint or other sacred person. Rituals reflect one's attitude and emotions towards a particular thing. According to Humphrey (1994, 64), a ritual is also a form of communication. In other words, rituals are based not only on a script or book regulating practices and actions and directing the way practices should be performed, but also on a form of practice that interprets a particular event and ideology. Torab (2007, 4) asserts that ritual activity is the means with which a person negotiates, redefines, or constructs new interpretations of a particular action. Rituals are techniques performed to express one's own inner desires and ideologies. Turner (1984) also advocates a performative approach to rituals. He presents rituals not as symbols with particular meanings, but as actions that involve the individual's abilities to express their inner feelings and attitudes towards a particular social phenomenon. This book follows this performative approach to rituals as an activity. Like the researchers (Sadiqi 2004; Humphrey 1994; Torab 2007; Turner 1984) articulation of rituals, I will develop Moroccan women venerators' rituals within the shrines and discuss aspects of this performative approach, and the way it shapes Moroccan women venerators' rituals as well as *murshidāt*. Venerators performed a variety of rituals within shrines and mosques not only as a way to revive their women saints' life stories but also to express their strong inner feelings and relationship to saints, to glean some of their women saints' *baraka* and to construct pious personalities.

The question that arises is: How do women saints and their venerators reorient themselves, in particular, their bodies, which have been trained to perform, according to cultural norms, in order to develop and perform rituals that negotiate their inner intentions and desires in a way that contradicts the local norms? Do their constructed religious personalities that their new cultural norms approve of impact their communities? This question leads us to a discussion of the concepts of embodiment and agency.

### 3.4 *Embodiment and Agency*

Embodiment is another important topic of debate among scholars. Strathern (1996) defined it as a way to embrace local cultural norms and to construct personhood. Mary Douglas (1970) and Marcel Mauss (1934) studied the concept of the human body in the context of religious systems of meaning. They emphasized the importance of "bodily techniques" for becoming a human being in a particular society, for constructing religious personhood, and for achieving communication with God. The body is modified by social categories through which a particular view of society is sustained. Embodiment, therefore, involves the body not as a material object, but as a concatenation of action, affecting and affected by cultures (Kugle 2007). The body is, thus, both a pre-condition for social action and a product of social and cultural contexts.

The concept of embodiment offers an understanding of the way the body is constructed and the way it reinforces or resists social dominant norms. It also provides activist researchers with a means to criticize the social patterns and norms that are judged to be oppressive. From this perspective, researchers in the field of gender studies are able to discuss, from a critical point of view, whether the body is or is not, in a specific case, the locus of a critique on patriarchal and oppressive gender relations. In this book, I assert that Moroccan women saints and their venerators embodied local norms to live their religion. Their embodiment of religious personalities (saints and Sufis) began with their ability to follow the techniques of piety that their culture encompassed, but ended with the construction of strong religious personalities that their culture approved of. Women embraced conventional norms and /discovered/ uncovered/ techniques to construct strong saintly personalities that empowered them to have access to power and authority. This means that Moroccan feminine sainthood emanated from the local norms. Their embodiment of sainthood and access to leadership received a positive response from the local conventions. The positive impacts of women's embodiment of sainthood, as I will explain in chapter 3, are clear in people's support and approval of their sainthood.

In order to elaborate the theoretical perspective regarding embodiment, let me refer to the French philosopher Michel Foucault who analyzes at length how power practices mold and shape the body, through what he calls a 'microphysics' of power. He analyzes how power and knowledge in the West have been intermingled since 1800, culminating in power practices through which human bodies are disciplined' and 'normalized'. He aims to show how all human bodies since then have been molded and standardized according to norms set by the human sciences, which determine what constitutes the normal subject, but also the abnormal subjects (Foucault 1979a). His theories on the disciplining of bodies, in particular, are widely used by feminist researchers who analyze how the female body is a locus of these power practices, as it is adapted to standards of how the normal female body should be and what it should look like. In what follows, I will briefly define Foucault's thoughts on ethical self-formation, which means the modification of one's self to reach a state of perfection and power.

In his final works, especially those written after 1980, Foucault contends that in all societies we find techniques, devices, ideas and practices which can be used tools to change oneself. Foucault (2007c, 154) contends:

> techniques which permits individuals to perform, by their own means, a certain number of operations on their bodies, on their own souls, on their own thoughts, on their own conduct, and this in such a way that they transform themselves, modify themselves, and reach a certain state of perfection, of happiness, of purity, of supernatural power, and so on.

Foucault's analytics of power focuses on what he calls its 'techniques', various operations that one performs to change one's self and make one's inner intentions and desires conform to one's outer performances (Ibid., 155). Foucault stresses the importance of the concept of techniques particularly in the process of ethical self-formation.

These techniques are to be found in every moral system, which as such, consist of a set of moral codes or prescriptive rules on the one hand, and of vocabularies that constitute the ethical relationship of the self to the self on the other hand. Through the latter, individuals constitute themselves as ethical subjects who act and behave in accordance with the codes or rules of the moral system at hand, with embodiment playing an important role in that constitution.

This ethical relationship of the self to the self always has four dimensions, according to Foucault. First, there is an element that he calls the ethical substance, i.e. the answer to the question *what* should be cultivated or transformed through the techniques. Second, a dimension of assujetissement (sub-jugation), i.e. the answer to the question *why* the cultivation or ethical transformation of the self is necessary. Third, the self-techniques that are to be used, i.e. the answer to the question *how* this continuous process of ethical self-formation has to be undertaken, and finally, the telos: *to what purpose* it should be undertaken.

To learn more about these concepts Foucault studied Greek and Roman antiquity, where he found ethical vocabularies that were designed to cultivate an ethical improvement of the self. In his view, these ancient ethical vocabularies that involved self-practice are characterized by a relative independence from moral rules or moral codes. The adherents to the various philosophical schools and religious groups in antiquity, where ethical self-formation practices were implemented, were invited through relatively independent ethical vocabularies to cultivate their own personal 'ethos' or ethical life. The term ethical 'freedom practices' was coined by Foucault to refer to this ancient understanding of ethics. Freedom practices stand for practices which exhibit the individual's freedom and autonomy rather than her or his submission to power relations. This concept of 'freedom practices', in Foucault's view, refers to the practices that create and shape a new self-ethical formation that involves a form of freedom and autonomy rather than submission to the rules of dominant local culture.[5] Foucault introduced this concept of 'freedom practices' because, in his opinion, it stands for practices that exhibit the freedom to recreate oneself in a manner that is different from the self-image promoted by the dominant discourse (Foucault 1997b, 281–82). He contends that the principle of this relatively autonomous ethical formation of the self is inherently critical of domination in the sense that the practices contain their own normative dimension. In this way, ethical freedom practices implicitly or explicitly work on the limits of social forms of domination of whatever kind (Ibid).

What is important in Foucault's approach to freedom practices is his consideration of these practices as not being "invented by the individual himself or herself. They are instead models that he finds in his culture and are proposed, suggested, or imposed upon him by his culture, his society, and his social group" (Ibid). Thus, for Foucault, as Karen Vintges puts it, freedom is not as an individual achievement. Rather, it is a thing which exists within the social dominant discourses which offer the tools and techniques for a care of the self. It is not something achieved but it is the outcome of discursive self-technologies, Vintges (2004, 281).

Thus, Foucault asserts, on the one hand, that the practical techniques of self-ethical formation, which entail an ethical relationship of the self to the self, are to be found in many moral systems and he offered analytical tools for studying the various dimensions of self-ethical formation within specific moral systems. On the other hand, he made it clear in several ways that his preference lies with ethical self-practices which are relatively autonomous from moral rules, such as was the case, in his view, in ancient times. Moreover, he pointed to several strands of Islam and Buddhism to argue that this was also the case in other moral systems, and not merely in the ancient Greek and Roman ones.

Through his concept of 'freedom practices,' Foucault emphasizes that individuals can activate their abilities to practice techniques of their own choice that enables them to create their own free state of being, through the availability of vocabularies that offer the tools for such choices. The self-ethical formation in such a context is undertaken by free choice, and this free management of the self consists of a conscious, continuous practicing of certain preferred

5 For more details see Foucault 1997c.

ethical self-techniques[6] within the context of a specific chosen life project. Foucault, then, advocates the freedom practices of the care of the self and human beings' development of ethos themselves, instead of submitting to conventional dominant power relations and discourses (Foucault 1997c, 291–92).

In what follows, I will pursue the direction opened up by this approach because I find it very rich and because, as I will explain in chapter 3, women's construction of sainthood includes freedom practices as part of their local culture. Moroccan women saints activated their abilities to practice techniques of their choices to achieve the freedom that their local culture encompasses. Their achievement of freedom as such empowered them to impact positively on their local communities. Foucault's analysis of self-formation that reveals freedom practices is very useful for understanding Moroccan women's religious agency and its impacts on society.

Judith Butler (1990) agreed with Foucault's articulation of self-formation. Butler is the most prominent feminist researcher who uses Foucault's theories in this respect, arguing that one's gender is always an embodied product of power relations and practices. Butler famously argues that gender is not an essence, but a contingent repetition of performative acts. It is through this contingent repetition that shifts in meaning, involving dominant gender practices and behavior, can take place. Combining both performative approaches, one regarding rituals, the other performance of gender, I will examine the ways in which religious women construct gender through their performance of religious rituals, within a context where gendered cultural norms are strongly emphasized. This composite performative approach will be applied to the rituals performed by Moroccan women saints and their women devotees, whose rituals exhibit their religious agency. Through practices and performances, women negotiate, redefine and construct new gender. Butler discussed the possibility of change through her concept of performativity: one's gender results from a series of performative bodily acts, the repetition of which can amount to openings and shifts in dominant patterns of gender behavior. I find Butler's definition of performativity very important. Indeed, my argument in this book is informed by it. Moroccan women religious agents embodied and submitted to the social norms and performed their religion that ended with the construction of strong religious and powerful personalities. Moroccan women succeeded in discovering the cultural tools to achieve a self-formation that performs freedom practices that are part of their local culture.

6 Mahmood does not use the term « self-techniques » in her book. Rather, she refers to a number of Foucault's concepts involving techniques of moral cultivation and ethical self-formation, and builds on the notion of bodily techniques in the creation of ethical subject.

Here a concept of 'agency' comes to the fore that is nowadays often used in feminist theory: the concept, agency, as opposed to oppressive gender patterns is embodied in the oppressive discourses through which it is constructed. As I have discussed earlier, many anthropologists have also applied this concept to their studies of non-Western cultures and religions. Anthropologist and former student of Butler, Saba Mahmood, has elaborated the concept of agency in this context, criticizing Butler and taking up Foucault's theories in the process. In constructing her concept of agency, Mahmood based her study of an Egyptian women's mosque movement especially on Foucault's final works on ethics. Her *Politics of Piety* is an important work that has attracted much attention from academics and researchers in various fields in recent years. Her book investigates the desires, motives, aspirations, and commitments of Egyptian women affiliated with a mosque piety movement in Cairo. The movement emerged when women with varying levels of formal and informal training began to organize meetings in the mosque, Islam's male-dominated religious ritual space, to offer sermons and lessons on a variety of religious matters. Based on qualitative interviews with some of the women of this religious movement, Mahmood examines their approaches to the different dilemmas and struggles that Muslim women in general and Egyptian women, in particular, face today in cultivating a pious self.

The *Politics of Piety's* theoretical discussions on feminism, women, and Islam have become very influential and deserves more discussion here. It remains a challenge to Western secular feminism and its conceptualization of gender issues in the Muslim world. Mahmood problematizes secular feminism and its inability to conceptualize women's agency and freedom in any terms other than resistance or subordination to patriarchy. Mahmood (2005, x) argues:

> … I was not interested in delivering judgments on what counts as a feminist versus an antifeminist practice, to distinguish a subversive act from a nonsubversive one. While acts of resistance to relations of domination constitute one modality of action, they certainly do not exhaust the field of human action. Rather, the aim of the book is to develop an analytical language for thinking about modalities of the agency that exceed liberator projects (feminist, leftist, or liberal). Politics of Piety, however, goes beyond describing these modalities of agency to focus on two related analytical and political problems that are more central to its architecture: (a) the kinds of capacities – embodied, rational technical – these various modalities of agency required; and (b) the conceptions of the body, personhood, and politics these capacities presuppose, enable, and construct.

Here Mahmood is thinking outside the conception of agency in terms of submission and resistance. She does not show opposition to the feminist liberal approach of the agency, an approach which defines agency in terms of practices that seek women's individual freedom and autonomy. In her view, female agency is anchored in other understandings of freedom than those implied by secular feminist discourses. Mahmood's (Ibid., 14) aims are to:

> Question the overwhelming tendency with poststructuralist feminist scholarship to conceptualize agency in terms of subversion of resignification of social norms, to locate agency with those operations on that resist the dominating and subjectivating modes of power

Mahmood invited scholars and researchers to think of constructing a new thinking of agency based on fieldwork in other contexts. She presented another important perception of agency which has another understanding of freedom, one which is different from that upheld by Western feminism. She argued that the notion of agency in Western feminist discourse usually sought the autonomy of the subject and the challenge of power relations. In her opinion, agency is interpreted as a form of performance, meaning practicing religion and examining the variety of ways women lived and performed their religious and cultural norms. In her view, Egyptian women internalized values and constructed daily life realities that were not different from those life realities that liberal feminists wanted to construct. As I will show below, Mahmood explained that Egyptian women had chosen to wear the *ḥijab* and embraced other feminine virtues such as shyness and to actively pursue this choice in the same way that they viewed women who consciously chose and actively pursued the exact opposite (Ibid). In her opinion, women in both cases were active agents.

Interestingly, Mahmood (2005) criticized Western feminists for imposing their concepts of individual freedom and autonomy at the global level, i.e. for seeking to rescue women in non-Western countries through global emancipatory projects. But the Egyptian women in the mosque movement do not have the autonomy or freedom that the Western feminists defined, Mahmood contends. They are, however, agents, and should be respected and treated as such. Their concern is to live their religion. In other words, Mahmood's concern is to highlight Egyptian women's agency that is 'entailed not only in those acts that resist norms but also in the multiple ways in which one inhabits norms' (Ibid., 15).

Looking at Mahmood's application of Foucault's approach to ethics in her book *Politics of Piety*, I found that she approved Foucault's concept of 'techniques', "the various mechanisms and strategies, through which power comes to be exercised at its point of application on subjects and objects" Mahmood (2005, 17). Mahmood (Ibid., 28) also says:

> Foucault ... allows us to think of ethics as always local and particular, pertaining to a specific set of procedures, techniques, and discourses through which highly specific ethical-moral subjects come to be formed.

Mahmood finds Foucault's approach to ethics very important in shaping women's pious practices.

As explained previously, Mahmood applied Foucault's approach in analyzing the ethical self-formation of these women through self-techniques, which are aimed at a certain telos, on behalf of certain values, and working on a certain ethical substance. I will only focus here on the dimension of ethical self-techniques that are used by these women and that Mahmood discussed at length. Mahmood (Ibid., 31) contends:

> In comparison with other currents within the Islamic Revival, the mosque movement is unique in the extraordinary degree of pedagogical emphasis it places on outward markers of religiosity – ritual practices, styles of comporting oneself, dress, and so on. The participants in the mosque movement regard these practices as the necessary and ineluctable means for realizing the form of religiosity they are cultivating.

In her analysis, Mahmood examines, the techniques for cultivating patience (*ṣabr*) and for veiling particularly closely, and the way the body is involved in the ethical formation of the self of these women is made clear. Mahmood shows that her respondents are engaged in practices which involve their individual agency (Ibid., 40). They are consciously training their bodies to embrace new attitudes and dispositions related to shyness and patience, and cultural practices such as veiling. For example, Nadia, one of Mahmood's respondents, when asked whether or not it was hard to remain unmarried in a place where marriage was so important for women, says: "you have to have a very strong personality for all of this not to affect you because you are not married" (Mahmood 2005, 170). Mahmood asked Nadia about her marital life and about being able to achieve a state of patience. Through Nadia's answer, one understands that *ṣabr*, which is considered a moral virtue in Muslim culture and in Islam, has to be cultivated by being exercised and practiced until the body embodies these practices and starts practicing them naturally and spontaneously (Ibid., 156). With regard to veiling, Mahmood described the same principle; it is an ethical self-technique used in the context of women's ethical self-formation. For Mahmood, veiling is not a form of submission. For these women, veiling means shyness and modesty. Veiling here is taken as a practice that trains the body to acquire it and other moral values (Ibid., 39). Therefore, the body is the instrument through which cultural norms are cultivated.

Egyptian women's agency is achieved through "repeated bodily acts" and by training one's memory, desire, and intellect to behave according to the established standard of conduct. The pious practices of the Egyptian Muslim women whom she studied exemplify their internalization of the rules of the concrete conventional patterns, in which they are embedded. In this sense, Mahmood presented agency as the capacity to perform discursive traditional norms. She says: "this kind of agency I am exploring here does not belong to the women themselves, but is a product of historically contingent discursive traditions in which they are located" (Ibid., 32).

More importantly, the movement participants whom Mahmood observed are active agents. They are 'doing' religion, and their performance of religion, Mahmood concludes, endows them with a freedom, a freedom which does not mean free action in opposing domination, as is the case with Butler and others, but a freedom that people can also actively inhabit dominant norms as agents. Mahmood wanted to highlight a type of agency here which was clear in women's choice to follow cultural practices. Women embraced feminine virtues, namely shyness, modesty, and others, as necessary conditions for their access to political and religious life (Ibid., 6). In the opinion of Mahmood, Egyptian women did not regard cultural model of behaviors as hurdles that hampered women's emancipation. Rather, cultural dominant norms remained tools through which a self-formation could be achieved. She considered the social norms as the ground upon which practices were lived. Mahmood (Ibid., 31) argues:

> The women I worked with did not regard trying to emulate authorized models of behaviour as an external social imposition that constrained individual freedom. Rather, they treated socially authorized forms of performances as the potentialities – the ground if you will – through which the self is realized.

This means that Mahmood approves her respondents' submission to certain forms of local norms as a condition for achieving the subject's potentiality.

In her view, freedom remains the cornerstone of feminist discourse. Besides the liberalist approach to freedom, Mahmood presented another face of Muslim women's agency, an agency which was experienced within the limits of Islamic tradition to achieve freedom. Mahmood, therefore, seeks to explore the way power relations can produce free subjects who do not follow the trajectories of liberal politics (Ibid., 14). Thus, the question that arises: how can we apply Mahmood's approach to pious women who are not affiliated to a religious movement? What is the meaning of Moroccan women saints' agency?

Moroccan historical women saints took the local culture as the ground upon which to create a pious self but ended up with a powerful self-formation that gained them power. These women faced male authority through their compliance with the dominant cultural norms and embraced the local values to create alternative ways to live their piety. Their exclusion from the male orthodox Islam pushed them to think of Sufism as a way to practice religion. Women and men were able to live their mysticism equally. Following Mahmood, Moroccan women saints here are labeled active agents. As I will show in chapter 3, the narratives of these historical women demonstrated that they had chosen to live Sufism, which is not a movement, and they followed the trajectories of conventional norms (Sufism) to be saints and Sufis. This is a facet of Mahmood which I personally found very useful.

In the same line of reasoning, I will try to extend Mahmood's interpretation of Muslim women's agency. In particular, my argument is that Moroccan women saints' and Sufis' agency are performative, meaning doing religion as Mahmood described, but it is also transgressive and liberal. I came to this conclusion because I found that Moroccan women saints' agency that was performative had positive impacts on their local communities. Women used their abilities, engaged with the conventional norms, to uncover the techniques of self-formation of their local culture and construct saintly personalities. These women saints' sainthood promoted them to leadership, power and authority. The narratives showed that their agency started by inhabiting cultural norms to practice religion, but it ended with the performance of actions and practices that impacted positively their communities. Their performance of piety and achievement of sainthood, and their access to leadership, was approved by their local norms and dominant social relations. I seek here to extend Mahmood's approach to Muslim women's agency and show that Moroccan women submitted to the social norms to uncover the techniques to practice religion and also to highlight their abilities to use their cultural tools to achieve a sainthood that empowered them to perform what Foucault calls freedom practices.

Moroccan women religious agents followed the norms of the local culture and lived a freedom similar to that advocated by feminists. Moroccan women religious agents revealed Foucault's concept of freedom practices that constitute part of Moroccan culture. My goal here is to highlight the other side of

Muslim women's agency, a side where the progressive values of the local culture reside. Therefore, it is Foucault's perspective, i.e. freedom practices, that informs my research.

### 3.4.1 Equality Effects and Egalitarianism

I make use of another concept, which I consider important in the exploration of the meaning of Moroccan religious practices, namely the concept 'equality effects,' as developed by the Dutch historian Siep Stuurman (2004). According to Stuurman, a history of equality can be written that focuses on the 'equality-effects' in discourses and texts that express notions and thoughts of equality without necessarily using the term or addressing the concept of equality as such. Referring to a concept used by Wittgenstein, Stuurman argues that there are 'family resemblances' between equality discourses and concepts in different languages and historical contexts. Equality can be expressed in a rational Enlightenment discourse but also in mythical or religious discourses. "We can recognize affinities and parallels (…). Stories may suggest similarity and equality without any explicit reference to them" (Stuurman 2004, 24–25).

Stuurman (Ibid., 26) adds that there is a difference between equality effects and egalitarianism.

> (I)t is useful to distinguish between equality and egalitarianism. Egalitarianism denotes the conscious pursuit of some specific variety of equality, while discourses and concepts of equality refer to specific senses in which persons are deemed equal in particular respects. The relation between equality and egalitarianism is one of potentiality: concepts of equality are not necessarily egalitarian. On the other hand it is obvious that ideas of equality can easily spill over into egalitarian discourses, which hold that when things are alike they should 'receive similar treatment'.

Combining Stuurman's perspective with Foucault's approach to ethical self-formation, I assume that it is not only possible to bring about equality effects and egalitarian effects through texts and stories in different historical contexts but also through life practices as well (Vintges 2007). I will investigate whether concepts that underlie the norms and effects of gender equality are expressed in life stories as well as in the embodied practices of Moroccan Muslim women in past and present.

I look at women's religious agency in Morocco in the past and present and pose the following questions. Are Moroccan religious women as agents merely conforming to the dominant moral system, or have we found agents here who transgress the dominant patterns of domination? Are we, therefore, dealing here with ethical self-formation in the sense of 'freedom practices'? Are the historical women saints working on the limits of their moral system when they undertake to develop their piety and spirituality and to cultivate moral self-hood? Similarly, I question whether their venerators are doing this, as well as the feminists I interviewed.

### 3.4.2 The Organization of the Book

In the five chapters that follow I will discuss and present my book as follows. In Chapter 2, Moroccan Islam is documented, and the basic principles of Sufism are explored more in depth, in particular in relation to the theme of gender. The chapter concludes that Sufism is a religious space where gender is neutral; it also elucidates the characteristic features of Moroccan Sufism and Moroccan hagiography. The third chapter examines Moroccan women and men saints' construction of sainthood, through an analysis of their self-techniques. It also discusses three famous Moroccan women saints, investigating their agency and empowerment as they are articulated in history and oral tradition. The fourth chapter studies the way women pilgrims and devotees understand/interpret/receive historical women saints' agency and explores the different rituals that pilgrims perform in the women saints' shrines and what these mean. In this chapter, I will analyze the ways Moroccan women devotees today benefit from their women saints' agency and become agents and empowered women. I will also discuss the extent to which *murshidāt* understand/experience/receive/ women saints as role models and as a source of empowerment. The final chapter investigates the way Moroccan Islamist and secularist activists interpret/ receive/ historical women saints and incorporate them into their discourses and assess whether or not feminist activists in Morocco today perceive historical women saints as a source of inspiration for their feminist agency and empowerment.

CHAPTER 2

# Sufism and Gender

To further contextualize Moroccan female sainthood, this chapter focuses on Sufism and its relation to gender. Its first section deals with Moroccan Islam. The second section will discuss the way it is approached by different scholars. The third section focuses on gender and its relation to Sufism. It examines how gender is approached in the mystical dimension of Islam and how the female presence is displayed in Sufism. The fourth section examines women mysticism in Islamic history. The final section involves Moroccan hagiography as a source of historical women saints. It also discusses its different properties.

## 1 Moroccan Islam[1]

Islam constitutes an important contributor to Morocco's identity. The 7th Century is marked by the invasion of Arabs who brought Islam to North Africa. ʿUqba ʾibn Nāfiʿ and his companions converted Berber[2] people to Islam, and Islam became the official religion of Morocco, and Malikism was its school of jurisprudence. However, Berbers were not converted in a simple way. There was a resistance and largely voluntary adoption of Islam on the part of the Berbers: and the subsequent spread of Islam in the region was mainly the work of Berbers. Morocco was completely Islamized by the end of the 12th Century, but until now it is not completely arabized.

The propagation of Islam and the Arabic language in urban spaces was promoted by the Idrisid dynasty (172–304 H),[3] the first Moroccan sharifian Muslim Arab dynasty. It was supported by only some of the rural Berber tribes. The Berber urban elites were the first to adopt Islam. They were the ones who

1 Moroccan Islam is an Islam which constitutes of the following bases. Besides ʾAshʿarī doctrine, Maliki religious law, commandership of the Faithful, Sunni Sufism has been recently considered another important cornerstone of Moroccan Islam Bekkaoui 2011. Sufism has been employed as a political dynamics to fight political Islam and transmit Moroccan moderate Islam and propagate its universal ethics of tolerance and peace inside and outside Morocco.

2 The word "Berber" is used instead of the word "*Amazigh*" because it is not a pejorative term in the Anglo-Saxon literature.

3 The Idrisid dynasty is the first Sharifian dynasty that ruled Morocco. Its founder is ʾIdris I. For more details see ʾal-Naṣirī (1954).

 | DOI:10.1163/9789004429895_003

enthroned the first Arab *sulṭān* (Idrīs I) and married him to a Berber Sufi woman (Kenza ʾal-ʾAwraba). The urban spaces became the centers of formal Islam and witnessed the intrusion of the Arabic language, which became the official language of the newly Islamized cities (Sadiqi 2003).

The Arabization and Islamization of Morocco were enhanced by the different dynasties that ruled Morocco over the course of its history. The six dynasties, Idrisids (172 AH–787/304 AH–990), Almoravids (434 AH–1042/557 AH–1185), Almohads (485 H–1126 CE/595 H–1226 CE), Marinids (614 H–1217 CE/869 H–1465 CE), Saʿadiyyīns (916 AH–1525 CE/1021 H–1603 CE) and Alawites (1664 CE to the present), ruled in the name of Islam.[4] Each dynasty contributed to the propagation of Islam in Morocco.

Morocco here experienced two major waves of Islamization. The first wave was initiated by the Arab sharifian dynasties. These included the Idrisids, Saʿadi and Alawite dynasties which initiated an effective Islamization of the Berbers. The second wave of Moroccan Islamization was introduced by Muslim Berbers dynasties, namely the Almoravids, the Almohads, and Marinids. These dynasties contributed considerably to the conversion of the remaining Berber tribes to Islam. The religious and spiritual masters of the Almoravids and the Almohads dynasties disseminated Islam among the dissident Berber tribes. They constructed a number of qurʾanic schools and religious centers in urban and rural spaces. They also constructed various religious educational missions that were launched under the patronage of Sufi and spiritual masters.[5] In conclusion, the dissemination of Islam was put under the patronage of Sufi scholars and Sufi political leaders during the different dynasties that ruled Morocco. The question that rises: what are the properties of Moroccan Islam?

Moroccan Islam is summarized in the following lines. Moroccan Islam is also called maraboutism, the local practice of Islam in Morocco in particular and North Africa in general. In other words, maraboutism, as Geertz (1968, 43) puts it, is a religion, which is based on the belief that a marabout, meaning a holy person, is "attached, bound, tied, perhaps the best word is shackled – to God." On marabouts' death, people built on their graves shrines where venerators celebrated different rituals.[6] In Morocco there are dozens of shrines and Sufi orders where Moroccans visit to live their piety.

---

4 See ʾal-Nāṣirī (1954); Ben Roched (2007).

5 One of the great masters of the Almoḥads and Marinide periods was Abū Meddyān Chuʿayb ʾal-Husayn (1126). His order was perpetuated by his disciple Abdessalam ben Machich whose *murīd*, the *shaykh* Abū l-Hassan Shādilī, the founder of the Shādiliya order. For more details on the religious and socio-political roles of medieval Moroccan *zawiya* see ʾal-Shādilī (1989).

6 See chapter 4.

History displayed the existence of two faces of Moroccan Sufism, namely orthodox Sufism and popular Sufism. Orthodox Sufism stresses the respect of the laws and traditions of the *Qur'ān* and prophetic tradition (Hadīth). Popular Sufism, however, includes activities associated with the worship of saints that I will discuss in chapter 4, and other non-Islamic rituals. Orthodox and popular Sufism are developed in response to the cultures in which they emerged. Sufism is practiced differently: each individual has his/her own personal way to live piously and spiritually. Sufism focuses on individual emotional and psychological experiences and intellectual understandings. These vary and can even be radically different from one individual to another within the same Sufi community, and from one Sufi community to another within the same cultural region or country. The variations and differences in terminology, beliefs, and rituals result from the individual's interpretations of Sufi doctrine and practice which are colored by local cultural and linguistic specificities. In this sense, popular Sufism can be seen simply as a further adaption to these specificities. These two types of Moroccan Sufism may, for my purpose, serve to define Moroccan women's agency both in orthodox and popular religious areas.

The central figure of Moroccan Sufism is *Walī Allāh* who played religious and political roles. He is referred to in Moroccan Arabic as *siyyid*. This term means lord or master, as well as possessor. Moroccans also use the Moroccan word *mūlāy*[7] when addressing a male *walī Allāh*. The Moroccan term *Lalla* is used to address a female saint, and finally the ecstatic (*majdhūb/majdhūba*) is a holy person whose mental capacities are affected by his/her intense attraction to and sense of intimacy with God. The term *majdhūb* emanates from the Arabic root verb *jadhb*, which means to draw out or pull out, Kugle (2007, 109) while the noun *jadhb* can be translated as ecstasy. A *majdhūb*'s behavior is excused and exempt from punishment. All of these Sufi figures belong to the same circle of believers who seek God closeness. They used their own methods, which conformed to their own nature, to be with God and to serve people. Therefore, there are different paths that the Sufis follow in journeying toward closeness to God, in pursuing divine union, in achieving sainthood, and in creating saintly personalities.

Saints built *ribāṭs*, spaces designated, on the one hand, for prayer and worship of God, and for preparing people for holy war against the enemies on the other hand Toufiq (1997). Sufis and saints founded, in the course of time, *ribāṭ* that came to be called zawiya. This word emanates from the root verb *zawā*

7 Concerning the transcription, I use Moroccan Arabic pronunciation when I refer to local Moroccan people, places and roles. But when I refer to people, institutions, and places that are not purely Moroccans, I use *fuṣḥā* words and their transcription.

meaning to gather in a corner to pray and to reconsider one's wrong deeds. *Zāwiyas* served politically, socially, economically and religiously people. Thus, *zāwiya* is the word used in North Africa to indicate a religious center which is founded by spiritual masters and where Sufis gather to perform their religious rituals and seek socio-political purposes.

There is a relationship between *zāwiya* and *ṭarīqa*. Each *zāwiya* belongs officially to a particular *ṭarīqa*. Saints' followers, *murīds* and admirers organized Sufi communities called *ṭarīqa*. The latter has two meanings. It is both a "way" to live religion and piety, and it is also an organization where the saint or the spiritual guide educates his/her disciples. Furthermore, a *ṭarīqa* also involves the perpetuation of the founder's method of practicing Sufism and transmitting religious knowledge and is thus often named after its founder. It is a space where socio-political and economic matters discussed.[8] In *zāwiya*, Sufis taught Islam and propagated it in spaces that Islam did not reach. They also organized meetings to teach people about their religion. They encouraged Muslims to participate in *jihād*[9] against the enemy, to organize trips to *ḥijāz* (pilgrimage trips), to safeguard commercial activities and to maintain social security among the tribes and central authority ʾal-Nāsirī (1954).

It is these saints' roles that made Sufism in Morocco a crucial civilizational and historical component, developed as it was in Muslim Spain in the heyday of Muslim *ʿulamāʾ*. The importance of the saints' role has been substantiated by different scholars' such as ʾal-Bādisī (14th Century) who said that in Morocco there were *ṣulaḥāʾ*, *ʿulamāʾ* and *fuqahāʾ*.[10] *Ṣulaḥāʾ*, (sing: *ṣāliḥ*) were saints, *ʿulamāʾ* (sing: *ʿālim*) were scholars and *fuqahāʾ* (sing: *faqīh*) were jurists. These people all had a Sufi background and authority in their communities. The

8 *Ṭarīqa* played important religious, economic and socio-political roles in Moroccan history. For many socio-political reasons, several *tariqas* invaded medieval Morocco. Members of *ṭarīqas* participated in the fighting against the Iberians and French colonialists during Morocco's struggle for independence; they also offered help to the poor, sheltered the homeless and instructed their *murīds* and other followers. They played a crucial role in the alleviation of oppression, discrimination and social injustice caused by the colonialists. In modern Morocco, most of *ṭuruq* (sing: *ṭarīqa*) have lost their power and ceased to play the roles that they used to. Their role today has become limited to the practice of religion and spirituality especially on particular occasions, such as in the sacred month (Ramaḍān) and the Prophet's birthday (*mulūd*, a Moroccan term that refers to the Prophet's birthday feast).

9 *jihād* in the Sufi discourse means fighting the evil soul and changes it into a peaceful soul.

10 *Fuqahāʾ* are also Muslim jurists specialized in the study of *fiqh* (jurisprudence). The latter is also known as *ʾusūl l-fiqh*, meaning the analysis of the origins, sources, and principles upon which Islamic jurisprudence is based. For details see *The New Encyclopedia of Islam*. ʾal-Bādisī (1982).

enormous number of saints, jurists and Sufis, and zawiyas resulted in Morocco being labeled *'arḍ 'awliyā'* (the land of saints) 'al-Tādilī (1997, 31). Their Sufism underlined the type of Sufism historical Moroccan women performed. It was a Sunni Sufism which is primarily based on the *Qur'ān*, Sunna, and Malikism (the Islamic school of jurisprudence (*madhab*) of the North African countries, as founded by Mālik ibn 'Anas (8th Century)). Its definition of the Sufi necessitated the unity of the juridical and spiritual competencies.[11] As I will demonstrate in chapter 3, Moroccan women's religious agency includes both Islamic law and Sufism.

My purpose in drawing this picture on Moroccan Sufism and its properties is to clarify the different religious public spaces where historical women saints and Sufis performed their piety and lived their spirituality. Moroccan history is pregnant with a number of examples of women saints and Sufis who were presented as *ṣāliḥāt, 'ālimāt and faqīhāt*. Their religious practices marked the different aspects of Sufism and sainthood and revealed their combination of *sharī'a*[12] and Sufism. In what follows, I will study the way Moroccan Islam is studied by Western scholarship.

## 2 Approaches to Moroccan Islam

Moroccan Islam constituted the debate of a number of Western researchers and scholars. Most of these scholars made a sharp distinction between orthodox and popular Islam in Morocco. Several issues are noteworthy in this respect. Most anthropological studied on Moroccan Islam equated orthodox Sufism with the religion of the *Qur'ān* and *Sunna*, as embraced primarily by the intellectual urban elite, and popular Sufism with the religion of the rural population, especially Berbers. In his study, *La Religion Musulmane en Berbérie*, Bel defined popular Sufism in terms of a fusion of Islam and Berbers' local cultural

11 *Qawā'id 'al-Taṣawwuf* (the Rules of Sufism) by Aḥmad Zarrūq (1992) is the most important source of *Maliki* jurisprudence, which still informs jurisprudence in Morocco. His book *Qaw'id 'al-Taṣawwuf* also elucidates 216 principles of Sufism. It is a compilation of instructions for teaching students the principles of mainstream Sufism. Zarrūq (14th Century) was one of the Sufi leaders of Fez, Marinid Morocco. His grandmother, 'Umm 'al-Banīn, was a *faqīha* and played an important role in the development of his Sufi orientation. Zarrūq developed a critical approach to Sufism. He introduced the ideology of *'uṣūli* Sufism that displayed the fusion of Sufism with the *sharī'a*. He sought the fusion of legal and saintly discourses within Sufism. He coined the word *'ālim ṣūfī* (Sufi scholar) meaning a Sufi who unites the juridical and spiritual competencies.

12 *Sharī'a* means Islamic law derived from the *Qur'ān*; whereas, *fiqh* is a body of laws interpreted and introduced by religious scholars.

beliefs and practices, including belief in the forces of good and evil, magical forces and saint veneration (Bel 1938, 37). The spread of popular Sufism in rural Berber Morocco is due, in Bel's view, to Sufi scholars who propagated Islam by adapting it to the belief system of the Berber population. This conclusion was influenced by a political goal, namely colonialism Dennerlein (2002, 131). Such an understanding of Moroccan cultural beliefs facilitated the propagation of French colonial dominance over the whole territory of Morocco. Geertz (1968), Eicklman (1981) and Gellner (1969) also studied Moroccan Islam and stressed the tension between orthodox and popular Sufism.

Interestingly, both Cornell (1998, 95) and Munson (1993, 84) criticized the assumption that there was a clear division between orthodox and popular Sufism. According to them, there was no sharp tension between popular and orthodox Sufism. They added that the anthropologists who studied Moroccan Sufism neglected the study of history, and therefore failed to recognize that the twentieth-century division between orthodox and popular Sufism did not exist in the past (Ibid). In Munson's opinion, anthropologists did not study religious rituals within shrines. These popular rituals, in the opinion of Tapper and Tapper 1987, more intertwined with orthodox religious rituals in the past than in the present. In line with Cornell and Munson, I found in my research on women's different religious rituals that orthodox and popular Sufism were homogeneous in history.

Throughout my research in *zāwiya* Butchīchiyya, for example, I noticed while Sufism entails an acceptance of the foundational texts, beliefs, and practices of orthodox Islam, it also includes additional beliefs and practices that Sufis believe are derived from and not in contradiction with the foundational texts. *Dhikr*, for example, derives from the command found in the *Qur'ān* to remember or mention God. Early Sufis turned this command into a ritual that was performed individually and communally. They also formalized a path (or method – *ṭarīqa* to follow) to transform the individual in ways that enabled him/her to cultivate character traits and attributes that the *Qur'ān* described as necessary to be a pious Muslim. Sufis developed the idea that individuals needed a guide to become pious Muslims. In other words, individuals needed spiritual leaders that had reached a level of advancement that showed them the way to do the same. These guides, who were venerated as saints, were recognized as having acquired special abilities or powers, some of which exceeded normal human capabilities, such as communication with disciples through dreams and the transmission of *baraka*. From my own experience and research, I thus found that popular and orthodox Sufism have been intermingled until this very day.

Most of the anthropological studies I mentioned earlier did not discuss the issue of gender explicitly. In his study of the Sharqāwa order in Bujād, Eickelman (1981) mentioned women's participation in the performance of religious rituals without, however, discussing or interpreting the meaning of their participation. Similarly, Crapanzano (1979) mentioned that women participated in Hamadsha ritual practices as well. But Crapanzano did not study the reasons and the meaning of their participation as he did with male participants.

These scholars disregarded the ways in which women engaged in Sufism and created saintly personalities that impacted their communities socially and politically, thus overlooking women's actual agency and fulfillment in the religious space. After having explored these general characteristics of Sufism and its different aspects, I now will discuss Sufism in its relation to gender.

## 3 Sufism in Relation to Gender

As I mentioned earlier, Sufism is gender neutral, it is open to men and women to live freely and equally their piety. The religious scholar Ibn ʿArabī made it very clear that women are included in the practice of Sufism. He explicitly stated that women could reach the highest stages of Sufism. Ibn ʿArabī thus believed in women's abilities to achieve strong piety and to become gnostic and a part of *ʾabdāl* (sing: *badal*), the highest stage of sainthood and mysticism. According to him, all the positions in Sufism, including those of *ʾaqṭāb* (sing: *quṭb* meaning great saint) and *ʾawtād* (sing: *watad* meaning spiritual protector), were accessible to women. Ibn ʿArabī approved that Sufism is a space where gender equality is highly visible. This is clear in the passage of his book where he described the different types of sainthood that he derived from the *Qurʾān* (*Sūra ʾal-ʾAḥzāb*). Ibn ʿArabī (1985) continuously included women as part of religious courses and practices. Some other names in this respect are Ibn Taymiya (14th Century) who met a Sufi woman called ʾUmm Zaynab Fāṭima bint ʿAbbās ʾal-Baghdādiyya[13] whom he introduced in his work not only as a spiritual leader of the *ribāṭ* ʾal-Baghdādiyya but also as *faqīha* (a jurist) and *muftiyya* (preacher). He explicitly approved her performance of sermons. Abd Raḥmān ʾal-Sulāmī (10th Century) and Farīd ʾal-Dīn ʿAṭṭār (12th Century) are other religious scholars who stressed women's role in Sufism. The Moroccan spiritual masters ʾal-Tādilī (12th Century) and ʾal-Jazūlī (16th Century) both

13 Baghdādiyya is related to Baghdad, the capital of Iraq.

included women as Sufis and believed in women's ability to achieve the highest stages of piety.

Sufi Hagiographers consistently employed a specific terminology in addressing their male and female saints. Ibn ʿArabī, who believed that the qur'anic virtues are accessible to both men and women, used the following phrase: *min rijāl wa nisā'* (including men and women) in his discussion of all saintly categories. Other Sufi spiritual masters like ʿAṭṭār, Ibn Taymiya and ʾal-Sulāmī coined words and expressions such as *rijāl* (actors) to refer to concrete men and women as actors of Sufism and religion. In his *'al-Tashawwuf*, ʿal-Tādilī (1997) continuously repeated the expression (*kāna/ [kāna- t] min 'ahl al-ʿilm wa al-ʿamal*) "he or she was among the people of religious learning and practice" while narrating their female saints. Thus, these scholarly Sufis included Sufi women in their compilations. They eliminated gender in their discussion of spiritual perfection. In as far as these male Sufis and spiritual masters referred to the qur'anic discourse for their reference to women, and their belief that the qur'anic virtues were accessible to both men and women, they clearly understood the *Qur'ān* as egalitarian in character.

Saʿdiya Shaikh (2009, 18) argued that these male Sufis created symbolic language to implicitly criticize the "dominant patriarchal concepts of gender within Muslim legacy."[14] According to her, the Sufis were conscious of the dominant *fiqh* that marginalized the quranic gender justice. The Sufis' believe in the equal spiritual capacities suggested that they were implicitly criticizing patriarchal communities where such equality was not approved. Shaikh (Ibid., 809) acknowledged that there is no distinction between men and women in the practice of Sufism. I focus here on these voices that are quite prominent in this area of research today. Shaikh (Ibid.) stated that patriarchy and patriarchal discourses, which existed in different societies, were responsible for many limitations placed on women's practice of religion. However, Shaikh argued, Sufi doctrine and practices were more open to women since they focused on the individual's inner state and not on his/her physical side. Sufi practices, in Shaikh's opinion, have served as a means to subvert the patriarchal ideologies existing in the dominant discourses of traditional societies, as these Sufi practices incorporated gender justice and equality (Ibid., 37).

14 Shaikh draws on Rita Gross's book, *Buddhism after Patriarchy* (1993). Gross calls for a feminist revalorization of the history of Buddhism to uncover the Buddhist female voices, which androcentric culture concealed. To do so, Gross calls on scholars to return to the past to explore historical Buddhist 'feminist' ideals that empowered rather than disempowered women. For more information see Shaikh 2009.

Shaikh's argument regarding the ideals of Sufism and its relation to gender equality is primarily based on Ibn ʿArabī's views. She underscored his conception of Sufi women as heroines of spirituality and chivalry. Ibn ʿArabī, Shaikh (2009, 18) asserted, criticised *fuqahā'* for interpreting Sufism and Islam in androcentric and patriarchal ways, stressing women's subordination and marginalization and making these processes appear intrinsic to Islam.

Likewise, other scholars stressed the gendered neutrality of Sufism. The Moroccan sociologist Abdssamad Dialmy, likewise argues that Sufism constitutes a space where gender difference is substantially disregarded Dialmy (2008, 123). He elucidates that the Sufi body's physicality melts while the Sufi is navigating in the realm of spirituality. Schimmel (1975, 426–35) also approved that Sufism includes women and men and that the Sufi body became free and emancipated from its gendered physical difference and sexual procreative functions. Thus, sexual and physical differences have no significance in the Sufi tradition.

According to these scholars, gender neutrality is a basic presumption of Sufism. To further discuss the relation of Sufism and gender, I have to take into account that Sufism is part of a broader movement of Islamic mysticism, which finds its basis in readings of the *Qur'ān* that emphasize its spiritual core. Interestingly, several contemporary authors have once more emphasized this spiritual side of Islam, such as to be found in the ethical message of the *Qur'ān*, discussing it in terms of gender equality like the Sufi masters implicitly did long before them.

In her influential book, *Qur'ān and Woman: Rereading the Sacred Text from a Woman's Perspective* (1993), Wadud studied the *Qur'ān* from a gender perspective. She explored the way a woman's position is portrayed in the sacred text. According to Wadud, the *Qur'ān* did not justify any oppression of women. She argued that God in the creation of humankind did not distinguish between man and woman. The *Qur'ān* presents both men and women as created from the same *nafs*. It also addresses the position of the individual in the hereafter not in terms of gender but in terms of the individual's actions and faith. The only distinction it makes is on the basis of *taqwā* (piety) of the person (Sūra 'al-'Aḥzāb, 34).

The *Qur'ān* also shows that the practice of religion was available to men and women. It referred to *muslimāt* and *muslimūn* (Muslim men and Muslim women), *mu'mināt* and *mûminūn* (the faithful men and faithful women) (Sūra 'al-Naḥl, 96). No restriction has been placed on women to acquire religious knowledge and to perform religious roles. Thus, Wadud stressed that her egalitarian reading of the *Qur'ān* did justice to the real spirit of the *Qur'ān*. Men's leadership and women's obedience are not Islamic but cultural constructs.

Muslim women's oppression and backwardness are due to patriarchal interpretations of the original sources of Islam, particularly the *Qur'ān* in the centuries following the death of the Prophet. Since then, women are discriminated, and not considered as being on the same level as male believers. Since then, Wadud argues, Islam is used as an instrument to restrict woman's function in society and to make her inferior to her male counterpart. Thus, a rereading of the *Qur'ān*, preferably by women themselves, is also important in fighting patriarchy.

Likewise, Barlas (2002) argues that the *Qur'ān* does not present men as superior to women. In her opinion, Barlas believes that the *Qur'ān* distinguishes between people only on the basis of praxis, which means faith and the practice of qur'anic instructions and not patriarchal gender. Leila Aḥmed (1992) also argues in similar ways and stresses that women's subordination stems not from Islam but from a patriarchal interpretation of Islam.

These new voices of believing Muslim women, who argue for a reinterpretation of the *Qur'ān* as a book in which women are seen as equals, have inspired many Muslim women today to turn to the *Qur'ān* and start reading the texts themselves. A precise evaluation of their arguments exceeds the scope of my research. However, from their arguments one can conclude that gender egalitarianism is not external to Islam. The works mentioned above argue for intrinsic gender equality in the heart of Islam, like some Sufi scholars implied in their works.

## 4 Women's Mysticism in Islamic History

Wadud discussed several stories in the *Qur'ān* on women who, as were presented as great examples of piety. Regarding the story of Maryam, I can add to Wadud's findings that in the Sufi literature, Maryam is taken as a symbol of the mystic's love and strong attachment to God who becomes pregnant with the divine light. Another woman mentioned in the *Qur'ān* is Asiya, Pharoah's wife, who prayed God to save her from Pharoah's injustice and to build her a house in paradise. In this respect she can be considered a mystic woman. In the *Qur'ān*, another woman comes forward, who is referred to as the maid of the governor of Egypt (*'imra'at 'azīz miṣr*) Sūra *Yūsuf*. This woman fell in love with the Prophet, Joseph. Her love for him was a symbol of her love for God. Her strong love for God made her lose her mind and walk on the streets in search of her beloved. Her story has become a symbol of the soul which engages in the Sufi path of poverty and love. Schimmel (1975, 434) included her in her list of female mystics because this woman totally devoted herself to the divine.

The authors above discussed the egalitarianism of the *Qur'ān* and did not go into the *Hadīth* at length, nor will I, since this is a topic that exceeds the limits of my study even further. I will only limit myself to a brief mentioning of several references in the *Hadīth* to women experiencing mysticism during the Prophet's life. In this context, I mention the Prophet Muḥammad's saying to his first wife Khadīja that the angel Gabriel (Jibrīl) sent her his greetings and promised her a house in paradise. In the Sufi literature, Khadīja is the first woman who experienced the mystical state that the Prophet was living during the first stages of the Islamic divine revelations. It is she who sustained and comforted the Prophet when he first met the angel Jibrīl. She lived with the Prophet at the time of his first mystical states, and she was the first woman who practiced religion with the Prophet and remained by his side. Being the first believer of the Prophet's divine mission, Khadīja was promised a place in paradise 'al-Bādisī (2004, 2). She, then, is often seen as the pioneer of female sacredness and as the first who opened the door for other Muslim women to enter the world of spirituality.

Likewise, the Prophet's daughter Fāṭima became one of the greatest pious women in the Islamic world. She was the only daughter of the Prophet and the only woman who inherited the Prophet's sacredness. The Prophet says: "Fāṭima is part of me, whoever makes her angry makes me angry too".[15] In another *Hadīth*, the Prophet said to Fāṭima when he found her ill because she found nothing to eat: "Oh daughter! Don't you want to be the lady of all women?" She said: "Oh father, what about Maryam, the daughter of 'Imrān?", the Prophet replied: "She was the lady of her time, and you are the lady of your time" (Ibid). 'Ā'isha was also a spiritual woman who was involved in the Prophet's divine revelations: she is reported to have seen the Prophet in the company of the angel Jbrīl Skalī (2007, 130). These exemplary pious women were heroines of stories that both written and oral archives contain. They show that the fundamental texts of Islam record the lives of men as well as of women whose piety lifted them to a heightened position.[16] The question that arises is: how history present women saints and Sufis?

The role of some women mystics in the history of Islam is highly stressed. Islamic history is pregnant with instances of women who played a role in their

15 'al-Bukhārī wa Muslim 2007, 1066. *Ṣahīh 'al-Bukhāri* is a prophetic tradition, or *Hadīth*, which were collected by the Persian Muslim Muhammad 'al-Bukhārī (d., 256 H) after being transmitted orally for generations. It is also considered as the most important trusted collections of *Hadīth* which covers almost all aspects of life in providing guidance of Islam.

16 For more examples of these historical Muslim women see *Nisa' hawla Rasūl* by M.Ibrahim Ibrahim.

societies. It is full of instances of women's scholarship and religious agency. As I will show latter on there are women who engaged in the Sufi path and reached the highest stages of piety and spirituality that empower them to have power and authority.

Islamic history refers to a number of other Sufi women who marked the Sufi world with their strong piety and religious knowledge. Fāṭima of Nishapur and Fāṭima of Cordova who succeeded in becoming religious scholars and participated in the education of renowned male Sufis. Fāṭima of Cordova whose faith and sainthood is reported to have bestowed youthfulness on her despite her old age. Her spirituality is said to have endowed her with divine beauty. Ibn ʿArabī considered her his spiritual mother. He argued that her divine beauty oriented his spirituality and made him perceive the divine through the medium of a woman. She used to tell him: "I am your spiritual mother and the light of your bodily mother". (Ibn ʿArabī 1985, vol. 3, 89). Her strong piety pushed Ibn ʿArabī to consider her instructions and to follow the right path to God. Fāṭima of Cordova thus was Ibn Arabī's spiritual master, who taught him Sufism. Thus, women for Ibn ʿArabī, reveal "the secret of the compassionate God" Helminski (2003, xxi).

Bayazid ʾal-Bisṭamī (8th Century), a known spiritual master, also referred to a saintly woman whom he encountered in the desert and whom he considered as his spiritual master. It is true that in his entry, ʾal-Bistamī's hagiographer did not give a detailed description of the role this woman played in ʾal-Bistamī's spirituality, but one understands from his approval of her as his spiritual guide who guided his piety and spirituality that she mastered him Schimmel (1975, 243). In what follows, I will discuss the way Moroccan hagiography presents women saints. My purpose from drawing a literature on Islamic hagiography below is to familiarize the reader with its major properties and to define the way hagiographers presented women saints and whether they respected the egalitarian sprit of Sufism.

## 5 Islamic Hagiography

Before I focus on Moroccan hagiography I will elaborate a bit more on the main characteristics of Islamic hagiography amidst other laudatory genres. As it is documented earlier, hagiography literally means writing about holy people. It is a historical discourse on virtuous individuals and their religious performances. Hagiography thus compiles memories of religious people aiming the survival of their legacies. Hagiographers preceded their entries on saints and Sufis in a traditional manner with a short introduction. In it the compiler mentioned his name, offered praise to God and asked for the bestowal blessing upon the Prophet. Hagiographers also explained the reasons for writing their compilations and their intentions behind narrating the saints' life stories. They opened each entry with *'isnād*, or a chain of previous transmitters, that is, the people who heard from someone else and could authorize the veracity of the sayings, as well as with the name of the saint's geographical origin. They also gave basic information on this place and its significance within his/her family and local community. After that, hagiographers recounted the way the saint was chosen to do the will of God.

Other laudatory genres are *manāqib* defined by lexical scientists in terms of 'al-*'akhlāq* (virtues) and qualities. *Manāqib* valorize traits of character and behavior. Their purpose is not only to record the person's actions but also to evaluate the virtues of the individual. *Manāqib* celebrate the qualities, virtues, talents and good deeds of a particular religious person. They are biographies that have a laudatory character and that praise the traits of an individual or a group of individuals.[17] *Manāqib* as virtues were celebrated on other forms of traditional writings, namely *sīra*,[18] biographical dictionaries[19] and hagiography. In the section that follows, I will discuss at length hagiography because it constitutes the major source of Moroccan women saints' life stories.

---

17 See Encyclopedia of Islam. Vol. VI, 333.

18 *Sīra* is an additional form that includes *manāqib* materials. It is a traditional biography of the Prophet that emerged with the growth of the Islamic empire characterized by a new socio-political context where multiculturalism flourished. To preserve the Prophet's cultural heritage, Muslims engaged in compiling the Prophet's life stories and those of his companions. They composed the Prophet's biography to preserve it for the subsequent generations and to perpetuate the essential foundations of Islamic identity. The pioneers of *sīra* were 'Urwa'ibn Zubayr (8th Century), Ibn 'Uthmān (8th Century) and Sharhabīl ibn Sa'əd (8th Century). These scholars constitute the first generation of Muslims who were interested in writing about Islam. The compilations of *sīra* on the Prophet were written down by Abū Muḥammad abd 'al-Mālik îbn Hishām (9th Century). The latter collected Ibn 'Ishāq's works, the genealogy of the Prophet and his divine revelations. Another important example of *sīra* is *Sīra 'al-Nabawiyya*. *Sīra* remained a fundamental reference of Islamic history. 'al-Buṭī 1993, 7.

19 Another genre of Islamic literature that competed with *manāqib* are biographical dictionaries. The latter appeared in the mid-seventh and at the beginning of 8th Century. Muslim biographers committed themselves to the writing of the Prophet's life as well as that of the Prophet's companions by relying on the *Hadīth* and the oral transmissions. As mentioned earlier, the growth of the Islamic *umma* and the expansion of Islam in various remote areas required further efforts in the gathering of other prophetic sayings and behaviors that Muslims sought to emulate. Muslims began to search for the Prophet's detailed utterances and deeds from the transmitters of the Prophet's tradition. Likewise, Muslim biographers recorded the lives of the *'imāms* or founders of the schools of Islamic jurisprudence and other important religious figures.

FIGURE 2 Islamic hagiographic manuscript
PHOTOGRAPH ANONYMOUS

Hagiography in the Muslim context is rooted in the Islamic tradition. The *Qur'ān* contains hagiographical material in as far as it contains stories of human beings known for their exceptional characters, traits and actions. The Prophets Adam, Abraham, Moses, Jesus and Muḥammad were mentioned, and there are stories of pious and spiritual women like Eve and Maryam bintu 'Imrān. The *Hadīth* is an additional source of stories about the Prophet Muḥammad. It is a compilation of the Prophet's deeds and sayings recorded orally by his companions during and after the Prophet's lifetime. The Prophet's companions also transmitted stories about the Prophet. Many tales celebrated the Prophet's acts and sayings from the time of his birth, during his infancy and childhood, as well as along his adult life when he received divine revelations and founded the Islamic religion.

The Prophet's Faithful Companions such as Abū Bakr Ṣaddiq and 'Umar ibn Khaṭāb experienced the company of the Prophet and miraculous events which took place in the Prophet's lifetime such as his receipt of divine visions, performance of wondrous deeds, interpretation of dreams, prediction of future events and communication with animals. Their accounts bear witnesses to these events. Their companionship with the Prophet impelled them to become compilers of this sacred tradition. The Prophet's companions were engaged in this compilation process not only to better understand the *Qur'ān* but also to find solutions to their contemporary crises and to preserve their Islamic identity, which began to be lived out in a competitive social and political environment. Thus, the companions' stories on the Prophet constituted an important model for the subsequent biographers and hagiographers who sought to record religious people's life stories.

In my study of women saints' life stories, I see that hagiographers described their practices and actions following the way the Prophet's companions did in writing about the Prophet. My purpose from drawing Abrahamic prophets, messengers and companions is to show that hagiography is rooted in the primary sources of Islam. I also want to show that entries on men and women saints were recorded following the model of the Prophets' and companions' life stories.

The rise of written hagiography was enhanced by the development of Sufism and the spread of religious centers in the Islamic world. In the eleventh Century, Islamic hagiography presented the lives of saintly people who were engaged in the world of Sufism and sainthood. Several spiritual masters appeared and various Sufi orders developed. The death of these highly respected spiritual masters impelled their disciples and followers to develop hagiographical and biographical anthologies. Among these hagiographical texts which presented the life stories of Sufis are *'al-Ṭabaqāt 'al-Ṣūfiya* (Sufi Generations) by Abd Rahmān 'al-Sulamī and *Tadhkirat 'al-'Awliyā'* (Remembrance of God's Friends) by Farīd 'al-Dīn 'Aṭṭār. These works are compilations about saints' and Sufis' life stories who were known by their strong spirituality and charismatic deeds. The properties I discussed earlier on Islamic hagiography are also the main characteristic of Moroccan hagiography. In the following section, I will study Moroccan hagiography and the way it presented Moroccan women saints.

## 6 Moroccan Hagiography

In Morocco, a variety of developments spawned the emergence of hagiograph ical writing. According to Halima Ferḥat (1986, 18), it is very difficult to locate its birth exactly because thousands of Moroccan hagiographies still languish in manuscript form and only very few are edited and published (Ibid). It is often assumed, however, that Moroccan hagiography originated in the 11th Century and flourished in the 20th Century when Morocco witnessed the expansion of Sufism. The increasing number of saints, Sufis and marabouts, holy men and women,[20] in urban and rural Morocco characterized many regions.

20 French anthropologists, who studied Moroccan Islam, coined the term marabout to name a holy men or a holy woman.

This proliferation of Sufi orders favored the emergence of hagiographical texts and historical records of spiritual masters and holy people. Their leaders engaged in writing entries on their faithful saints and Sufis.[21] The Moroccan hagiographer Ibn Zayyāt 'al-Tādilī (12th Century) composed his compilations following the model of 'al-'Aṣfahānī (11th Century)'s *Ḥilyat 'al-'Awliyā' wa ṭabaqāt 'al-'Aṣfiyā'* (The Ornament of the Saints and the Generations of the Pure). This work constitutes a storehouse of information on the utterances and deeds of the pious. Like Eastern hagiographers, Moroccan hagiographers compiled their narratives on saints by drawing on professional narrators, other scholars, predecessors and family members. Thus, the main sources used by Moroccan hagiographers in composing their texts were scholars and people of confidence whom they considered to be authentic sources of information on Moroccan saints.

Most of Moroccan hagiographical entries have a similar structure, compared to each other and to hagiographies from the other regions. In addition, the general texture of Moroccan hagiography includes a variety of devices such as lengthy narratives about the saint's miracles, passages describing the saint's physicality, personality and piety. The entries usually end with the death of the spiritual hero. Hence, Moroccan hagiography has a chronological texture. Moroccan hagiographers compiled saints' life stories to propagate the moral and ethical messages that they contained. Saints' entries served to guide religious education and spiritual orientation. Hagiographers intended through their exposition of saintly figures to strengthen the moral character of their communities to which saints belonged. The description of the lives and characters of religious people buried in different parts of Morocco served the pedagogical aim of erecting models of ethical conduct. Saints' educational messages still find expression in the religious performances of the current generation. Moroccan saintly moral messages deriving from saints' life stories impel people to respect the saints' conducts. Hagiographers and their followers cherished their favorite saints' spiritual and social status. Consequently, the devotees of the saints inherited their saints' religious and social actions, practices and attitudes, and they sought to emulate them. This practice turned out to be part of the daily rituals that they have still celebrated in the saints'

21 The sharifian dynasties also played a role in documentation in the form of hagiographical works. Almoravids and Almohads dynasties were led by Sufis and saintly kings such as Yūsuf Ibn Tāchafīn and Ibn Tumart. Each of these patron saints authorized the production of hagiographical manuscripts, family documentations and biographical dictionaries to preserve their saintly life stories. Moroccan hagiographers followed the model of Eastern hagiographers such as that of 'al-Sulāmī, Abi Nu'aym 'al-'Aṣfahāni (11th Century) and 'al-Qushayrī (11th Century) and their ways of documenting hagiographic record.

sanctuaries to this day. As I will discuss in chapter 4, venerators of women saints transform their women saints' ethics into rituals to underpin the survival of saints' hagiographical reference.

Furthermore, Moroccan hagiographic records constitute a window through which one could see the life stories of women saints' and the local values and norms of their communities. Hagiography is a tool through which one could acquire knowledge about the religious collective consciousness and the general worldview of the period in which the saint lived Hefferman (1988, 15–16). In other word, saints reflected the religious ways of life of their contemporary community, and, through their entries, hagiographers indirectly made reference to the women saints' historical environment and to the impact of the local historical events on their pious lives Ferhat and Triki (1986, 18). I found this very important because the hagiographic stories of the women saints I selected to study give us a picture of the environment where they constructed sainthood and of the context that empowered them to reach power.

The first hagiographic literature that appeared in Morocco includes the following. The hagiographic dictionary *'al-Minhaj 'al-Waḍih fī Karāmāt Abi Muḥammad 'al-Ṣāliḥ* (14th Century), which was unfortunately lost, is one of the most important hagiographic references on Moroccan saints. *'al-Tashawwuf ilā Rijāl 'al-Taṣawwuf* (Insight into The Tradition Bearers of Sufism) by the Sufi scholar Ibn Zayyāt 'al-Tādilī, also constitutes another primary source on Moroccan men and women saints, and one of the important compilations I consulted. *'Al-Tashawwuf* is a source for the first generation of Moroccan saints and the early phase of Moroccan sainthood and its development. It contains 279 hagiographic notices devoted to the Sufis and saints of Southwestern Morocco during the Almoravids and Almohads periods. 'al-Tādilī recorded the lives of the saints he encountered during his life or heard about. *'al-Tashawwuf* remains a key reference for future scholars of hagiography. Huwat 'abī Rabī' Sulaymān (13th Century) is a hagiographer who wrote on Fassi saints, based on oral stories only. Another hagiographic work, from the fourteenth Century, is *'Uns 'al-Faqīr wa'izz 'al-ḥaqīr* by Ahmad ibn 'al-Aziz 'al-Qusṭanṭinī who is known by the name of Ibn Qunfudh. It is a hagiographical compilation of saints and Sufis belonging to the 14th Century Maghrebin countries. Ibn Qunfudh wrote his hagiographic work during his journey across Maghrebi countries to describe the phenomenon of sanctity and to compile the entries of saints and Sufis who were disciples of the axial saint Abū Madyān 'al-Ghawth (13th Century).

Another hagiography is *Dawḥat 'al-Nāshir*, written by the Sufi-scholar Ibn 'Askar 'al-Shafshāwunī (16th Century). It deals with the lives of the Northern Moroccan saints and Sufis. Other Moroccan hagiographers are Muḥammad

ʾal-Huḍaykī (18th Century) and Mukhtār ʾal-Sūsī (20th Century). ʾAl-Huḍaykī is one of the great Sufi scholars of the Sūs region. His *Ṭabaqāt* is a compilation of hagiographic entries on 813 Sufis. ʾAl-Sūsī accounts mostly on ʾal-Huḍaykī and oral stories for his compilation on Sufi saints of the Sūs region.

Another hagiography is the one of Jaʿfar ʾal-Kattānī (20th Century). In his *Salwat Anfās*, ʾal-Kattānī devoted more than 1,100 pages in his three volumes to present extensive data on Fez, its holy people and religious scholars. ʾAl-Kattānī compiled entries on the great saints of Fez by borrowing narratives from other hagiographers such as Huwat ʾabī Rabīʿ Sulaymān (13th Century) and historical narrators of stories on residents of Fez. He arranged his compilations according to the location of the saints portrayed. He started with the saints whose tombs are located in the center of the urban space before proceeding toward the city's outskirts. All these hagiographic works rely on ʾal-Tādilī's *ʾal-Tashawwuf* for their entries on *ʾawliyāʾAllāh* living before the 13th Century. Therefore, his work is prominent in the following section, where I go into the main characteristics of Moroccan hagiography.

## 7 Diversity, Hierarchy and Authenticity

In what follows I will take a closer look at the content of the main Moroccan hagiographies, specifically the ones of ʾal-Tādilī andʾal-Kattānī. Throughout my study of Moroccan hagiographic records, I notice that hagiographers recorded a diversity of religious styles and modes of religious authority in their compilations. In *ʾal-Tashawwuf*, ʾal-Tādilī refers to different types of religious figures, Sufis, saints and pious individuals, as well as people who followed the path of blame, known as the Malamatiya (*malama* means to blame) meaning people who never cease to blame themselves in front of God and those characterized as *majdhūb*. He seems to aspire to completeness rather than to a strict division and opposition between literate and illiterate saints or between orthodox and popular religious people.

As a hagiographer, ʾal-Tādilī was interested in Sufi *ʿamal* (religious practice) and *ʿilm* (religious knowledge). He stressed that in his book he refrained from dealing with the sciences. Instead, he argued that he provided information about *rijāl*. ʾAl-Tādilī thus included in his compilation jurists (*fuqahāʾ*) (Sing: *faqīh*), ascetics (*zuhād*) (Sing: *zāhid*), pious believers (*ʿubād*) (Sing: *ʿābid*) and the like. He was concerned with all Sufis whose religious practices empowered them to be friends of God. This is clear in his continuous reference to particular terms in his description of saints. For example, he repeated in each entry the expression "*kāna*/ [*kānat*] *min ʾahl ʾal-ʿilm wa ʾal-ʿamal*" (he or she was among the people of religious learning and practice). As I documented earlier, this statement signifies the combination of legal sciences with the manifest pious practice and virtuous conduct associated with the Sufi way of life, particularly asceticism, *zuhd*. Thus, ʾal-Tādilī stressed the importance in using this expression to define the way individuals constructed sainthood.

In his *Salwa*, ʾal-Kattānī (1900) adopts ʾal-Tādilī's definition of sainthood in his work. His compilation likewise includes biographies of scholars and virtuous figures, *ʿulamaʾ* and Sufi ascetics and *majādhīb*. Like ʾal-Tādilī, ʾal-Kattānī seems to aspire to completeness and inclusiveness rather than exclusiveness or establishing a strict division between literate and illiterate, between orthodox and popular saints. He presented life stories on saints that he derived from written hagiographies and oral sources. He classified the saints' entries according to their lineage, starting with the *shurfa* followed by scholarly saints and finally by holy people.

Abdellah Laroui (1997, 109) described ʾal-Kattānī's organizational structure as follows: the *shurfa* were placed at the top of the list, classified according to the purity of their genealogy and the miracles ascribed to their lineage. They were followed by the learned and knowledgeable saints such as the *ʿulamaʾ*. The latter were followed by the more or less illiterate *ʾawliyāʾ* and *majādhīb*. But this ranking of saints, in the opinion of ʾal-Kattānī (1900), was non-oppositional, meaning there was no tension between orthodox and popular saints. In spite of their different genealogies, degree of sainthood and scholarly education, Fassi saints shared a power and authority that put them in harmonious relationships and that entailed cooperation among them. Through his compilation, ʾal-Kattānī presented saints who provided insight into the construction of religious authority. ʾal-Kattānī maintained that orthodox saints, such as *ʿulamāʾ*, and popular saints, such as *majādhīb*, constituted forms of religious power and authority that did not exist in opposition in late 19th Century and beginning of 20th Century. Each saint whether literate or illiterate had a sacred power that impacted people on different spiritual levels. Therefore, ʾal-Kattānī thus drew on different religious styles and shaded light on their authoritative status and emotional appeal.

Moroccan hagiographers like ʾal-Tādilī (1997) and ʾal-Kattānī (1900) thus approved of the complementarity of *fiqh* and Sufism in the construction of saintly personalities. ʾal-Tādilī referred to a number of Sufis and jurists who stressed the importance of *ʿamal* alongside *ʿilm* in achieving sainthood. An example from ʾal-Tādilī's was the Sufi ʿAbd ʾal-ʿAzīz Tūnsī, who constructed himself as a celebrated Maliki jurist who taught jurisprudence to the Maṣmūda Berber people of the High Atlas in a *ribāṭ* in Aghmāt. In the course of his religious teaching, he found out that those of his students who did not study and practice

Sufism attained worldliness (*dunyā*). He disapproved of teaching *fiqh* without the practice of Sufism fearing that his students would be involved in worldliness and lost the knowledge of right and wrong (*'al-ḥalāl wa l-ḥarām*). As a consequence, Tūnsī stopped teaching jurisprudence because it was a way of gaining worldly benefits. He decided to consecrate the rest of his life to Sufism in his *ribāṭ* 'al-Tādilī (1997, 34).

By depicting sainthood through descriptions of their *'ilm* and *'amal* and other practices, Moroccan hagiographers highlighted the traits, characters, virtues and practices that made saints into friends of God. They revealed that many saints chose to be not only jurists and orthodox religious figures, but also Sufis, two distinct, but interconnected professional branches and spiritual pathways, which complemented each other in the construction of their saintly personalities as well as impacted the communities.

In the description of saints, hagiographers also employed a variety of terms. In *'al-Tashawwuf*, words like *kabīr sha'n* (great importance) and *kāna min 'ahl 'al-'afrād fī waqtih* (he was among the peerless of his time) were widely used (Ibid). Hagiographers also used the same expressions to describe women saints. Muniya bint Maymūn 'al-Dukkālī (12th Century) was presented as one of the elite (*kānat min 'ahli 'al-'afrād*) (Ibid., 136). In addition, she was described as being among the miracle workers (*aṣḥāb karāmāt*). I can conclude that another indication of Moroccan hagiography's inclusive and non-oppositional account of forms of spirituality, sainthood and authority, is its inclusion of women.

Both 'al-Tādilī and'al-Kattānī included them as spiritual exemplars and authority figures. They referred to a number of women saints, Sufis, ascetics and *majdhūbāt*. They recognized women's abilities to create their own specific religious style and included stories on their lives. Women were considered to be among the *rijāl*, meaning ideal actors of sainthood, exemplary persons of spirituality and models of moral selfhood.

'Al-Tādilī's and 'al-Kattānī's compilation of saints also focused on axial saints, both men and women. The latter achieved spiritual status and authority through knowledge or piety, which impressed the great axial Sufi jurist'al-Tādilī, as well as other hagiographers who offered them a space in their scholarly writings. 'Al-Kattānī's compilation included fifty Fassi women saints and holy women who belonged both to higher and lower social classes. In spite of their lower class origin, these exemplary women were part of the elite, in the opinion of 'al-Kattānī, because they achieved strong saintly personhood. Thus, these Moroccan hagiographers could be interpreted as people with a gender consciousness.

Finally, it is noteworthy that Moroccan hagiography presented male and female saints' entries differently, in that the women saints were introduced with more details on their family relations and marriage than male saints. The main hagiographic sources of this study all were similar in this respect. A brief look at two of these can illustrate this different approach of male and female saints.

In his *Salwa*, 'al-Kattānī without exception described women saints, Sufis and *majdhubāt* in terms of their family situation. He presented them, next to their being saintly scholars, and great mystics, as married women, wives, mothers and as relatives in large families, which were usually headed by male saints and Sufis. For example, the great Sufi 'Ā'isha bint Shaqrūn 'al-Fakhār (17th Century) was described as the daughter of the great saint Sidi Shaqrūn 'al-Fakhār (16th Century) and as the wife of the male saint, Aḥmad ibn 'Abdullah 'al-Ma'in. She was also presented as the mother of the female Sufis: Ruqayya bint Muḥammad ben 'Abdullah 'al-Ma'in (17th Century), 'Ā'isha bint Muḥammad ibn 'Abdullah 'al-Ma'in (17th Century) and Sayyida Safiya bint Sidi Muḥammad ibn 'Abdullah 'al-Ma'in (17th Century). Furthermore, 'al-Kattānī presented 'Ā'isha's three daughters as sisters, wives and mothers who were very faithful to their husbands, families and relatives. Another example is 'al-Kattānī's record of the life of another Fassi woman saint called Faṭima, who was introduced without any surname, merely as the wife of the axial male saint Muḥammad 'al-Qādirī.

In contrast, 'al-Kattānī (1900) never described male saints and Sufis in terms of family relations and marital situations but only in terms of their public activities. He presented them not as husbands, fathers and brothers, but rather as performers of public miracles, and in terms of their public relationships to other great male saints and Sufis. The male saints were only described as jurists, teachers, scholarly saints and Sufis. Examples are the many male saints in Fez, such as Shaqrūn 'al-Fakhār whose family status and marital situation is absent in his entry. 'Al-Kattānī also described Shaqrūn 'al-Fakhār's high educational level, deep knowledge of religion, spiritual practices and scholarly talents. He stressed his preaching and teaching people both in Fez and other Moroccan regions.

Likewise, 'al-Tādilī (1997) gave a list of male saints' entries describing only their scholarly knowledge and public miracles that highlighted their public status in their communities. In *'al-Tashawuf*, 'al-Tādilī never referred to these male saints' family situation. An example was Muḥammad 'Abdssalām Tunsī, whose entry described his deep public piety, spirituality and miracles, all of which impressed his people and presented him as an axial saint. 'Al-Tādilī (1997, 110) made no reference to his family situation. In his reference to women saints, 'al-Tādilī presented some of his women saints as married women and mothers. For example, he mentioned the woman saint Muniya as the daughter of a man called Mimūn Dukālī. He called her Muniyya bint Mimūn Dukālī, and he presented her as a mother (Ibid., 316). Hagiographers described women saints and Sufis in terms of their family relations, because that was the way women in general were defined in the Moroccan rural traditional communities, and this definition should not be interpreted in terms of male dominance. This also does not mean that hagiographers are misogynist people and their definition of women in family relations could be interpreted in terms of male dominance. The argument here is simply that hagiographers respected the traditional way of presenting Muslim women and men without rejecting women's and men's spiritual egalitarianism.

In this respect, Kugle (2007, 115) distilled from the hagiographer's different approach to male and female saints that they wanted to show that these women could not achieve sainthood without the assistance of their male relatives. But in what follows, I will show that hagiographers, who believed in Sufism as gender neutral, in no way belittle the women saints, presenting them instead as scholarly saints and Sufis who marked written history. Hagiographers' introduction of their women saints in terms of family relations seemed to only mirror the conventions in their environment that did not influence them.

Moroccan hagiography originated according to its authors from authentic oral and written sources. ʾAl-Tādilī (1997, 20), for example, claimed to rely on narrators who were known for their truthfulness and uprightness. He mentioned his father as the primary source of data for many of his prominent saints. He also wrote on contemporary saints and Sufis with whom he shared saintly lineage, family relations and strong friendships. Hagiographers were also saints and their achievement of God closeness laid at the basis of their belief in the authenticity and veracity of what they wrote about the saints, their miracles and extraordinary actions.

Nevertheless, the authenticity and veracity of hagiographies constituted a major source of debate, in particular due to their legendary nature. Many entries included actions that called into question their authenticity, such as walking on water, talking to wild animals and flying in the air. This might mean that hagiographers' strong attachment and deep relationship to saints made it possible for them to believe in all that was said about them whether real or unreal (Zeggaf 1991). Cornell (1998) acknowledged the difficulty of distinguishing in a precise way whether hagiographic narratives were based on fact or fiction. He added that pre-modern Moroccans believed in their saints' narratives because both saints and their followers lived in a sacred cosmos in which the transcendent, not the material, represented their reality. What is important to Cornell (1998, xlv) is that, whatever our modern and postmodern assumptions of hagiography may be, hagiographies remained true to the saint's subjects' cultural space and time. This requires that one acknowledges that the *walī Allāh* is both a transmitter of spirituality and an agent of the miraculous. Rather than being concerned about the veracity and authenticity of hagiographies, Cornell (1997) thus concentrated on their presentation of saints as agents of miracles. In spite of the fact that the authenticity of the stories about saints was questionable and could not be verified, hagiography remains an important source, because it reveals so much about the way historical people understood and constructed sainthood. Hagiography in Morocco, too, has recently come to be perceived as a source of materials that reflects important features of societies within which they were composed Kaḥḥāla (1982); Toufiq (1997).

The hagiographers – believing in all the dimensions of their saints' sainthood – revealed materials from different historical eras concerning the abilities, character traits, attitudes, personality types and other features, they felt characterized exemplary religious people. Since historians marginalized women in their writings, I hardly found anything on religious women in historical records. Historical stories on women saints are rare. I relied on hagiographic records more than historical and biographic literature, because the former contains rich material in comparison to other sources. Thus, hagiography is the main source on women's religious roles in history.

My aim here is to investigate the ways female saints are portrayed as subjects of hagiography. I am not concerned with determining whether hagiographic stories are factual or fictional. What concerns me is the ideal laboratory hagiography offers for analyzing the saints' practices and the phenomenon of sainthood. Therefore, I have drawn on hagiographies and oral traditions as the major sources for my next chapter on female Moroccan saints and the way they reached sainthood.

This chapter discusses various views of Islamic mysticism from a gender perspective, one of them being that Sufism as articulated in the primary sources is gender neutral. Sufism's emphasis is on the heart, and the purification of the heart cannot be achieved without the knowledge of Islamic law. Sufism, as it is presented in the primary texts, stresses the inner side of the Sufi's body rather than his/her gender. Similarly, I have studied several discussions of the qur'anic message from a gender perspective from which I can conclude that Sufism reflects the heart of Islam; in as far as it invites the Sufis whether males or females to achieve a spiritual education that enables them to reach God.

Moreover, women's religious participation is more visible in Sufism than in orthodox Islam. Sufism opens its door for women who are marginalized by orthodox religious institutions. It invites women to express their religious desires and to construct religious personhood. From hagiographic and oral narratives: how did Moroccan women saint reach sainthood? What were the techniques they used to become saints?

CHAPTER 3

# Moroccan Female Saints

The first section of this chapter consists of a presentation of exemplary female and male saints in the Moroccan context through a discussion of the various self-techniques they applied, which are discussed in separate sub-sections. Several saints are coming to the fore throughout this discussion, such as *ṣāliḥ, faqīh*, and *majdhūb*. As will be seen, women are to be found among all of these.

From this first section, I get an impression of how female saints, as narrated, lived and achieved sainthood next to their male counterparts. Both men and women come forward from the narratives as creating sainthood through their application of self-techniques, most of which come forward as gender neutral. The self-techniques the women used turned out to be basically the same as men's, with some minor exceptions. The second section of this chapter inventories how, from the narratives, the women saints transgressed the social limits that were imposed on them, and refused the conventional patterns that they were supposed to embody. The third section of this chapter illustrates this transgression, by focusing on the lives of three notable women saints: ʿAzīza, ʿĀʾisha and Fāṭima.

## 1 The Construction of Sainthood

As further indicated in chapter 1, my research focuses only on female saints who have a Muslim background. From what I discussed in chapter 2, Sufism did not make any distinctions between men and women in as far as both could enter the Sufi path and acquired sainthood. From the written hagiographies and oral stories in Moroccan contexts indeed found that there were basically no differences between men and women where it concerned the main self-techniques that they undertook in order to become saints. This will become clear in the following sub-sections, which discuss exemplary cases of saints, male and female, with a focus on women saints. To elaborate on their position as not being different from the one of their male counterparts, sometimes non-Moroccan female saints are highlighted. This is then indicated in the text.

### 1.1 *Piety*

Some main self-techniques used by Sufis, as I have already discussed in the previous chapter, are the practice of piety, acquiring learnedness, the performing

 | DOI:10.1163/9789004429895_004

of miracles, and practicing *jadhb*, as will be discussed respectively. The practicing of piety begins with some first steps of initiation into the Sufi path.

One of the most important actions a Sufi performs at the beginning of her/his initiation into the process of developing piety and spirituality was repentance (*tawba*), a word that describes the person's desire to change his or her life. *Tawba* signifies not only turning away from sin and worldliness, but it also conveys a person's total transformation of selfhood Ibn Manzūr (no date). As it is documented earlier, hagiography presented Sufi women, like men, experiencing an internal desire to radically change their material existence and to lead a pious life. In Moroccan hagiography, I found many narratives of women and men undergoing initiation into mystical life.

One enlightening example of this initiation is found in ʾal-Tādilī's hagiographic entry of the female saint ʾUmayya bint Yaghrūshin (12th Century), one of the greatest spiritual women of ʾAghmāt. One day when she visited shaykh Abdssalām Tūnsī (12th Century), she found people waiting in front of his door. They all wanted him to pray to God for them. When her turn arrived, she asked him to pray to God for her as well. She said to him: "Oh Saint! Please pray to God for me". He replied: "God has forgiven you". She left him and went to her house where she took off all her clothing and put on a coarse woolen garment. She confined herself in retreat in a cave, where she led a lonely mystical life until she died ʾal-Tādilī (1997, 112). ʾUmayya entered in a Sufi life, leaving behind worldliness to pursue piety and spirituality, exactly like her male counterparts did.

Like ʾUmayya, the male saint ʾAbū Zakariyyā Ṣanhājī (12th Century) expressed a strong desire to become initiated into the mystical life. He was one of *ʾumarāʾ* (sing: *ʾamīr*) (a prince) of the Ṣanhāja,[1] who was impressed with the *walī Allāh*, Tūnsī and wished to become one of his *murīds*. He thus willingly submitted to his master's instructions. Ṣanhājī followed his orders immediately. Tūnsī was so pleased with his *murīd*'s behavior that he named him: "*malik zuhd*" (the king of asceticism). When Tūnsī died, Ṣanhājī left Telemcen (Algeria) for the desert where he lived in complete solitude.

Adherence to *ribāṭ* as a step of initiation is referred to in hagiographic literature with regard to men and women. In *ʾal-Tashawwuf*, ʾal-Tādilī refers to the *ribāṭ* Shākir.[2] He argued that many *ʾawliyāʾ* (Sing: *wālī*) sporadically in *ribāṭ*

1 "Ṣanhāja" refers to the Berber tribes located in the South of Morocco. It is actually Marrakech, Tansif ʾal-Haouz.

2 *ribāṭ* Shākir was built in the 10th Century by the Muslim Shākir in the region of Marrakech to propagate Islam among Maṣmuda Berbers and discuss different socio-political matters. Toufiq (1997).

Shākir to instruct *murīdūn* (sing: *murīd*). Women Sufis also visited *ribāṭ* Shākir to learn about religion and undertake the stages of initiation. One of these women Sufis is the famous Berber woman Muniyya bint Maymūn Dukkālī (12th Century), who continually came from Marrakech to visit and participate in the religious activities of *ribāṭ* Shākir. She met ʾIbrāhīm ʾAzadī ʾal-Baṣṭī (12th Century) there and said to him: "I have never seen a place like this before, and I wish you were here" ʾal-Tādilī (1997, 316). In his entry, ʾal-Tādilī acknowledged that ʾal-Baṣṭī approved Muniyya's strong piety and continued participation in *ribāṭ* Shākir's activities. He said: "I saw Muniyya in *ribāṭ* Shākir, I guided her prayer and that of other *murīd*, and then I went away" (Ibid., 112).

As narrated, Muniyya recorded that there was a large number of Sufi women in the gatherings in *ribāṭ* Shākir. She contended: "one thousand women saints visited *ribāṭ* Shākir this year" (Ibid). Moroccan women's strong desire to become religious and Sufis impelled them to seek spiritual guidance offered by Sufi orders. They participated in religious meetings and ritual gatherings to learn about, and undertake, the stages of initiation and piety. Women, like men, adhered to a public religious space like *ribāṭ* to undergo initiation and to develop their spirituality and to take part in the socio-political discussions that *ribāṭ* Shākir observed.

According to Abū Barik (2010, 146), there are some women saints, such as Fassi women saints, who preferred to live their piety within their private families and close to their Sufi family members. Abū Barik called these women saints private saints, saints who had chosen to live their lives as ordinary women and showed submission rather than non-submission to the conventional norms (Ibid). These private women saints, in the opinion of Abū Barik, wanted to live secretly their sainthood and make it nonpublic. The Sufi path and Sufi lifestyle were inward-looking by nature. These Sufi women perhaps considered the interior nature of the soul and the process of spiritual introspection to be at their best in the domestic sphere. From the stories on them, Sufi women asserted that the home was a place where piety and spirituality could best be experienced, as the distractions of worldly existence were left outside. ʾal-Tādilī described FāṭimaʾAndalusiyya (12th Century) confining herself to her home where she performed daily and nightly prayers and remembrance (*dhikr*) ʾal-Tādilī (1997, 331). She refused to go out and join her Sufi male counterparts, such as Muḥammad Aḥmad Zanāti (12th Century) who invited her to experience with him his spirituality.

ʾal-Sulāmī (10th Century) referred to a female saint from Persia,[3] Umm Aḥmad, and to her son, the Sufi Abdallāh ben Khafīf, both of whom spent the

3 Persia is the modern day Iran.

*laylat 'al-qadr* (the 27th night of Ramaḍān) in prayer, but she remained in her home while her son prayed in the mosque. Once they finished their prayers, they learned that they both had experienced the same practice internally and externally, and both realized that the internal practice of piety was as fruitful as the male's external mystical practice 'al-Sulāmī (1993, 88).

Women's desire for piety in the domestic sphere might be explained in terms of women's refusal of public spirituality. The latter held the potential for haughtiness, which was frequently observed among Sufi males. Such a public way of practicing piety appeared perhaps undesirable to some women, being an occasion for displaying arrogance, which was detrimental to the mystical and spiritual life. Rabī'a rebuked a male Sufi for his public preaching because it revealed his penchant for worldliness.

An example is the Moroccan woman saint Mu'mina 'al-Tilimsāniyya (14th Century), who according to her hagiographer, Ibn Qunfudh (14th Century), lived out her piety alone, inside her home in the *medina* of Fez Ibn Qunfud (1965, 85). She refused invitations from her male Sufis to practice public piety with them because, according to her, it displayed their haughtiness and arrogance. 'al-Tādilī (1997, 94) also referred to some women saints who spent their lives in caves and isolated spaces to live their spirituality.

Sufi women's piety in the domestic sphere might be evaluated in terms of social limits and gendered constraints and seen as following the dictates of the conventional norms that underscored woman's presence within private spaces, in contrast to the male's presence in public spaces. However, these accounts should not be taken as recommendations about the appropriate location of women's practice of piety, but as admonitions to other men who might not consider women's spiritual endeavors and achievements merely because they were not undertaken in public spaces. Sufi women's indoor piety, meaning their practice of piety within their houses, did not hinder them in their agency as Sufis. It was believed to be rewarded with the same *'ajr* (religious merit) as that of men's public piety, as was clear from the story on Umm Aḥmad above, and from many other hagiographic stories which placed them on the same level as men. The active nature of women's participation emanated from their engagement in strategies to construct piety. One of these strategies was making the body submissive to the spiritual demands of the soul.

In hagiographic and oral narratives, the Sufi body was subjected to certain rules and conditions for developing piety and spirituality. As I explained earlier, the renunciation of worldliness constituted the primary condition that Sufis sought to attain. Men and women Sufis were described as similarly purifying their bodies and constraining their emotions and feelings against material desires. They were also presented as training their bodies to adapt to the hard ways of life that they chose to endure, in order to cultivate a pious personality. Through asceticism, prayer, remembrance, fasting, nightly invocations and austerity women's bodies, like men's, became inhibited and damaged. An example was given by ʾal-Tādilī (1997) when he described Muniyya bint Maymūn Dukkālī's physical body. He explained that through self-denial, her body became very thin. He wrote that when he visited her [Muniyya], she was old, and through *mujāhada*, she became thin and her skin stuck to her bones ʾal-Tādilī (1997, 316).

The non-Moroccan hagiographer ʾal-Sulāmī also referred to an ʿIraqi Sufi woman called Muʿāda bint ʿAbdallāh ʾal-ʿAdawiyya (9th Century) who had chosen to perform nightly prayers instead of sleeping. She overcame her body's desire to sleep by walking around the house. She remained that way until daylight ʾal-Sulāmī (1993, 88). Their bodies became the means for achieving God's closeness, and signs of their successful embodiment of piety and spirituality.

In other instances, men and women Sufis forced their bodies to submit to their spiritual needs and to their hard spiritual life. Many descriptions presented concrete Sufi women as performing daily and nightly prayers and *dhikr*. Both their emotions and physical organs were engaged in an eternal servitude and remembrance of God. Their bodies experienced an endless invocation of the divine. ʾAl-Kattānī described a Sufi woman's spirituality as follows: She invoked God continuously. She said that when she slept, her veins continued invoking and remembering God ʾal-Kattānī (1900, 319).

This reminded me of a Sufi woman I met in one of the shrines of the women saints I selected to study. I saw her sleeping next to *Lalla* ʿAzīza's grave, but her fingers were moving. When she woke up, I asked her why she moved her fingers while she was sleeping. She replied that it was her body which continued remembering the names of God she started reciting before she had fallen in sleep. The body here reflected the woman's piety and continued performing *dhikr* and invocation on her behalf after she had lost consciousness either through sleeping or fainting (*ʾighmāʾ*). The Sufi body, then, submitted to the power of the pious soul during its navigation in the world of spirituality.[4]

In similar ways, hagiography provided references to male Sufis who trained their souls and bodies to construct pious personalities. They used asceticism, prayers, fasting, and austerity to purify their bodies from worldliness. They were in the continuous struggle against the evil dimension of their souls. ʾal-Kattānī (1900) described a Sufi who quarreled every night with a woman whom he had beaten severely. His neighbors heard him shouting at her and biting her. Later on, the neighbors discovered that the Sufi man was celibate and that he spent

4 For more details on saints and their bodies see Kugle 2007.

the entire night rebuking the evil dimension of his soul for its penchant for worldliness Ferhat (2000, 547). ʾal-Tādilī (1997, 145) also referred to a number of Moroccan male saints who trained their bodies to achieve *taqwā*. He described the Sufi Abū Muḥammad ʿAbdallāh ʾal-Malījī (12th Century) that his body became like a thin burning stick (*jismu-hu ka ʾal-sufūd ʾal-muḥtariq*) and his skin stuck to his bones. There are others who even destroy their physical properties to achieve spiritual illumination. This is true for the *majdhūb*. The divine attraction destroys his mental abilities.

Women saints, like their male counterparts, not only ignored their physical need, but also chose other ways to destroy the physical properties of their bodies. Women and men saints experienced biological crises, which empowered them to put an end to their conventional roles. These physiological crises are *jadhb* and foolishness or insanity (*junūn*), which made Sufis behave freely and without social constraints, as will be dealt with in a separate section below.

Hagiography contains examples of Sufi women and men whose strong desire for God ever impelled them to put their bodies to death, with the destruction of its life as the ultimate stage of their annihilation in the divine. Sufi women and men saw death as a way to free themselves from the body and its material desires. In the Sufi discourse, the body is sometimes considered not a means to reach God but as a burden that prevented Sufis from reaching God, and that they had to get rid of to be with divine Geoffrey (1998, 127). In life stories, many women saints prepared their graves when they felt their death was near. Nufisa, a Sufi woman, would continuously read the *Qurʾān* inside the grave she prepared for herself. They even longed for death as the ultimate desire to deliver themselves from their sinful bodies, which hindered them from meeting with God. Thus, for the sake of God's closeness, women saints inflicting harm on their bodies through praying, fasting and starving.

Crying constitutes another technique that the Sufi employs to achieve God's closeness. It emanates from an inner state that reflects the Sufi's internal feelings while addressing God, such as love, shame, fear, and even passion. During the Sufi's journey to the divine, his/her eyes do not stop shedding tears. In Islam, crying and weeping are highly respected as behavior which expresses one's *taqwā* (piety) and *khushūʿ* (submissiveness) (*Sūra ʾal-Māʾida*, 83). Many Prophets were described in the *Qurʾān* crying while asking for God's mercy and salvation, such as the Prophet ʾAbū Shuʿayb whose eyes did not stop crying until they lost the capacity for sight.

Similarly, Moroccan friends of God also expressed their desire for God by crying. Abū ʿAbdallāh Muḥammad ʾal-Barādiʿī (12th Century) feared *Allah*, and his eyes never stopped crying. Abū ʿAlī Sharishī (12th Century) was another saint who had an alternative name, which was *bakkāy*, meaning one who cries a lot. Women also used crying as an utterance to express their desire for God and for his salvation. Ibn Qunfudh (1965, 115) made reference to an anonymous pious woman who never stopped weeping such that her eyes were stricken by blindness. He added that one day the Sufi 'Abū Hassan bin Yūnus Ṣanhājī (12th Century), visited this pious woman in her cave. After she welcomed him, he started weeping. Then, he fell dead on the ground (Ibid). 'Al-Hudaykī (2006, 173) referred to ḥawwā bint Aḥmad 'al-Hudaykī (18th Century), a very pious woman saint who was always shedding tears to express her fear of God.

Men and women Sufis cry not only out of their desire for God but also out of fear for God's punishment in the afterlife. Abū Yaḥya 'abū Bakr ibn Fakhīr 'ābidī (12th Century) was described as crying and continuously slapping his cheeks (*laṭma 'al-khudūd*) as signs of his repentance for his dreadful sins and of his fear of God 'al-Tādilī (1997). While the spiritual master Hassan ibn Yusuf Ṣanhājī was delivering his lectures, he cried and made his attendees cry too. When Ibn Qunfudh saw him crying, he said to Ṣanhājī's disciples: "This man will die from crying" Ṣahrawardī (1999, 340). Although crying afflicts the body by causing Sufis to be stricken by blindness, Sufi men and women used crying as a performance to construct piety and to express publicly their strong spirituality, all for the sake of God.

The standard cultural interpretations of weeping, which portray women's crying positively and men's tears negatively, are not applicable to Sufis. In the field, I saw men venerators shedding tears while supplicating God and while kissing the graves of their favorite saints. Women's public crying is an accepted practice because it is culturally related to their gender, like other forms of excessive emotional expression, while men's crying is seen as a negative expression as it displays their weakness Buffault (1986), and is not relevant in the mystical space. The Sufi women and men discussed above found in shedding tears a remedy for their social and spiritual crises.

The Sufi, on his/her Sufi path, engages in celibacy and avoids marriage to reserve himself/herself exclusively for God. Marriage in Islam is important because it has many advantages such as the preservation of chastity, procreation, and the growth of Muslim *'umma*. But marriage is not praised worthy in Sufism. It is a worldly life that hinders the spiritual life Ibn Qunfud 1965, 115. 'Al-Tādilī (1997, 327–28) mentioned a number of male saints who preferred celibacy to marriage. He also referred to anonymous male and female saints who led celibate lives to live freely their spirituality. He also mentioned married male saints who divorced their wives and abandoned their families to live the Sufi path, such as 'Abū Muḥammad 'abd Razzāq 'al-Jazūlī and Mālik ibn Dīnār (12th Century). Many though not all, Sufi men considered women a possible source of temptation that must be avoided. Women who embodied the dominant norms and patterns, such as matrimony, were understood as a part of that worldliness that Sufi males found necessary not to take into account. The questions that arise: Did women also consider marriage an obstacle to their spirituality? Did they interpret their male partner's company as a source of worldliness?

Celibacy also characterized other women saints. In *'al-Tashawwuf,* 'al-Tādilī refers to a number of women saints who chose celibacy over marriage. Ibn Qunfudh (1965) also included in his compilation the life story of the urban woman saint Mu'mina Tilimsāniyya (14th Century). He lived near her in Fez, and observed her daily actions and expressions of piety and spirituality. He contends that she was a very pious woman. Her spirituality attracted the attentions of orthodox religious scholars such as Abū ʿAbdallāh 'al-Maqarī and Sharīf Abū 'al-Qāṣi Sharīf 'al-Tilimsānī (14th Century). Throughout her life, she rejected the presence of the Sufis and spiritual masters who came to her door seeking her friendship and love. Instead, she had chosen to remain a lonely female saint but faithful to her Lord Ibn Qunfud (1965, 86). Thus, Mu'mina Tilimsāniyya preferred to remain a solitary publicly recognized Sufi saintly figure.

From the hagiographies, Sufi women considered men to be seekers of sexuality and persons who soiled the purity of their bodies (*mudnis li-ṭahāra-ti-hā*). These Sufi women found in their celibacy a refuge for living their spirituality peacefully. This, however, did not mean that marriage constituted an obstacle for all women to achieve piety and spirituality.

There are exceptions. Some married women saints successfully developed not only their own piety but also that of their partners. This is the case with the two women saints, Fāṭima Muhadūz and ʿĀ'isha 'al-Idrīsiyya, whom I have selected and will discuss in the final section of this chapter. Ibn Qunfudh (1965) mentioned in his compilation a pious woman saint whom he met in Azmour and who guided the piety and spirituality of her husband, *shaykh* ʿAbd 'al-Wāḥid Ṣanhājī (13th Century). Her followers said to her hagiographer that, thanks to her, her husband ʿAbd 'al-Wāḥid became a spiritual master (Ibid., 131). The rural Moroccan Sufi woman, ʿĀ'isha bint Sāliḥ bin Masʿūd (19th Century) developed strong piety and sainthood that impressed her husband Muḥammad bin Masʿūd (19th Century), one of the greatest spiritual masters of the Sūs region (South Atlas). Mulkhṭār 'al-Sūsī said that her husband built her a shrine 'al-Sūsī (1960, 152). Another female worshipper in this context was doing her nightly vigils and prayers while her husband was sleeping. She rebuked him for his laziness and for his lack of worship of God ʿal-Jawzī (1985, 40). The Moroccan Sufi jurists Zarruq's mother Umm 'al-Banīn guided his piety and spirituality. These examples demonstrated that a married woman was able to live her piety in the company of her husband. Matrimonial relations enabled her to live her spirituality and to guide that of her partner and her children. Women, whether married or unmarried, succeeded in living their piety and playing the role of the spiritual master in guiding their male counterparts' spirituality and that of their family members.

I have demonstrated thus far that women, like men, lived their piety through the performance of a set of techniques. They engaged in the initiation and in the annihilation of the body through crying and starvation. They trained their feelings and bodies to reach God and to construct piety and sainthood. In this sense, the practice of Sufism and the construction of sainthood are gender neutral. Both men and women were free to follow the path of Sufism and articulate the same practices to reach God. In addition, the search for knowledge was another self-technique that both men and women employed to achieve saintly personalities, as will be discussed in the next section.

### 1.2 *Learnedness and the Quest for Knowledge*

Sufi women, like their male counterparts, marked their personalities within orthodoxy through the quest for knowledge. They engaged in fighting their illiteracy and learning different sciences. Narratives were pregnant with examples of women mystics who were interested in education. There were some who founded educational centers and built schools and universities from their own money. This was the case of Fāṭima 'al-Fihriyya (8th Century) who built in Fez 'al-Qarawiyyīn the first mosque and religious educational center in North Africa. Zaynab 'al-Nafzāwiyya (12th Century) also built many schools in Morocco and in the *mashreq* to teach women about Islam and the Islamic sciences 'al-Tazī (1992, 24). There is also the woman saint, Sa'īda 'al-Tiṭīliyya (12th Century). She studied the *Qur'ān, Hadīth* and *fiqh*. Her desire to propagate her knowledge to students and other people enhanced her to become a *nāsikha* (copier of books).

In *'al-Tashawwuf,* 'al-Tādilī gave examples of knowledgeable women saints. He contended that his friend and spiritual master Abī 'al-Mahdī (12th Century) met a woman saint in a cave in the Atlas Mountains. She trained him in the Islamic courses that he did not know. 'al-Tādilī (1997, 266). 'Al-Sūsī's mother, Ruqayya 'al-'Adūzī (19th Century) was another woman saint who always held a board on which she wrote *Qur'ān* verses to learn by heart. Wherever she went, she held her board showing people her strong desire to learn the divine text 'al-Sūsī's (1960, 39). Women were able to achieve an educational level that enabled them to be instructors of Sufism for others. They succeeded in changing themselves into knowledgeable women.

Another example is again that of Mu'mina. According to Ibn Qunfudh (1965), her quest for religious knowledge enhanced her status as a female axial saint (*quṭb 'al-'aqṭāb*). She was a disciple of Abū Madyan 'al-Ghūt (13th Century), one of the greatest spiritual masters of the Maghreb. Her axial status attracted her contemporary Sufis such as Ibn Qunfudh and Ṣāliḥi 'abū 'al-Hassan, who became her students and devotees; 'Abū 'al-Hassan, for example, wrote on her slate (*lawḥ*) and brought it to her. Ibn Qunfudh studied religion under her guidance. The Sufi scholar 'Abū 'al-Qāsim Sharīf Tilimsānī wanted to be her student and devotee to learn from her knowledge and spiritual aptitude. All of these Sufi scholars sought to be her disciples and benefactors of her knowledge and religious expertise Ibn Qunfudh (1965).

Another example of a woman who achieved the sanctity of sainthood through the acquisition of knowledge is the woman Sufi *Lalla* Maḥilla (12th Century). According to Janbūbī (2008, 172), Maḥilla dedicated her life to the quest for religious knowledge and the study of the Islamic sciences. Her strong desire for learning impelled her to reject marriage. She spent entire nights reciting the *Qur'ān* and the names of God. Her nightly and daily prayers convinced her father that she was possessed by an evil spirit. He urged her to marry as a remedy, but she rejected the marriage he arranged for her. He consulted with 'al-Qāḍī 'Ayāḍ (12th Century), one of the greatest seven spiritual masters of Marrakech, about Maḥilla's behavior. 'Al-Qāḍī 'Ayāḍ understood her desire and asked one of his students to train her in religion. Maḥilla soon achieved the status of a scholar. Her reputation spread throughout Marrakech and many people admired her expertise and status. She spent the rest of her life as a religious scholar and instructor of religion. Her shrine was erected beside 'al-Qāḍī 'Ayāḍ's and still enjoys considerable popularity. Therefore, like Mu'mina, Maḥilla created a saintly personality through the pursuit of knowledge and education.

In a non-Moroccan context, we find Fāṭima Nisabūriyya (8th Century), one of the pious, ascetic and knowledgeable women of Nisabūr. 'Al-Baṣrī sought her advice on doctrinal matters. Dhu Nūn'al-Miṣrī was also impacted by her knowledge and considered her his teacher (*'ustādīh*) 'al-Sulāmī (1993, 144). Ibn 'Arabī was a disciple of another female spiritual master called Fāṭima bint 'al-Mutanā. She was his teacher and spiritual guide. Ibn 'Arabī served her like a *murīd* serves his *shaykh*. He learned from her Sufi secrets Ibn 'Arabī (1985, vol. 2, 364–65). Women saints' relationship with their disciples was, however, different from that between the male spiritual masters and their disciples. The male *shaykh* usually exercised a cold, strict authority towards his disciples Hammoudi (1980). He was rarely observed behaving like a father who should bestow his affection and love on his children (followers). And if he employed fatherly care towards his students, it was just to impose his power and authority Abū Barīk (2010, 110). The male spiritual masters' care was cold and not as intense as that of female spiritual masters. Women saints had a religious authority, which was characterized by motherly affection and care. We already saw that Ibn ʿArabī described his spiritual master Fāṭima bint ʾal-Mutanā as his mother. Whenever she wanted to call him, she used the following words: *waladī qurrat ʿaynī* (my son, my sweetheart) Ibn ʿArabī (1988). Fāṭima as a spiritual master had a relationship with Ibn ʿArabī, which was based primarily on spiritual love more than on the authority, which is found intensively in the *shaykh*'s relationship with his *murīd* (Ibid). I can concur, however, from all examples mentioned above, that for women, like for men, knowledge and education opened the door to become saintly and knowledgeable persons.

### 1.3 *Miracles*

As I mentioned earlier, the Sufi engaged in the Sufi path until he/she reached God's closeness, which endowed him/her with divine grace, enabling him/her to perform miracles (*karamāt*), i.e., extraordinary actions that an ordinary Muslim cannot perform. From the hagiographies, women were also able to perform different kinds of miracles that advanced their saintly personalities. Healing constituted one of the important *karamāt* that Moroccan holy women performed widely. In one hagiographic narrative, Muḥammad Abdallāh ibn ʿabd ʾal-Mālik ʾal-Bayyānī (12th Century) went to visit ʾAbū Yaʿzā (12th Century), one of the greatest saints of Moroccan religious history, to cure her blindness. Abū Yaʿzā said to him: "Go to Fulāna ʾal-ʾAndalusiya and asked her to spit in your eyes" ʾal-Tādilī (1997, 237). ʾAbū Yaʿzā, who himself was a very powerful healer, thus advised the ill Sufi ʿAbd ʾal-Mālik ʾal-Bayyānī to request the holy woman Fulāna ʾal-ʾAndalusiya's divine grace to regain his sight. This means that Abū Yaʿzā believed in Fulāna ʾal-ʾAndalusiya's miracles, which were more powerful than his own. For this reason, he advised ʾal-Bayyānī to visit her and to benefit from her strong divine grace. Besides healing, there are other miracles that women performed, such as foreseeing the future, flying in the air, walking on water and others. ʾAl-Hudaykī (2006, 474–75) described Fāṭima teleporting to Arabia to do her prayers in Mecca and saving persons in difficult situations.

The Moroccan saint Muniya bint Maymūn Dukkālī, whom I have already introduced, was a woman whose miracles prevailed even after her death. One day the spiritual master Muḥammad ben Yahaya visited her tomb and said that he saw a vapor rising from her grave, and it covered the light of the sun ʾal-Tādilī (1997, 317). This light symbolized the spiritual power of a woman saint that displayed the power of her spirituality and faith. Women saints were pictured as being able to perform miracles that exceeded those of their male counterparts.

Another woman saint from Sūs who played the role of a Sufi *shaykh* was called Tin Slāmt (a Berber word meaning "the peaceful"). Tin Slāmt (12th Century) was another spiritual master with miraculous skills. She was one of the fourteen women saints of the Maṣmūda region,[5] many of whom were able to fly or be transported over long distances. In his discussion with other saintly figures on the topic of Moroccan saints who had the miraculous ability to fly, *shaykh* ʾAbū Yaʾzān ben Wibdān ʾal-ʾIlānī ʾal-Qadər (19th Century) said that in Maṣmūda region there were twenty males saints and fourteen women saints who could fly or have themselves transported (ʾal-Sūsī 1960). *Shaykh* ʾAbū Yaʿzān referred to Tin Slāmt as being among these women, which meant that they had achieved the highest spiritual level like their male counterparts. Her great saintliness enabled her to be the spiritual master of her male saint counterparts. *Shayk* Abū Bakr ʾal-Huwayrī admired her spiritual skills and status as a saint bearing the miraculous ability of flight. He served Tin Slāmt for eight years because he wanted to know how saints fly. She advised him to ask God's forgiveness and do a lot of fasting. Abū Bakr ʾal-Huwayrī was not the only saint who sought her instruction and blessing. *Shaykh* Sajmāt also admired her and came to visit her from time to time. Her devotee, Abū Bakr ʾal-Huwayrī, saw him in her tent conversing with her. *Shaykh* Sajmāt said to him that he had chosen the right *shaykh* (ʾal-Sūsī 1960). Tin Slāmt was a saintly master whose spiritual knowledge caused her to be surrounded by male and female saints and disciples. Therefore, spiritual leadership is not limited to males but also belongs to women.

## 1.4 ʾal-Jadhb

In Moroccan hagiography there are many stories of women and men who were stricken by *ʾal-jadhb*. These were called *majdhūb*s and *majnūnāt* or *majdhūbāt*. They were considered to be in this state because God attracted their minds and hearts to Himself, and they longed for Him in such a way that it caused their mental destruction.

ʾal-Kattānī presented a number of *majdhūbāt* in Fez such as Ṣafiyya Lubāda (19th Century), whom we have already met. She was called Lubāda because she

---

5 Maṣmūda is a Berber tribe and one of the largest Berber tribes in Morocco. It is composed of several sub-tribes like Berghouata and Ghomaras. Its residence is in Aghmat, the High Atlas Morocco. ʾal-Nāṣirī (1954).

fabricated *lubbād* (traditional woolen carpets used for praying). She was very pious and spent entire nights weaving carpets and remembering the divine until she was attracted to God and stricken by mental infirmity. As a *majdhūba*, she left her family and roamed the streets of the *medina* of Fez. When she went deeply into ecstasy, she took off all her clothes and started to foretell future events ʾal-Kattānī (1900, vol 2. 10).

Another *majdhūba* of Fez was Fāṭima bint Khāwa (18th Century). She was a Sufi who would sit on the threshold of a public gate in the *medina* of Fez called *bāb ʾal-maḥrūq* (the burned door). She put many multi-colored scarves on her head carrying all her stuff with her (Ibid., 309–10). Her sister ʾĀmīna, who was known by Manāna ʾal-Bastyūniya (18th Century) was an absent-minded woman saint. She frequently put on long rugs. She used speech and sign language. When she met people, she asked them a number of questions such as: Where are you coming from? And where are you going? Some people understood her words but others did not (Ibid., 192).

ʾĀmīna bint ʾal-Qāḍī (19th Century) was also a mad woman saint. According to her hagiographer ʾal-Kattānī, ʾĀmīna belonged to the prestigious Ibn ʾal-Qāḍī family of jurists and scholars from the city of Meknes. The family moved to Fez to take up official positions in the royal palace. ʾĀmina gave up her juridical family, preferring to wander the streets and perform miracles. She fell into trance, gave reports on unseen matters and rebuked people for their wrong deeds. ʾĀmīna was an admirer of ʿAlī Ṣanhājī, a *majdhūb* in Fez. She divorced her husband and took care of Ṣanhājī, proudly roaming the streets of the *medina* with him. She wandered through the market places with him. Her family once locked her in a room and restrained her with chains to prevent her from going out of the house. When she saw Ṣanhājī standing in the middle of the house saying to her: "Oh ʿĀmīna," she answered: "Yes my lord". The chains suddenly fell from her, and she left the room and walked out of the house with him while her family watched, unable to stop them. When their attempts to change her unconventional habits failed, her family decided to leave her alone (Ibid).

From a non-Moroccan context, there is the story of Maryam ʾal-Baḥriya from Baṣra (Iraq) (11th Century). She was one of the *majdhūbāt* of her time. Whenever she presented lectures on divine love, she went into ecstasy. Her spleen ruptured and she eventually died ʾal-Sulāmī (1993, 85). Another case in this context is the example of Dakkāra, a holy woman from Baghdād Iraq, whose acts and words were full of wisdom (Ibid).

This is another indication that the *majdhūbs* are not mad in the normal sense, i.e. mentally ill. Oral tradition is another source of Moroccan female *majdhūbs*. Oral stories also convey accounts of Moroccan women and men known for their mad holiness. In the field, I met a *majdhūba* sitting in the shrine of *Lalla* Maymūna in the North of Morocco. She wore tattered clothes and many strings of beads around her neck and hands. I was told that she used the string of beads to recite the names of God. When she fell into trance, she started rebuking people. She roamed the streets with her unkempt hair uncovered. My respondents said that she was stricken with an intense attraction to God at an early age. Her holy madness made her distribute all that she owned to people. She liked to be with male *majdhūbs*. One of these male mad saints whom she liked to be with was *Mūlāy* Hafīð 'al-Majdhūb. His age exceeded seventy. He had a thin, black body, and preferred to wear white *jellaba* (Moroccan traditional dress for men and women). He was married and had children, but he never stayed with his family. He was always traveling. People said that *Mūlāy* Hafīð 'al-Majdhūb was attracted to God in his early years. I saw him putting his saliva on his admirers' heads to bestow his blessing on them. He also distributed money to the poor.

Furthermore, women and men were attracted by a madness that endowed them with a sacredness that impacted their environment. Their irrational behavior bestowed sacredness upon them, which enabled them to be highly admired and greatly respected by people. Their relationship with the sacred world shed a positive light on their foolishness and madness. For this reason non-conventional behavior, such as public nudity, public rebuke, and other actions performed by saints were accepted by the local population. This ill behavior did not lead to women's punishment. Ṣafiyya Lubāda deserted her family and her private space to roam the streets of Fez. She rebuked people but no one tried to stop or blame her. Similarly, *Mūlāy* Hafīð 'al-Majdhūb exposed his madness; he left his family behind and chose to live his life freely. Thus, despite their madness, *majādhūb*'s sacredness made their unconventional behaviors highly appreciated in their communities.

The *majdhūb* here presented a new picture of Fez, the city of spirituality and orthodox religion. Fez was described in history as the city of *'ulamā'*. It is believed to be the center of orthodox religious and Islamic sciences in North Africa. It is also believed that popular religion left no traces in Fez. However, the historical presence of *majdhūbs* and *majdhūbāt* in Fez showed the opposite, namely that this urban space was not only the location of institutionalized orthodoxy but also of popular religious practitioners. The city belonged not only to the orthodox *'ulama'* but also to popular saints and mad holy people, who left their mark on its religious spaces. The *majādhīb* (plural of male *majdhūb* and female *majdhūb*) decorated Fez with their shrines, which still enjoy great veneration.

### 1.5 *Social and Political Roles*

The *majdhūb*'s and *majdhūba*'s sacredness was highly evident from their attitude to the political corruption of their times. As it is mentioned earlier, Ṣafiyya Lubāda rebuked people for their corruption. This concerned not only common people in the street, but the ruling elites as well. When she fell into trance, she would run to 'al-Qarawiyyīn mosque, stand next to its door and start shouting: "*yā 'ulamā'! yā-ẓalama* (oh religious scholars! oh the unjust!)." 'al-Kattānī (1900, vol. 2,10). According to 'al-Kattānī (1900), Ṣafiyya meant that the members of the ruling elite of that time were unjust political leaders.[6]As I will explain in the final section of this chapter ʿAzīza is another example of women saints who opposed the political elite. In addition, the woman saint Mu'mina Tilimsāniyya, whom I have already met, resisted the political elite of her time by refusing to participate in the orthodox male Sufis' meetings. She rejected invitations from Ibn Qunfudh and Abū ʿAbdallah 'al-Maqarī, one of the 14th Century great Sufi jurists of Fez. She also refused to meet some of the greatest religious scholars of Fez, such as the famous Sufi scholar Abū 'al-Qāsim Sharīf 'al-Tilimsānī. The urban woman saint Mu'mina did not submit to her contemporary political Sufi masters because of their injustice and corruption.

Similarly, 'Āmīna bint 'al-Qāḍī (19th Century), rebuked the unjust political leaders of her time. Her political role was clear in her resistance to the unjust political elite. In the market places, in the company of other *majādhīb*, she rebuked the ill political leaders of the Marinid dynasty. 'Āmīna's political role was also clear from her participation in *jihād* against the Iberians (Spanish) and against their invasion of Moroccan port cities. One day, 'al-Kattānī contended that she found herself awake in bed covered with miraculous wounds as if she had been participating in *jihād* 'al-Kattānī (1900, vol. 2, 10). She was symbolizing the injured Moroccans who participated in fighting the Iberians. She was symbolically called to arms in the male-dominated public spaces of Fez. Her wounded body showed how women displayed resistance to the Iberians. According to her hagiographer, Khadīja Tamgdushtiya (19th Century) was a leader of her tribe. She headed a war against another tribe for more than thirty years 'al-Sūsī (1960, 304). Thus, these women saints participated in the struggle for the country's independence.

Other pious women who played political roles were Zaynab 'al-Nafzāwiya (12th Century). She was a holy woman and the wife of Yūsuf 'ibn Tashāfīn, the *sulṭān* of Almoravids. She helped the *sulṭān* in ruling his country. Suḥāba 'al-Raḥmāniyya (16th Century) was the grandmother of Abd Mālik Saʿdi, a

---

6 For more details on the socio-political situation of Morocco at 18th Century see 'al-Nāṣirī 1954.

*sulṭān* of Sa'diyyīn. She was a holy woman who played the role of an ambassador 'al-Murākushī (1983, 58). Khnata bent Bakār (17th Century), the wife of the *sulṭān Mūlāy* Ismā'īl, was a Sufi woman. She also helped her husband in ruling his empire and secured her son's succession of the throne. The question that arises: what about Moroccan women saints who preferred to live their sainthood only in private spaces?

## 1.6 *Private Sainthood*[7]

I do, however, find in the literature a number of other women whose spirituality and sainthood did empower them to reach divine closeness and who remained faithful to the spiritual performances that conventional norms advocate. These women chose to live their sainthood within their private spaces and among their family members. Such is the case with the woman saint 'Ā'isha bint Shaqrūn 'al-Fakhār (19th Century) 'al-Kattānī (1990, vol. 2, 330). She was a worshipper, invoker, ascetic, charitable and self-denying woman. She is the daughter of *Shaykhh* Sīdī Muḥammad Shaqrūn 'al-Fakhār (19th Century) and the wife of the *shaykh* Sīdī Muḥammad bin 'Abdallāh (19th century). 'Al-Kattānī (1990) said of her that she loved her father and her husband. She served them like a *murīd* served his *shaykh*. When her husband called her in the night, she came to him, lit the lamp and provided him with anything he wanted. She prayed the dawn prayer with him. Her piety was so strong that her husband said of her: "She was among those women who deserved to be venerated." (Ibid).

Her daughters, Ruqayya and 'Ā'isha and her sisters, 'Āmīna, Fāṭima and Ṣafiyya, were described as pious women who were always in the company of their male Sufi relative saints, such as their grandfather and their father. In a non-Moroccan context, I already demonstrated how 'al-Sulāmī described Umm 'Aḥmad bint 'Abī 'Uthmān 'al-Hīrī (10th Century) as a mother who was very pious and faithful to the education of her son *shaykh* 'Aḥmad. He said that she confined herself to their home for more than fifty years 'al-Sulāmī (1993, 218). These women preferred to practice Sufism and to study religion with their relatives and within their private domestic spaces.

Female, domestic saints were wives, mothers, sisters, and daughters. 'Ā'isha, as referred to above, presented the ideal wife whose behaviors conformed to the conventional norms. She was an example of a wife who was devoted to the service of her husband and of a mother who took care of her daughters. These women saints could be considered private or domestic saints because they

7 Some Moroccan women saints refused to make their sainthood public, but instead lived it in secret or privately. I refer to these women saints as private saints.

followed the model of their mothers, serving their male Sufi relatives within their house. These women saints considered their homes to be a kingdom for their piety and a realm for the construction of sainthood, which they refused to make public.

Another type of private sainthood is that which is achieved through inheritance. In the field, I met an old woman healer called Mannāna. She was specialized in curing ill children for more than twenty years. According to her story, Mannāna was an orphan. When her mother died, her grandmother, a woman saint, and healer, accepted to be in charge of her. Mannāna started to serve her grandmother and to learn from her the way she cured ill children. She said that learning her grandmother's utterances and deeds is not sufficient to become a woman healer. She added that when her grandmother was on her deathbed, she ordered her to swallow her blessed saliva. Mannāna thus told me that she gained sainthood through inheritance and through serving others. This, however, did not mean that Mannāna was passive and did not construct a saintly personality. Mannāna said that her grandmother transmitted her sainthood to her. As I have discussed earlier, private and domestic women saints stood in contrast to the *majdhubāt*, who displayed an outer spirituality and lived internally and externally her piety that endowed them with public recognition.

The stories discussed earlier showed both men and women taking piety and mysticism as realms where they could achieve sainthood. Both expressed their deep devotion to God through similar means such as crying, weeping, loneliness, and renunciation of worldliness. Both chose learnedness and the pursuit of knowledge and orthodox religious education to become *faqīhāt*.

## 2 Types of Agency

What kind of agency did the self-techniques of Moroccan female saints, as inventoried and discussed in the previous section, yield? The next section discusses the various types of the agency which these women saints from the narratives, display.

### 2.1 *Ethical Self-Formation and Effects of Equality and Egalitarianism*[8]

From the previous section, the female saints were applying basically the same self-techniques as their male counterparts. Drawing from our discussion in chapter 1 of the concepts of Mahmood – following Foucault – I conceive of

8 See chapter 1.

these self-practices as the means through which these saints tried to achieve an ethical 'telos', which was piety at the level of sainthood. Their work on themselves, i.e. applying all kinds of the techniques, thus took place in the context of a project of ethical-spiritual self-formation (Interestingly Foucault used the term 'spiritual' in the context of antiquity's ethical self-practices, to indicate that not only the mind was involved, but body, heart, and soul as well). Women saints trained their bodies as well as their souls, these being the ethical substance of their ethical spiritual self-formation (see chapter 1). They did so on behalf of their worship of God, which was another characteristic of their project of ethical self-formation (see chapter 1). It is this type of agency that I found among male and female Sufi saints. It was the discourse of Sufism which enabled the women to develop their own spirituality and realize themselves as saintly personalities.

Moroccan orthodox religious spaces in the past hardly offered any opportunities and means for women to live their piety and religiosity. They marginalized women. For this reason, women sought a space where they as persons could live their religion. Sufism became a means by which they satisfied their religious needs and developed spiritual skills and abilities. The hagiographic narratives demonstrate the extent to which women forged personal religious paths, and defined their religious selves.

The female saints used similar self-techniques as their male counterparts. Their ways of life as narrated in the discourses on them, thus entail effects of equality which sometimes even spill over into effects of egalitarianism. The gender-neutral self-techniques I found often implied the breaking of conventional rules and values. The hagiographic accounts about women saints were pregnant with instances of their non-conventional behaviors. Their choice of mysticism as a strategy to practice piety and to construct saintly personalities differed in many ways from the standards that their local traditional culture imposed on them. These women entered the Sufi path to become more than their cultural socialization wanted them to be. As it is documented previously, there were some women who chose to achieve this purpose in the privately domestic sphere, through their relationship with their Sufi relatives, remaining under their instructions and supervision. Their sainthood did not have a public dimension, but they nonetheless remained challengers to the conventional construction of femininity.

Another strategy women employed in constructing saintly personalities was spiritual marriage with a saintly male figure, which consequently entailed rejecting conventional marital relations. Fāṭima ʾal-ʾAndalusiya left behind her family in *ʾal-ʾAndalus* and came to Morocco to meet her spiritual master ʾAbū

Madyān 'al-Ghawth. Likewise, *Lalla* 'Ā'isha 'al-Baḥriyya came from the *Mashreq* in search of the *shaykh*, Abū Shu'ayb (12th Century) to study Sufism with him Janbubī (2008, 93).

Another way of breaking conventions was through *jadhb*. Women and men who were attracted to God were able to give up their gender roles. The examples of male and female *majdhūb* described above such as Ṣafiyya Lubāda, 'Āmīna bint Khawā, 'Abū Rawayin, and *Mūlāy* Hāfiẓ 'al-Majdhūb showed how they left their families and rejected conventional roles so as to live freely their saintly personalities and spirituality. Mannāna's family convinced her to marry. When she gave birth to her first child, Mannāna was afflicted by *jadhb*. Eventually, she left home to roam in the *medina*.

Sufi women also explicitly destroyed the beauty of their bodies, and compelled them to non-material desires and needs. Their strong devotion to and affection for God made them disregard the beauty and health of their body parts. Their bodies became so thin and weak that they attracted piety and disapproval instead of admiration and love. This was another way of breaking with the social standards for women, particularly conventional marriages. Sufi women's deep passion for God made them refuse proposals for conventional marriages from their male counterparts. Rābi'a outspokenly refused to marry the male Sufi Hassan 'al-Baṣrī. 'Al-Tādilī (1997) also referred in his compilation to a number of Sufi women who had chosen celibacy over marriage. The celibate young anonymous woman he met in one of the caves of the Atlas Mountains is an example of a Sufi woman who succeeded in forging her own way of life. These women saints thus consciously showed their desire to live a form of piety of their own making. Intellectual forthrightness constitutes another way through which women achieved independence. In the literature, there are cases of women who had access to orthodox education. 'Āmīna Zubādiyya learned the *Qur'ān*. She spent her life writing copies of the *Qur'ān* and distributing them to people. Fāṭima of Nishapur was called *'ustādh*. This means that women proved themselves capable of acquiring an orthodox education, which was thought to be limited only to males and to have impacted only their male counterparts.

Where these women saints come forward as breaking the conventions for women of their time, behaving and developing themselves in ways similar to their male counterparts, I can conclude that their (narrated) ways of life entail effects of equality. They conveyed that women and men are equal, without using the notion as such. And when one heard Rabī'a rejecting a marriage proposal she received, by saying: "God can give me all you offer and even double it ... So farewell" Smith (1984, 11), it is hard not to conclude for effects of egalitarianism as well.

## 2.2 *Ethical Freedom Practices*

In the context of the patriarchal patterns in which women saints lived I can conclude that their ethical self-practices, [i.e. their applying of ethical self-techniques in the context of ethical self-formation], can be called freedom practices. Ethical freedom practices, as I explained in chapter 1, invent positive ethical ways of life which implicitly or explicitly oppose domination. From what we have seen above, I can conclude that Moroccan female saints invented alternative – publicly visible – ethical ways of life for women, to the dominant patterns. That is: they worked on the limits of the conventional patterns they lived in.

Many Sufi women took advantage of the flexibility of Sufism to free themselves from societal constraints. Through Sufism, they challenged the dominant orthodox religious system and cultivated an independent and personal spirituality. It is in that sense that I can speak in terms of freedom practices. The example of Rābiʿa, who devised her own mystical way, encouraged other women to create their own personal spiritual paths as well. Women's independence is evident not only in their choice to lead a mystical life but also in the definition of the type of relationship with God that they chose to establish. Sufi women such as Ṣafiyya Lubāda and ʿĀmīna ʿal-Bustyūnia loved God so intensely that they chose to roam the streets expressing publicly their sense of intimate proximity to the divine, as discussed above. The power of this feeling of proximity empowered them to reject their conventional roles (wives, mothers, and daughters) and to live a free mystical life.

Women's decision to live a personal mystical life of piety and solitude did not contradict the norms of their local environment. Cultural norms approve women's practice of mysticism. Fāṭima ʿal-ʿAndalusiyya, *Mūlāy* Hāfiẓ ʿal-Majdhūb, ʿAbū Rawayin and others proved themselves able to re-orient their religiosity and to cultivate their piety in their own way. They sought and acquired the power to reject the religious style of their local space and to refuse to be led by conventional and traditional norms and values. Thus, Sufi women had the power to forge their own spiritual life, a way of life that was an alternative to the dominant patterns for them.

Women's religious leadership is also clear in other respects. Ṣafiyya *ʾal-Majdhūba* freed herself from her family's control and faced the *ʿulamāʾ* of the ʾal-Qarawiyyīn mosque, openly criticizing their injustice and corruption. As I mentioned earlier, many people gathered around her seeking her divine blessing. Rābīʿa was an important heroine of Islamic mysticism. A former slave she became one of the founders of Sufism. She was well known for her instruction to people that God had to be loved for His own sake and not out of fear of hell Smith (1984, 98–99).

Rabīʿa again had religious authority and power. While traveling to Arabia to make pilgrimage ritual to Mecca, she was delayed so the *kaʿba* (the holy shrine in Mecca) rose up and went out to meet her. Seeing this, Rābīʿa said: "What have I to do with the house, it is the Lord of the house I am seeking". When ʾIbrāhīm ibn ʾAdam, Rābīʿa's contemporary male Sufi, traveled to Mecca to perform the ritual pilgrimage, he found the *kaʿba* was not in its place. He was told that the *kaʿba* went to meet a woman. ʾIbrāhīm ibn ʾAdam felt defeated when he saw the *kaʿba* approaching in the company of Rābīʿa (Ibid., 140). Women saints' spiritual expertise and strong faith empowered them to impose their strong saintly personalities on their contemporaries.

Women saints' power and authority were recorded in oral and written sources. Through attaining strong saintly personalities they had – and still have – an impact on people. It was this impact that inspired hagiographers to preserve their life stories. They not only developed into spiritual leaders, but into political and social leaders as well. As I explained earlier, women saints became leaders of their tribes. And in this respect, it is also noteworthy that many tribes are named after saints, such as *Lalla* ʿAzīza tribe in the Atlas, the Maymūna tribe in the Northwest, and the Taʿlat tribe in the Southwest.

Effects of equality and even egalitarianism of women saints' ways of life as spiritual and political and social leaders once more come to the fore, to such a degree that one can affirm Leila Ahmed's conclusion – based on Rābīʿa's independent and powerful way of life – that "the beliefs on which feminism rests are an endemic part of Islamic civilization (just as they are an endemic part of Western civilization before the development of the political idiom of democracy)" Ahmed (1989, 144). From my study of Moroccan women saints' construction of sainthood, I can conclude that Ahmed's conclusion is applicable in the Moroccan context as well.

In what follows, I will study the life stories of three selected women saints and once more evaluate the types of agency they performed, in line with my classification of the female saints' types of agency above.

## 3 Women Saints: ʿAzīza ʾal-Saksāwiyya (14th Century), ʿĀʾisha ʿal-ʿIdrīsiya (16th Century) and Fāṭima Muhdūz (19th Century)

In this section, I focus on the life stories of three women saints, namely ʿAzīza, ʿĀʾisha and Fāṭima. Each one of them represents different groups of female saints. ʿĀʾisha represents the female saints of the North of Morocco. She is an example of Moroccan-Arab, urban, married women saints who engaged in Sufi life and constructed a pious and saintly personality. She also represents North

Moroccan-Arab female saints whose conventional roles as wives and mothers did not confine them to the domestic sphere, but who instead actively developed a public spiritual personality. ʿAzīza represents the rural Berber women saints of the Atlas. She is an example of Berber women saints who renounced marriage, fertility and family life, and challenged traditional life. Her aim is to seek the knowledge of God. She is also a representative of Moroccan saintly women who played political roles. Finally, Faṭima represents Southwestern rural Moroccan women saints and Sufis, in particular Berber *majdhūbat* and rural married women of this region. She exemplifies women who refused to stick to their conventional roles, such as wifehood and motherhood, through becoming a *majdhūba*, leaving behind their children, husband, and family to live freely their piety and spirituality.

The selection of the three women saints is also based, as I mentioned earlier, on the detailed information their hagiographic and oral life stories encompass. In comparison with other entries of female saints, theirs are more detailed. The relative abundance of details enabled a more in-depth discussion of their lives, in particular in terms of the different self-techniques they used to transform themselves into saintly personalities.

## 3.1 *ʿAzīza ʿal-Saksāwiyya (14th Century)*

The primary hagiographic story of ʿAzīza is the one found in the hagiographic work entitled *ʾUns ʾal-Faqīr wa ʿizz ʾal-Ḥaqīr* (The Intimacy of the Sufi and the Greatness of the Denigrated) by the Sufi scholar ʿAbd ʿal-ʿAzīz ʾibn ʾal-Khaṭīb who is known by the name of Ibn Qunfudh. His hagiographic record is a compilation of saints, Sufis and holy people belonging to Morocco and other Maghrebian countries. It included only saints who were disciples of the axial saint, ʾAbū Madyān ʾal-Ghawth. ʾIbn Qunfudh collected his entries from other hagiographic records such as *ʾal-Tashawwuf* and from narrators. He also recorded life stories of the saints he met and lived with. One of these saints was ʿAzīza whom he met in the Atlas.

Ibn Qunfudh (1965, 86) contended that he heard of her in ʾal-Qarawiyyīn University in Fez. He then recorded that he traveled to the Saksāwa tribes in the Atlas and met ʿAzīza there:

> I heard of her in ʾal-Qarawiyyīn mosque....
>
> I saw Lalla ʿAzīza on a mountain called Qihra (free). She blessed me with her divine grace. I stood with her, and I studied with her. Then, she left me to meet her tribes' men and women. I saw her putting a veil on her head before she got out to meet her people. She delivered a lecture to men and women who were always around her. She was eloquent in speech

FIGURE 3 Lalla ʿAzīza ʾal-Saksāwiyya's shrine in Imintanout
PHOTOGRAPH BY AZIZA OUGUIR

> and in preaching. Abū ʿĀmir ʾal-ḥanṭaṭī, the governor of Marrakech who headed an army of six thousand soldiers, had arrived planning to conquer the Saksāwa tribes. He was advancing with his armies, but Lalla ʿAzīza stopped him and engaged with him in a long conversation. When he finished his conversation with her, he came to me and said: Oh! faqīh! What a surprise? This woman is a wonderful person. She answers me before I ask her anything. She knows in advance what I have in my mind. She knows my ideas and my thinking. I have never seen a person like her. I find myself unable to reject her demands. Indeed, her arguments are so pertinent and convincing that I decide to leave the Saksāwa tribe in peace.[9]

Her living descendants whom I encountered in her shrine were still chanting her story to her pilgrims. They reported the following oral story:

> Lalla ʿAzīza was born in the Saksāwa tribe and grew up in a Sufi family. From childhood, ʿAzīza learned God's words, commands, and rules. She

9 The translated hagiographic and oral stories on women saints mentioned in this book are my own translation.

> worked as a shepherd for her family. She used to guide her goats to the mountains where she prayed to God and lived peacefully in retreat. The Sufi girl was continuously scolded by her father for leading the goats to mountain slopes where there was no grass. One day her father followed her to the mountains and found her praying to God. He shouted at her because she did not guide the goats to the banks of the river where the grass was in abundant. "Father," *Lalla* ʿAzīza said, "Look at what your goats are eating." The father turned to the goats and found their mouths full of herbs. From that time on her father and the whole tribe believed that *Lalla* ʿAzīza was a "*tagurramt*," (a Berber word meaning a woman saint) sent to them by God.

The narrator stopped for a while, then carried on reciting the story:

> It is said that one day, Lalla ʿAzīza was alone with her goats in the mountains and a young man who wanted to marry her followed her. The young man wanted to kidnap her, but she suddenly disappeared. The sulṭān of Marrakech also heard about her sainthood and invited her to live in his castle. There, Lalla ʿAzīza continued to study religion. People said that she even traveled to Tlemcen to study in ʾAbū Madyan's zāwiya, and when she came back to Marrakech, her sainthood had grown and was propagated. The sulṭān proposed marriage to her, but she refused his proposal, so the sulṭān threw her in jail and ordered her jail guardian to offer her a poisonous food, but she refused to eat. Since Lalla ʿAzīza could not stand the hunger, she decided to eat the poisonous food offered to her. She said: "In the name of God I will eat it, and for the sake of God I will die." It is also said that after her death, the sulṭān ordered his servants to build her two shrines, one in her native tribal territory and the other in Marrakech.[10]

Both the oral and written stories thus provide some details about ʿAzīza's mystical development and experiences.

### 3.1.1 Ethical Self-Techniques

As the narratives show, ʿAzīza undertook different techniques to become a saint. She was forward as overwhelmed by a desire for spirituality since an early age. She was presented as a Sufi girl who lived in a Sufi family, but who desired to be in retreat. This is clear from her insistence to be alone with her cattle in the mountainous areas, where she enjoyed God and His universe. Her

10 Interviews, venerators, Imintanout, 2010.

strong desire for spirituality and piety was also clear in her resistance to her father's orders. She followed her desire for retreat, and did not respond to her father's commands but remained alone in the mountains. ʿAzīza came forward as striving to develop her own piety, taking the mountain as space where she could live in the company of the divine. Another aspect of ʿAzīza's piety was her ability to perform miracles. From the stories, ʿAzīza had developed miraculous skills since her childhood. Her devotees narrated that she made her goats healthy and their mouth full of herbs and grace. Her father and his tribesmen were surprised because they wondered how the goats became so healthy though they were always in mountainous spaces where there was no grass. They wondered how the Sufi girl succeeded to have this miracle.

Miracles related to shepherding and protecting the cattle indicate the importance of this woman saint since in rural society cattle constituted the most important source of economic income. For rural people, women saints' miracles were very powerful since they met the hardships of their rural lives. ʿAzīza's miracles allowed her to successfully fulfill the role of shepherd and to support her family economically. Her extraordinary skills and miracles made the whole tribe consider her a saint who deserved to be worshipped.

The stories above also described ʿAzīza's rejection of conventional marriages, thus using celibacy as a self-technique to develop her sainthood. She was presented in the stories as a beautiful Sufi girl, the *sulṭān* and many tribesmen proposed to her, but she refused them all. She was able to live the life of a married woman, but she did not want to. She had chosen celibacy to live exclusively for God.

Another equally important self-technique was ʿAzīza's pursuit of knowledge to achieve sainthood. Her overwhelming desire for religion impelled her to leave her family home, which was located in rural Saksāwa tribal territories, so as to move to Marrakech to study religion. She even traveled to Tlemcen in Algeria to study Sufism in Abū Madyān's *zāwiya*. This shows that ʿAzīza refused to remain an ordinary woman. Instead, she chose to satisfy an overwhelming desire to learn about Islam and Sufism. Her quest for knowledge and education empowered her to become a preacher, enabling her to maintain followers and disciples who benefitted from her knowledge. Her hagiographer, Ibn Qunfudh, acknowledged her scholarly status, having already heard of her in ʾal-Qarawiyyīn University. Her religious knowledge endowed her great fame and a positive reputation that seemingly reached orthodox religious centers like ʾal-Qarawiyyīn. He also confirmed his respect for her status as a knowledgeable and capable teacher, by personally studying with her and seeking to learn from her. His recognition of her as being superior to him in intellectual and spiritual respect enhanced ʿAzīza's reputation as a scholar and saint, and contributed to making her sainthood and religious expertise is more widely known and publicly visible and accessible. By means of all the self-techniques mentioned earlier, ʿAzīza undertook a lifelong project of ethical self-formation. In what follows I will see that her ethical self-formation did exceed the limits of the conventional norms and patterns that were imposed on her and that she succeeded not only in transgressing them but in developing alternative ways of life as a woman in society.

### 3.1.2 Ethical Self-Formation as a Freedom Practice

I have concluded that through their ethical self-practices, Moroccan female saints developed alternative ways of life for women, in working on the limits of dominant, oppressive patterns and practices. The life stories of the three saints I selected showed exactly this.

First of all, ʿAzīza's life stories stressed women's abilities to achieve a Sufi self-formation that resisted the dominant order. Like other women saints, ʿAzīza refused women's submissiveness to the dominant conventional norms. Her stories above showed how she created a pious personality and how she believed in her abilities to achieve a personal pious life. The stories showed that her desire to become a Sufi personality increased since her childhood and developed in the course of her life. Since her childhood, ʿAzīza wanted to improve her spiritual status, and she was determined to live the different stages of Sufism that her local norms approved and be involved in training herself to reach an advanced stage of piety. She engaged in retreat, *dhikr* and the recitation of the *Qurʾān* as well as charitable actions.[11]

Her endeavors to live the hard Sufi path are visible in her success in reaching proximity and God's union. Her proximity and sainthood did not prevent her from serving people. Rather, her saintly personality empowered her to be close to her people and serve their needs. ʿAzīza's new personality made her very aware of her people's problems, and she decided to use her knowledge, piety, and service to meet her people's needs. Her stories portrayed her as a knowledgeable woman who delivered her knowledge and education to her tribesmen and as a political leader who sought people's help, sustenance, justice and peace for her community.

ʿAzīza's saintly status and image, which resulted from the way she reached sainthood, empowered her to have and exercise public power. Her saintly personality permitted her to have an impact on the common people as on the elite. These people had great respect and admiration for her. This is clear from the admiration and respect evident in Ibn Qunfudh's descriptions of her being

11 See the story above.

surrounded by the men and women of her tribe. ʿAzīza succeeded in achieving a form of popular sainthood that extended into the countryside and urban centers. The power of her sainthood enabled her to play the role of the political leader of her tribe. Her method for dealing with her people when they encountered crises and problems demonstrated her skills in the political arena. She made her tribe a center of refuge, security, and reconciliation. She took on the role of the arbiter saint who not only defended tribal territory against the *maghzen*, but also among tribes in a context where controversial relations over water, lands, and animals prevailed.

Although women were denied political rights and access to decision-making procedures and positions, ʿAzīza constituted an exception. She proved to the dominant society her abilities to be a political leader, which was particularly notable in a rural context, where women's rights and living conditions were significantly disregarded in comparison to those of women in the urban centers. She was the exact opposite of those women saints who confined themselves to caves and private spaces and of those male saints who in vain tried to attain public power. ʿAzīza achieved a mode of orthodox sainthood that empowered her to have access to leadership and authority.

To understand ʿAzīza's political empowerment, I need to place her story in its historical context, i.e., from the end of the 13th Century until the end of the 14th Century. ʿAzīza lived during the last years of the Marinid dynasty. In this era, the Saksāwa tribes were like most other Berber tribes in dissidence (*sība*), meaning opposing the official authority. Confrontations between dissident tribes and the central authority were increasing. The fall and the decay of Marinid central authority in Marrakech urged people to seek refuge in dissident tribes. The latter became a space of refuge for the poor, homeless and refugees. People who fled from the *makhzen* turned not only to dissident tribes but also to *zāwiya* for security. The Iberians had also started to conquer the coastal regions and port cities. Under these conditions, the Waṭāsid dynasty had defeated the Marinid's weak political system and conquered Fez ʾal-Nāṣirī (1954).

From her hagiographic record, ʿAzīza was engaged in *jihād* against the political leaders, not against the Iberians but against the central authority and against its plan to place the Saksāwa tribes[12] under its control. As a leader of her tribe, ʿAzīza challenged ʾal-ḥanṭāṭi, the governor of Marrakech, and his plan to conquer the Saksāwa tribe. She defended the autonomy of her tribe. She acted on behalf of her tribesmen and tribeswomen to eliminate the threat to their

12 Saksāwa tribes remained for two centuries in dissidence. See ʾal-Naṣirī 1954.

stability and autonomy. With her rhetorical speech, she inhibited ʾal-ḥanṭāṭi's power and its political intentions. Her miraculous religious rhetoric impelled this man of great authority to submit to her demands, change his plans and leave the Saksāwa tribes in peace. Although Ibn Qunfudh did not transmit exactly what ʿAzīza said to ʾal-ḥanṭāṭi, it is possible to assume that she called for respecting God's instructions and the values of love, peace, respect, and mutual assistance among Muslims. ʿAziza here instructed the governor that respect for life was essential. She likely performed the role of a preacher who spoke out against violence, war, and destruction. ʿAzīza's success in influencing the powerful elite with her strong spiritual image and religious speech, and convincing them to withdraw from their destructive plans, emanated from the saintly power that she had developed and that empowered her to defeat peacefully her enemies.

Another instance where ʿAzīza's political power was displayed was in her resistance to the *sulṭān*'s injustice. The story above shows that the *sulṭān* was impressed by ʿAzīza's sainthood and therefore invited her to his palace. But the growth of her sainthood and its popularity made the *sulṭān* fear her. The *sulṭān* put her in jail. This sheds light on the traditional and controversial relations between the political corpus and religious people, which were current in 14th Century Morocco. It also revealed the oppositional relations between, on the one hand, the Sufis and saints, whose power emanated from their divine grace and impelled people in pre-colonial Morocco to respect them, and, on the other hand, the political rulers who had begun to lose their legitimacy. The *sulṭān* failed to realize that ʿAzīza's popularity was due to her developed saintly personality that appealed for justice, love, peace, and non-violence. Her resistance to the *sulṭān* showed that a rural Berber woman from the mountains could counteract the power of the political system. She indirectly instructed the *sulṭān* and taught him moral lessons, such as the way to gain God's love and people's admiration and support. The *sulṭān*'s failure to follow ʿAzīza's example resulted in his use of violence against her, which entailed her imprisonment and death.

ʿAzīza's resistance to the *sulṭān* is exemplified in her choice to die rather than to submit to his wishes and desires. The *sulṭān* tried to make her eat poisonous food. She first resisted him by refusing to eat the poisonous food, but she later resisted him by choosing death rather than living a life of humiliation, injustice, and oppression and by imposing on the *sulṭān* the way he should bury her sacred body. The *sulṭān*'s decision to build her two shrines one in Marrakech and the other in her tribe, demonstrated the power of her saintly personality, which retained its great power even after her death. Having two shrines dedicated to her shows the power of the sainthood ʿAzīza developed which remained an eternal force among not only the elite but the common people as well.

ʿAzīza's ethical spiritual self-formation thus involved that she changed herself religiously, socially and politically. Her religious knowledge empowered her to access the political sphere. From her hagiographic and oral life stories, ʿAzīza was selected by her dissident tribesmen as the leader of the Saksāwa tribes so as to settle her people's conflicts and attend to their needs. She proved to the public that women were able to reach political leadership that women in modern Morocco are denied. ʿAzīza achieved political personality that impressed her male followers who showed her respect and submission. Her hagiographer, Ibn Qunfudh, witnessed how she managed to successfully preserve her tribes' freedom against the Marinid government that sought to put the Saksāwa tribes under its control.

Her ethical self-formation entails not only her remarkable self-transformation into a political and social leader but also her development as a religious scholar. ʿAzīza belonged to a Sufi lineage. The latter marked the history of her region Saksāwa by knowledge and the status of scholars (*ʿulamāʾ*). She lived in an orthodox religious space that was dominated by men and ignored women. Through Sufism, she, as a woman, succeeded to follow the path of knowledge and achieving an orthodox religious education that used to be assigned only to males. ʿAzīza's example is but one among others of highly educated women in Marinid Morocco who had chosen education as a tool to change themselves. ʿAzīza was influenced by her scholarly religious environment and engaged in the search for knowledge. As her story shows, she wanted to change herself, following the model of Sufis traveling from one space to another to search education and religion. She achieved the status of *ʿālima* through her continual traveling to Marrakech and searching *ʿilm* (science) from highly scholarly *ʿulamāʾ* such as Abū Madyān ʾal-Ghawth and others. She represented the *Sunnī* Sufism in Morocco which stressed the embrace of *sharīʿa* and *ʾal-taṣawwuf*. She combined sciences and Sufism in a manner Zarrūq stressed as crucial for the formation of a Sufi personality. ʿAzīza was able to develop her own spiritual path. Sufism enabled her to develop a style of spirituality that, working on the limits of the dominant patriarchal patterns, culminated in an alternative way of life for a woman. In other words, I can conclude that she was able to develop ethical self-formation in terms of an ethical freedom practice.

From these descriptions of the self-techniques that ʿAzīza followed to achieve sainthood, she was not different from male counterparts, such as her master 'Abū Madyān 'al-Ghawth (12th Century).[13] His strong desire for religious knowledge likewise impelled him to leave his family and go to Marrakech and later to Fez. From the brief description of 'Abū Madyān's life story, I learned that 'Azīza and 'Abū Madyān 'al-Ghawth underwent similar experiences. Both were employed as servants and shepherds by their families, both experienced an overwhelming desire for religious knowledge, which suddenly arose inside them, and both left their families to study and teach about Islam and Sufism. Another point of commonality shared by Abū Madyān 'al-Ghawth and 'Azīza was that they both relinquished their gender when they entered the Sufi path. Their life stories portrayed them as having given up the traditional male and female social roles. In order to devote themselves to the contemplation of God, 'Azīza refused to marry and become a housewife and mother, and 'Abū Madyan 'al-Ghawth avoided the conventional roles of husband and father. Both of them also founded *zāwiya* to train *murīds*, feed the poor, shelter the homeless and rebuke the unjust. Thus, 'Azīza was equally experiencing and constructing sainthood as men in her time.

## 3.2 *'Ā'isha 'al-'Idrīsiya (16th Century)*

One century after the death of 'Azīza, another interesting woman saint appeared, as is recorded by her son, the hagiographer Ibn 'Askar 'al-Shafshāwunī, one of the greatest Sufi scholars of the 16th Century. He wrote a compilation of biographies of Moroccan saints and Sufis of the North of Morocco, entitled *Dawḥat 'al-Nāshir*. Based on oral and written sources, his hagiography includes entries only on the male saints he encountered, lived with or heard about. In *Dawḥat 'al-Nāshir*, Ibn 'Askar (2003, 30–33), however, also writes on his mother 'Ā'isha:

> Among their numbers is the female saint my mother 'Ā'isha bint Aḥmad bin 'Abd Allāh bin Muḥammad bin 'Umar bin 'Abd Allāh bin Ḥassan bin 'Alī bin 'Abī ṭālib. She was a ṣaliḥa of sharifian descent. She was always consistent in nightly prayer and dhikr. In her zāwiya in Shafshāwun, she preached to people and recited the Qur'ān to them. She fed the poor and sheltered the homeless. She learned the Sufi path from the great spiritual

13 According to 'al-Tādilī 1997, Abū Madyān 'al-Ghawth was an important contributor to the development of Sufism in the Maghreb. He was an axial saint, and his doctrine of Sufism spread across North Africa. He was born in Ceuta (Spain). He was an orphan and his cruel brothers forced him to serve as a shepherd for their cattle. He founded a *zāwiya* in East Algeria.

masters such as ʾAbū ʾal-Baqāʾ ʾal-Ghazwānī, Sīdī Muḥammad ʾal-Habṭī, ʾabū ʾal-Hassan ʾal-Hāj ʾal-Ghazwānī, and others. Shaykh ʾal-Ghazwānī said to me that he used to put his hands on *Lalla* ʿĀʾisha's head, when she was still a child and said: "This young girl will have great importance (*shaʾn ʿaẓīm*)." *Lalla* ʿĀʾisha also cured ill people. She put her saliva on the pained part of the patient's body, and it soon became healed.

She was a woman with good ethics and baraka. Her intercession was much desired by people. Many people asked her to interfere on behalf of them to God to achieve their needs. They also asked her to secure them. Through her, God guided people to the right path. My father told me that when he and his friend were kept by the enemies in Tangier and put in a jail under the ground, they lost hope to ever be free again. They spent ten days in the jail. My father suddenly said that he heard the voices of my mother and of her friend, ʾUmm Raysūnī, saying to him: "never mind, God will soon release your imprisonment." After a while, my father said, the jail keeper came to them and opened the door of the jail and ordered them to leave. The commander of the jail asked them to return to their country because they were free. When my father returned home, he told his story to my mother. She answered him: "I met shaykh Abū Muḥammad ʾal-Ghazwānī in a dream and told him about your situation, and he said to me: 'go with ʾUmm Raysūnī, to your husband and get him out.' I got up and I called him from my place of prayer and God answered my praying."

I had a misunderstanding with Muḥammad bin Rashīd, the governor of the North of Morocco. The sulṭān ʾal-Ghālib bi Allāh ʾabū Muḥammad Shafshāwunī appointed me as a jurist and preacher in Qaṣr Katāma. My mother *Lalla* ʿĀʾisha refused to move with me to Qaṣr Katāma, and she decided to remain in her own zāwiya in Shafshāwun. From time to time, I travel to Shafshāwun to visit my mother. Since I was busy, I sent just my servant at my place to visit her and meet her needs. Ibn Rashīd was envious and thought the messenger I sent to *Lalla* ʿĀʾisha was a spy. So, he went to Lalla ʿĀʾisha and said to her: "Either you cut your relations with your son or you follow him to Qaṣr Katāma." *Lalla* ʿĀʾisha answered: "God does not allow the breaking of relations among relatives. So, I am going to leave Shafshāwun once and for all." ʾIbn Rashīd regretted his wrong deed, and he asked her pardon and to remain in her zāwiya. But *Lalla* ʿĀʾisha refused. ʾIbn Rashīd said: "We have caused ourselves a serious offense. We hope for God's forgiveness". When the sulṭān ʾal-Ghālib bi Allāh heard about Ibn Rashīd's wrong deeds towards *Lalla* ʿĀʾisha and other people, he ordered his army to put him in jail. ʾIbn Rashīd fled to the Middle East, where he was killed and ripped into pieces.

In spite of her hagiographic story and her name and reputation, ʿĀʾisha's life story is forgotten in most regions of Morocco. However, she still enjoys great fame in Qaṣr l-Kabīr and Shafshāwun cities. She had an alternative name, which is *ʾal-ʿĀliya* meaning "the highest". During my fieldwork, I asked her devotees about her alternative name. According to the *ʾimām* of the mosque nearby, this woman saint was called *ʾal-ʿĀliya* because "*she was ʿāliya fi dīn,*" meaning she had a high level of piety and religion. While I was leaving the mosque where her shrine is located, I heard a child screaming. I rushed to the door, and I found a forty year old woman holding a sick child whose age did not exceed three years. The woman ran to the closed door of ʾal-ʿĀlya's sanctuary, dropped on her knees and put her sick child against the wall of the shrine. Both the mother and the child were weeping, supplicating God and the holy ʿĀʾisha to save the child's life. All the female visitors did this to find favor with ʿĀʾisha and secure her assistance. Later on, I understood that ʿĀʾisha was a woman healer. Ghita a sixty years old woman and a seller of clothes in one of the shops attached to the mosque, says: "*Lalla* ʿĀʾisha is a *ṣāliḥa* and a woman healer. This is what I know about her." Most of the people I interviewed reported that they knew nothing about this woman saint's life except that she was a pious woman healer.

### 3.2.1 Ethical Self-Techniques

The story of ʿĀʾisha informs me of the way she constructed a pious personality. ʿĀʾisha's sharifian origin cultivated the seeds of sainthood in her, enabling her to become pious and spiritual. Her sharifian origin made her and her family part of the elite who were highly respected in the hierarchal society they lived in. Her piety emanated from her childhood. Her father is *shaykh* ʿujāl ʾal-Ghazwānī, and he predicted her future sainthood during her early childhood. He read in her eyes her ability to construct sainthood, which she developed during the course of her life as her story shows. Her piety, as described in the story above, included the self-techniques of continuous performing of nightly prayers, *dhikr* and reading the *Qurʾān*. Furthermore, she made her *zāwiya* a space for leading a pious existence with other women, as well as a center for offering social services to the needy. Her charitable acts such as feeding the poor, helping the needy, healing the sick, and curing the injured also marked her sainthood.

ʿĀʾisha was surrounded in her *zāwiya* by people who sought her blessing and advice. ʾal-Ghazwānī visited her to glean some of her *baraka*, and advised his disciples to visit her to benefit from her *baraka* too. Her sainthood impressed orthodox *shaykh* such as ʿUjāl ʾal-Ghazwānī's son, *shaykh* Muḥammad ʾal-Ghazwānī. Her piety empowered her to successfully carry out the role of wife and mother, faithfully serving her husband and family. She brought up her son and supervised his education until he became one of the important official orthodox jurists of Morocco during the Saʿdiyyīn dynasty. She proved herself to be a dedicated servant of her family and devotees in her *zāwiya*, successfully reconciling private and public responsibilities. This is evident from her desire to remain in her *zāwiya* and not to move to Qaṣr l-Kabīr to live a prestigious life with her son. Her devotion to God and to the service of the people was so strong that she decided to remain a servant of the devotees in her *zāwiya*.[14]

Another aspect of ʿĀ'isha's sainthood was her political role as an opponent of Ibn Rashīd's unjust political system, as I explained before. ʿĀ'isha lived in the 16th Century during the reign of Saʿdiyyīn dynasty. The country was under the threat of Iberian colonial rule, which had begun to wield power on the coast. Its port cities, which were invaded by the Christian missionaries, became the site of confrontations between the central authority and dissident Berber tribes. Under these conditions, Moroccans turned to marabouts and holy persons for refuge and help 'al-Nāṣirī (1954).

Furthermore, ʿĀ'isha served as a *mujāhida*, according to her hagiographer. She did not participate in battle, but took part in the *jihād* by treating and healing the injured. She would put her blessed saliva on the injured body parts of the *mujāhidīn* and their wounds would soon heal. She also cured the ill and rescued prisoners who had been captured by the Iberians.

ʿĀ'isha's political role also took the form of resistance to the political elite, which was headed by 'Ibn Rashīd. This was clear in her reaction to *'al-ʿĀliya* Ibn Rashīd, the governor of the North of Morocco. Here ʿĀ'isha had a strong attachment to her *zāwiya* and to her people. She refused to live with her son because she wanted to be close to her followers and to serve the *mujāhidīn*.[15] She sacrificed her son's company for the welfare of her *zāwiya* and people. As a consequence, she faced the governor with great courage. She taught him an ethical lesson that stressed the importance of the respect of social bonds, norm, and *sharīʿa* instructions. The power of her threat was clear when 'Ibn Rashīd felt coerced to regret his wrong deeds towards her and her son and went to her *zāwiya* asking her pardon. From the story above, Ibn Rashīd nevertheless died. His death could be caused by ʿĀ'isha's *baraka* which she bestowed on him in a negative way.

ʿĀ'isha's stories showed how ʿĀ'isha undertook a lifelong ethical self-formation. This process was clear in her strong desire to become pious and

14 See the story above.

15 *Mujāhidīn* are people who participate in *jihād* against the colonizer.

in the tools she employed to achieve a pious self. She benefited from her Sufi family, which helped her to become spiritual. But the story described her continuously practicing self-techniques such as retreat, *dhikr*, recitation of the *Qur'ān* fasting and praying rituals to develop her faith in God. Here ʿĀ'isha engaged in the Sufi path to improve her ordinary religious self, and she reached an advanced level of piety that empowered her to play religious and socio-political roles.

### 3.2.2 Ethical Self-Formation as a Freedom Practice

ʿĀ'isha stands for literate mothers who played important social roles. She represented the mothers who educated themselves to fight their illiteracy. Her strong desire to learn about religion was clear in her continuous attendance of her fathers' Sufi friends' lectures and in her interest in listening to their sermons. Like ʿAzīza, ʿĀ'isha took education as a tool to change her ordinary personality. ʿĀ'isha represented the educated mother who could give her son, Ibn ʿAskar, an important education. She highlighted the importance of literate mothers who gave birth to educated children. She most likely transmitted to him her knowledge and what she learned. This probably helped him to become an important scholar of his time. In her *zāwiya*, she preached to men and women about religion. She did not want mothers to remain illiterate. Rather, she wanted them to be literate mothers able to read and write. ʿĀ'isha is the symbol of educated women whose literacy and knowledge are important for themselves as well as for their families and the whole society. ʿĀ'isha changed herself and wanted people to change themselves as well.

## 3.3 *Fāṭima Muhdūz (19th Century)*

The hagiographer of Fāṭima Muhdūz is 'al-Sūsī who wrote a compilation of Moroccan rural saints of the Sūs region, Southwestern Morocco, entitled *'Afwāh 'al-Rijal*. He gathered their life stories from oral and written sources, such as 'al-Hudaykī (2006) and others. The compilation is composed of male and female saints' entries. One of the Susī women saints mentioned in his compilation is Fāṭima. 'Al-Sūsī (1963, 56–59) contends:

> Fāṭima was a rural Sufi woman from Tiznīt. She heard the spiritual master Sīdī Saʿīd Sūsī 'al-Maʿādrī discussing the actions an individual had to undertake to become a saint one day during his visit to her husband. "Good intention (*niyya ḥasana*), faithfulness, confidence and self-denial", Sīdī Saʿīd sʿīd 'al-Maʿādrī said, "are the conditions of sainthood." Fāṭima Muhdūz heard him explaining these conditions to her husband and said:

> "I decide to become a saint (…) if my husband fails to be a saint, I will succeed to be so." She said again: "I get up from my place (…) I know I am still menstruating, but I forget about the husband, children, and the world."
>
> The following day, Fāṭima confined herself within a room for a number of days. She refused to talk, eat or even feed the child she had just given birth to. Her husband was worried about her and about the child who needed his mother's breast milk. He brought her many *fuqahāʾ* to cure her, but her illness appeared to be incurable. To save the child, the father brought him a *murḍiʿa* (a wet nurse). But Fāṭima remained in this condition until ʾal-Maʿādrī visited her husband again. The latter told him about Fāṭima's situation, and ʿal-Maʿādrī entered her room to examine her. After many months of silence, she started to talk to him about her strong desire to become a saint. After he had left her room, he advised her husband to leave her on her own and left the house.

Fāṭima's venerators still preserve her life story. Most of the venerators report what follows:

> Our female saint Fāṭima is our '*tagurramt*'.[16] She was a pious and holy woman. She was also a shepherd and her goats were always in a healthy state even in time of drought. She lost her parents in the early years of her life. When her piety and sanctity were spread among tribes, people respected her. The great male saints of Sūs such as Sīdī Aḥmad Oumoussa, Sīdī bin Yaʿqūb, Sīdī Sīd, and Mūlāy bin Ibrāhīm came to visit *Lalla* Fāṭima in her house. She also visited them and other saints in Ilīgh *zāwiya* to do *dhikr* and give her *baraka* to people.[17]

### 3.3.1 Ethical Self-Techniques

Fāṭima undertook different techniques to become a saint. Her story described above gives us an insight into the way Fāṭima constructed her saintly personality in a rural environment that was purely patriarchal. As it is mentioned earlier, she was directly interested in the conditions of sainthood that *shaykh* ʾal-Maʿādrī explained to her husband. She was at that moment an ordinary housewife and mother who was faithful to her conventional responsibilities toward her home, husband, and family. When she eavesdropped on her husband's conversation with his guest, her husband to whom the discourse on

16 *Tagurramt* is a Berber word, meaning a woman who has great importance and high status.

17 Interviews, venerators, Shtouka ʾait Baha, 2010.

the construction of sainthood was addressed did not take the *shaykh*'s speech into consideration. The *shaykh*'s discourse was formulated in gender-neutral terms he did not exclusively or explicitly address males. Fāṭima was listening to his discourse and took it upon her. At the outset of her Sufi path, Fāṭima, as the story above shows, experienced psychological turmoil and anxiety. The visit of *shaykh* 'al-Maʿādrī to her home and her overhearing his discourse about the construction of sainthood coincided with her menstrual period. It was the blood that prevented her from purifying herself and performing her religious rituals. She, therefore, found herself in a situation of humiliation from which she could deliver herself only through the performance of *dhikr*. Since menstruation kept her from performing prayer and fasting rituals, she recited God's names until she saw the light. Peace and tranquility came over her, and her body stopped bleeding. Thus, she entered and began to experience the Sufi path.

One of the important features of her new spiritual life and its impact was the change of her domestic and conventional roles. She stopped being an ordinary woman who took care of her husband, children, and home. Instead, she became a transformed woman who insisted on the fulfillment of her spiritual desire. The spiritual illumination that she began to experience distanced her from her family and the child she had just given birth to. Fāṭima had reached an advanced stage of spirituality and involvement with God, which requires renouncing worldliness and conventional roles. Fāṭima's new spirituality was interpreted by her family in terms of *junūn* (madness) and not in terms of spiritual illumination.

Her inner spirituality was understood only by Sufis. It is a hidden and lonely spirituality that mystics experience. It required the expertise of a Sufi *shaykh* who easily understood that Fāṭima was on the path to the divine and had begun to experience spiritual illumination. He was the source of her confidence, and she finally accepted to talk to him about her crises. The *shaykh* was the one who detected her distress, which could be cured only by the fulfillment of her spiritual desire (see the story above).

Fāṭima's illness and physical hardships, which were the first states that the Sufi body experienced, have meanings. Physical crises such as illnesses showed the transition of the body from one state to another. Fāṭima left behind her ordinary life, and in her process of self-transformation and ethical self-formation, she experienced a transitional state at the physical and psychological level. Her ill body enabled her to live the transitional life a Sufi experiences between the material and the spiritual worlds. It empowered her to contact the spiritual world. Weakness and illnesses enable the body to have a special position, in as far as visitation, consultation, and healing rituals are undertaken. Fāṭima experienced these situations, which demonstrated that her illness was psychological, not physical.

Fāṭima's life story encompasses all the aspects that relate to women's mysticism and their conscious construction of sainthood. The most important aspects of her mysticism included her success in achieving spiritual illumination and sainthood and in fulfilling the instruction of sainthood that her husband failed to undertake. She proved herself able to create a saintly personality that impacted not only her familial environment but also her venerators who continue to offer her appreciation and respect.

### 3.3.2 Ethical Self-Formation as a Freedom Practice

Fāṭima Muhdūz's story describes a process of ethical self-formation and self-transformation that challenges the passive role of women. Though she was an ordinary woman faithful to her conventional roles, she refused to remain passive. She wanted to achieve a new self-formation by her engagement with Sufism where men and women were culturally allowed to develop new religious personalities. Her self-transformation into a Sufi personality involved practices on the limits of the conventional patterns she lived in. As a Muslim woman, she wanted to develop her faith and become a strong pious woman. Her desire for piety empowered her to revolt against gendered rules, confining herself in retreat and remembering God until she reached the spiritual light. Her male counterparts in the Sūs region were impressed by her religious personhood and religious leadership, and they gave her a space in their memories.

The selected women saints, ʿAzīza, ʿĀʾisha and Fāṭima, succeeded in creating an ethical way of life through the various techniques that the discourse of Sufism as part of the local culture offered them. These women who belonged to different Moroccan historical eras undertook techniques such as *jadhb* and the quest for knowledge so as to become ethical spiritual subjects. ʿAzīza, ʿĀʾisha and Fāṭima lived in spaces that were even more traditional than modern Moroccan society. In spite of this, these women succeeded to change themselves and to achieve ethical personalities that impacted their communities. Such change of the self and its positive impacts on the local community were culturally approved.

Their self-techniques helped these women not only to be close to God but also to make their closeness to God public and at the service of His people. Women saints were expressions of the "Muḥammadan paradigm" Cornell 1998, 233, which takes the Prophet as a model, encompassing the spiritual, social and political spheres. They were active persons who achieved great integration in the socio-political spaces of their times. They created ethical personalities, which played a role not only in religion but also in socio-political contexts. Women's inner spirituality empowered them to become public saints and to exercise their authority in the social space. Therefore, these women saints' life stories discussed in this chapter entail effects of equality – in the sense that the women came across as equally worthy and capable as men. As argued before, their ways of life could also be qualified as ethical freedom practices.

Other Moroccan researchers who studied women's mystical lives in history, mostly focused on whether these women's religious actions created modes of behavior that contradicted or conformed to the dominant norms. As it is documented earlier, Moroccan feminist Mernissi interprets female saints as ideal persons who refused to submit to local traditional norms, and who constructed saintly personalities that contradict the conventional understandings of masculinity and femininity Mernissi (1977, 112). According to Mernissi, the female saints' personalities did not challenge the dominant order. Their role remained that of a therapist who offered her services to people to cope with the formal power structure. Mernissi's approach to historical women paved the way for me to analyze the way Moroccan historical women saints constructed saintly personalities, and I discovered that these historical women followed the collective culture that included Sufism and employed its techniques to uncover its progressive values. These progressive values were clear in their abilities to achieve sainthood and construct an independent self that empowered them to power.

Mernissi argues that women's deep attachment to and involvement with saints in North Africa are linked to their dissatisfaction with existing society, this being the reason why more women visit saints than men do. Women seek the saint's *baraka* to save their social problems. Mernissi considers the saints' sanctuaries a permitted space where women could live freely their religious rituals and the cults of saint veneration. In her opinion, women live a rebellion against oppressive gender relations and social injustices. Mernissi's argument concerning women saints' and women venerators' inability to change the dominant social order, does not take into account their concrete roles in history. The challenging agency of these historical women saints would come more to the fore.

Another study on Moroccan women and religion, dealing especially with the Moroccan female saint ʿAwīsh and her veneration, is van Beek (2002). The aim of this study is to uncover women's presence within Islamic mysticism. Van Beek signals a scarcity of sources on women saint, since most researchers on Moroccan sainthood have focused only on male orthodox saints.

Van Beek focused not only on writing but also on oral sources on 'Awīsh in order to highlight the female presence within Islamic mysticism and the significance of women's religious practices.

Van Beek analyzed the mystical symbols mentioned in the legends as well as in the rituals celebrated around *Lalla* 'Awīsh Beek (2002, 203). On this basis, she described 'Awīsh's piety merely as a tool to achieve the divine unity. Van Beek thus did not take into account the techniques *Lalla* 'Awīsh employed to change herself into a saintly personality and the struggles she had to engage in to do so.

Another contribution to the discussion on women's religious agency is Bartels (1993). She investigated the significance of saints for Tunisian women. Bartels focused on whether these women, through their veneration of saints, protested against their subordinate position in society. She sought to demonstrate that this was the case, and discussed whether that protest was a threat to the existing order.

Both the saints and their venerators played active roles in Bartels' opinion: saints transmitted divine blessing to their troubled venerators Bartels (1993, 101). Female and male venerators performed certain religious rituals to get the saint's *baraka*. Bartels also discussed some parallels that existed between saints and women. Where the saint, as Bartels puts it, was the center of the whole tribe or even the whole region, women were the centers of their families. The saint helped the venerators to cope with their troubles; women likewise satisfied their husbands' and relatives' needs. Bartels further contended that sexual equity was visible in the space of sainthood and that sexual difference was not a criterion of sainthood.

Bartels argued for the double face that saints have. She argued that saints were rebels as well as upholders of the existing order in which men were dominant (Ibid., 44). Women saints as well as women venerators protested against the patriarchal order and affirmed at the same time the patriarchal system to which they were bound. They were, as Bartels puts it, 'loyal towards both the dominated and the dominant' (Ibid., 114). From her fieldwork on Tunisian women's rituals and their symbolism, she concluded that saints had a double face. Like Bartels my research will show that Moroccan women saints submitted to the dominant culture. But unlike Bartels my research women saints used their dominant culture to uncover its techniques of self-formation to perform freedom practices that displayed their transgression of the conventional order.

My book draws on the approach of Mahmood (2005; 2001) by discussing the agency of Moroccan women saints, namely through studying the self-techniques that they followed to become saints. I build on Mahmood's new approach of religious women as agents who practice ethical self-formation.[18] As such my study sheds new light on female saints as active agents, and on their impact on their communities. They were agents who followed the conventional norms of Sufi discourse and discovered its techniques to become saints and got power and authority. They sought a change from within the local culture that revealed freedom practices. The impact of their agency is also visible in the venerators' worship of these women saints. These saints' lives have considerable psychological impacts on women today who consider them as role models, as will be discussed in the next chapter.

18 See chapter 1.

CHAPTER 4

# Moroccan Women Venerators' Reception of Historical Women Saints

My research explores the various ways women exercise agency in the religious sphere in Morocco's past and present. In the preceding chapter, I discussed the exemplary lives of female saints. In this chapter, I explore the impact these devoted women have on contemporary Moroccan women. For that purpose, the focus will be on four types of contemporary Moroccan female religious agents: the functionaries (women working at female saints' sanctuaries), the women who visit and venerate female saints, contemporary women preachers (*wāʿiẓāt*) and spiritual guides (*murshidāt*) and the attendees (the women who attend the preachers' instructional sessions). I research the active ways these women transform themselves to achieve a new level of moral selfhood – i.e., self-ethical formation and the role of their holy predecessors in this process.

This chapter is made up of three sections. In the first section, I will discuss the different female agents, custodians, and visitors, and the various rituals performed within women saints' shrines. How do the women concerned judge the ways in which female saints and saint veneration impact their lives? The second section will explore *wāʿiẓāt* and *murshidāt* and their religious and social roles inside and outside mosques. I will pay particular attention to the way they receive women saints as historical female preachers. The chapter concludes with an investigation of women attendees' reception of these modern religious guides and women preachers.

## 1 Devoted Women, Shrines and Saint Veneration

In Morocco, both the mosque and the shrine are public religious spaces. In each one of them, a particular set of prayers and religious practices take place. While the mosque visitors try to focus on a direct relationship with the divine, in the shrine the visitor can establish an extra, indirect relation with God through the saint Hoffman (1995, 104). A shrine is also space where religion is practiced through different performances such as words, songs, and ecstatic dancing Andezian (1997, 211). This stresses the central role of the shrine in the achievement of a private and liberal relationship with the divine. In the shrine, the relation is more personal and tangible than in the mosque. The holder of

 | DOI:10.1163/9789004429895_005

divine grace is present, the pilgrims have access to the saint Gibb (1997, 30), and, if necessary, the functionaries of the shrines (*muqaddamāt* and others) help them to enhance and improve this relationship. Moreover, oral stories and legends about the saint's miracles can be heard. These accounts could be found in written historical sources, but are part of the local oral history. The shrine functionaries and venerators have preserved them for generations and perpetuate the rituals that they inherited from their ancestors.

Women employ both the mosque and the shrine to experience their spirituality, renew their piety and construct religious personalities. However, Moroccan women are marginalized in the mosques. They are given small spaces for their prayers and religious activities (Mernissi 1977; Tapper 1990). They are not permitted to view the *ʾimām* while listening to his prayers and sermons. They could not have access to *ʾimām*'s speech and sermon. They also feel constraints in mosques, finding themselves obliged to follow the instructions for attending *masjid*. Especially in the past, they were not supposed to do more than pray and leave. Today, their number is still small in comparison to their male counterparts. In the countryside, this discrepancy is even strong. Although this situation is slowly changing, as I will show in what follows, their marginalization in mosques has forced women to turn to the shrine to live out their religiosity. Moroccan women's relationship to shrines of both male and female saints is very strong. Because of the specific character of these shrines, they feel more at ease.

The shrines of male and female saints in Morocco have similar characteristics. They consist of saints' tombs that are located in the center of the sanctuaries. Over the tomb of the saint, there is a *darbūz* (sarcophagus), which is covered by a green cloth. There is a cupola supported by white walls and decorated with *Qurʾān* verses and large candles. On the floor of each shrine, there are multicolored carpets, sheepskins, and pillows for pilgrims and devotees to sit on. The shrines consist of several rooms, including public kitchens filled with utensils for pilgrims to use in ritual. Most shrines are attached to mosques.

The sanctuaries of holy men or women are surrounded by different objects that have a role in their sacredness. In the courtyard one often find large fig trees, which have tattered pieces of cloth tied to their branches, exemplifying votive rituals performed by devotees. There are also shops where people can buy items such as bread, sugar, tea, oil, sweetly scented incense sticks for ritual burning, *tasbīḥ*'s (strings of beads; rosaries) and other necessary items for the performance of *ziyāra* rituals.

Some saints' shrines are attached to traditional religious schools. The gender of the saint is no hindrance, as the example of Taʿlat's shrine shows, but only male (Sufi) disciples and students are allowed to study the *Qurʿān* and *fiqh* there. The schools offer preliminary training for lower level positions and prepare for more advanced study of the *Qur'ān* and other Islamic sciences at the Qarawiyyīn University in Fez.

### 1.1 *Similarities and Differences*

The research here focuses on the shrines of the three selected female saints that were discussed in the preceding chapter – 'Azīza, 'Ā'isha and Fāṭima, for the following reasons. They are all popular and have a large number of venerators, whereas other women saints' shrines are rarely visited by women or men. Moreover, the custodians and/or the numerous venerators of the selected women saints were willing to give me a chance to observe different rituals and religious practices. Next to the similarities, differences exist between the shrines and veneration of the women saints concerned. The shrines of the three saints are all simple, but 'Azīza's shrine is considerably larger. Having living blood relations is a significant difference between these female saints. Women saints in the Sūs region of southwestern Morocco like 'Azīza and Fāṭima have descendants, who maintain strong relationships with them. This relationship impels the descendants to actively take care of the shrines and to organize a *musim* in honor of their women saints. By contrast, women saints in the North have no known descendants organizing annual festivities; they have even recently started to witness a reduction in the number of visitors to their shrines. This is the actual case of the woman saint 'Ā'isha. No one visits her sanctuary. Clearly, different dynamics have been surrounding saints in the North and South.

The explanation for the recession in saint veneration activities in the North is orthodox religious education, which has started to gain popularity among educated Moroccans there. Orthodox Moroccans consider religious hierarchy and the veneration of saints to be un-Islamic practices. By propagating their views, they have started to weaken the relationship between saints and their devotees. This, however, does not mean that people in the North have ceased to venerate saints altogether. It is true that 'Ā'isha's shrine was closed, and the rituals performed around her tomb were reduced. But many people taking part in saint veneration still feel esteem, respect, and love for their female saints.

In the South, the situation is completely different. Orthodoxy has much less influence on the people. Southwestern Berber women saints still enjoy great popularity. They are part and parcel of their religio-cultural and ethnolinguistic background. Saints venerators believe that these female saints, who are friends of God, are able to offer assistance to people in need. They are intermediaries between the believers and God and also have curative powers themselves. In their pursuit of healing, pilgrims also live moral assistance and refuge at a sanctuary. How does this work in practice?

### 1.2 *Rituals*

A visit to a sanctuary is called a *ziyāra*. Pilgrims undertake daily, weekly, monthly and annual visits to saints' shrines. People's visits to saints are primarily enhanced by the power of *baraka*. As discussed in previous chapters, *baraka* in Morocco is the quality of sacred grace and salvation that saints possess and are able to transmit to others. It is a force that endows women and men with capacities to meet their daily troubles and to protect themselves against misfortunes such as evil eye, bad luck, illnesses, and accidents. Regular visits and various rituals aim at a strong relationship with the saints to enhance the achievement of this sacred supernatural force that they incarnate. Moroccan women actively participate in these rituals. In shrines more than in mosques, their religious agency becomes highly visible. This is especially the case on Fridays, *l- yum l-mbarek* (the blessed day), when hundreds of women visit saints' tombs, and the number of females far exceeds that of males. In all the shrines I visited, the women performed similar rituals, including trance rituals, *dhikr*-rituals, sacrifice rituals, marriage and fertility rituals, next to the celebration of mainstream religious activities. Venerators are free to choose the ways to pay respect to their women saints and to perform the rituals they need.

Researchers interpret the rituals of *ziyāra* related to saints as therapy that cures physical and psychological conflicts (Mernissi 1977; Crapanzano 1981). Trance is a special cure that is called *ḥaḍra* in the Moroccan native dialect. This Arabic word emanates from the root verb *ḥ-ḍ-r* meaning "to be present." *ḥaḍra*, then, is a religious expressive performance for seeking the divine presence. The participants submit to the rules of the rituals and put their physical bodies at stake. They cry, scream and faint, hoping to meet the spirit of their women saints. The women believe that they are possessed by the spirit of the woman saint or by other supernatural beings. Therefore, the trance is a way to experience the spiritual world, to glean some of its divine grace and to be cured of different illnesses.

Besides, women's acts and deeds, women's utterances in the trance are equally important. Women in the North and in the South chant religious ritual texts in their gatherings in the shrines. The texts reveal women's Sufi orientation by their expression of disinterest in the material world and the wholehearted devotion and love for God, the Prophet and the community of holy men and women. The significance and impact of positive relations between relatives and members of the whole society are also emphasized in women's

FIGURE 4 Devotees participating in Imma Hugga Ali's *musim* in Assoul

poetic texts. Altogether the songs express their desire for spirituality and good social relationships.

### 1.3 *Women in Shrines Today*

The women I will discuss in this section are women functionaries at shrines and women venerators. Not only women saints but also female functionaries at shrines are important because they help pilgrims to perform the rituals of saint veneration. They are *muqaddamāt* (custodians), *fqīrāt* or *ḥaḍḍārāt* (pious and/or Sufi women in charge of trance dances) and healers. All functionaries display women's leadership and mediation in rituals and the centrality of women's active religious agency.

The *muqaddamāt* are crucial. Whether or not they are descendants of women saints' and heirs of their *baraka*, *muqaddamāt* are all empowered to behave as the overall leaders of most of the shrines' activities, as the guides of the venerators' rituals and worship, and the teachers of women. They help women in crises and satisfy their needs. They serve God and people by respecting the instructions of religion. The *muqaddama* Rqiya[1] confirms that she played a wide range of religious and social roles such as leading prayers

1 Interviews, *muqaddama*, Imintanout, 2010. I have used pseudonyms to avoid recognition.

and other rituals.[2] I saw Zayna, another *muqaddama*, in action when a family brought a ram as an offering. In Southwestern, Morocco pilgrims offered sacrifices during their visits to saints. The sacrificing of an animal was referred to locally as *ʾal-maʿrūf*. Before the slaughtering of the ram started, the *muqaddama* painted the ram's head with *henna* and its eyes with *koḥl* (antimony). These acts, in the opinion of the *muqaddama*, increased the amount of *baraka* and *ʾajr* (religious merit) obtained by the sacrifice. As she explained, this embellishment and the healthy state of the ram were necessary for the veneration of saints. According to her, the spirit of the saint would be very pleased and satisfied and her blessings would be bestowed in great amounts on the supplicants.[3] In short, the *muqaddamāt*'s practices were supposed to generate more powerful effects for the pilgrims.

In other instances, I observed pilgrims whose financial situation did not allow them to offer a ram as a sacrifice. Instead, they sacrificed a chicken. The old male descendants were the ones who slaughter the sacrificed animal. When the ram was still bleeding, I saw the *muqaddama* taking a bowl and filled it with this blood. She then asked the family that offered the animal to sprinkle their hands with some of this blood and to expose the rest to the sun until it became dry. She advised them to use the dry blood as an amulet against the evil eye. The descendants cut the right shoulder of the sacrificed animal and offered it to the family that brought the animal to the woman saint. Then they cut the rest of the ram into pieces and distributed them to poor people and other venerators. Some of the pilgrims cooked the offered meat and ate it. Others had chosen to take their portions of meat to their relatives.

Other women in the sanctuary asked the *muqaddama* to say a prayer for relatives who were absent. One of these women explained that she came to the saint for her sister who was living abroad. The woman gave the *muqaddama* her offerings such as a large green cloth as a cover for the saint's tomb, and other items like bread, date, tea, and milk. Then, she leaned over and whispered to her her sister's wishes and needs. She asked the *muqaddama* to pray for her unmarried sister and transmit her wish to the saint.

Mediation roles may also be played by female healers. Rqiya, a descendant of Fāṭima and a healer at her sanctuary, explained that in order to cure ill venerators she bestowed her holy foremother's *baraka* on them. She did so by spitting at pilgrims, like all saints and their heirs used to do.

*Fqīrāt* (Sing: *Fqīra*) are Sufi women who lead the trance dance and prayer rituals. They may also be called *ḥaḍḍrārāt*, after the '*ḥaḍra*', as for example, in the

---

2 Interviews, *muqaddama*, Imintanout, 2010.

3 Interviews, *muqaddama*, Imintanout, 2010.

shrine of ʿAzīza: both in the North and the South of Morocco trance attendance was much larger on Friday than other days. On Friday women living near and far went to shrines or *zāwiya* to participate in the *ḥaḍra*. The room where these trance dances were held was so crowded with women that no empty space was left to stretch out one's legs. It started in the early hours of the afternoon and lasted until sunset prayer. The *muqaddama*, as the leader of *ḥaḍḍārāt*, ordered women to prepare musical instruments such as *bindīr*'s (circular frame drums with a skinned covered surface), drum and *taʿrija*'s (small tambourines). Each used a particular instrument while waiting for their *muqaddama* to open the session. The *muqaddama* started with the recitation of *sūra fātiḥa*. Afterward, she began to drum and chant religious poetic texts. Some women used musical instruments, and others chose to clap their hands. When the rhythm of the chanting quickened, women got up, formed a circle and started moving up and down. A middle-aged woman whom I called Nejma got in the center of the circle of women and started to jump up and down. I was told that she was in the trance. Her helper held her *jellaba* from the back to break her fall. The other women carried on their chanting and ecstatic dancing. Nejma was left in a corner to have a rest. No one paid attention to her anymore. Women carried on repeating their poetic verses *Allah ḥay'* (God is alive) following the new rhythm of chanting. Other women collapsed and sank to the floor too. Their stretched bodies occupied the whole space. Once the trance was finished, sweet tea with mint was served with a piece of bread.

### 1.4 *Women Venerators of Female Saints*

Women venerators of female saints covered a wide range of categories: young and old, illiterate and literate, sick and healthy. Most of them were in the midst of an emotional or social crisis; many had failed to meet the requirements of the conventional roles. For instance, marriage plays an important role in Moroccan culture. It is a religious and social duty that enabled men and women to be labeled real adults and mature Muslims. Marriage is especially important to women. It brings them status. Unmarried women, whose independent lives are not accepted, occupy a third-rate position on the social ladder of Moroccan society. However, the same applies to married, but barren, women. Women in Morocco always consider themselves primarily to be the cause of failures of fertility and reproduction, whereas men always regard themselves as fertile. Married women may also have problems with their co-wives and their husbands' families. Many women fear divorce because divorced women become subjected to negative designations. The position of women who are left behind is also a precarious one.

All these women's problems and inabilities to live up to the cultural norms urged them to search for spiritual comfort, peace of mind, and relief from daily life pressures. Many rural, illiterate women with no financial means find in the veneration of women saints a budget solution to their health problems. The women visitors in the sanctuaries explained in concrete terms that they came in pursuit of divine blessing and favors such as a good marriage partner, a conception of a male child, and a safe delivery. Other temporal wishes might include a cure from an illness, a good harvest, success in studies, employment and finding lost relatives. Of course, there were also women who had no problems. These women simply sought to practice their spirituality.[4] In addition, the daily routines in the sanctuaries of Taʿlat and Fāṭima provided an insight into the endeavors of women venerators to achieve all these purposes.

Orthodox rituals equally took place around saints' tombs. Most of the women within the shrines performed the ritual prayer (*ṣalat*). There were women who had chosen to perform prayers of either two, four or even more *rakaʿāt* (sing: *rakaʿa*, prostration). Its meaning differed from that in the ordinary mosque since women considered the shrine a holy place where the *ʾajr* (religious merit) of prayer ritual was doubled. I also observed women fasting and breaking their fast in the sanctuaries. They all chose to celebrate their *ʾIfṭār* close to their favorite women saints.

While venerators of women saints visited the shrine to strengthen themselves to cope with daily life issues, they also used the cults for spiritual self-development. They might learn a lot from the functionaries in the shrines, who in many cases experienced a period of growth and learning themselves. Raḥma swallowed her grandmother's blessed saliva, and her life changed. She became more pious than before, and she started to assign all her time to people's needs. She became a holder of divine grace, and it was this divine grace that enabled her to learn by heart the *Qurʾān* and to teach it to people. The *baraka* that Raḥma passively inherited from her saintly foremother empowered her and made her feel responsible to actively search for more knowledge and to have other women profit from it.

Fāṭima, the *muqaddama* of ʿAzīza's shrine, offered another powerful example for women venerators. During my fieldwork in that shrine, I forged a deep friendship with the fifty-year-old Fāṭima. The latter had completed secondary

4 Men also take parts in the performance of rituals. They are primarily concerned with finding solutions to their social and psychological problems of sexuality, fertility, masculinity, and other crises. In fact, their stress hinders them in the performance of the typical male roles. See Crapanzano 1981, 9.

education, was married and had two children. During my continuous encounters with her in the shrine, I came to know that Fāṭima has been the *muqaddama* for more than twenty years. She appeared to be very experienced in the art of saint veneration. She also called herself an expert in the teaching of the cult of saints and in the teaching of religion. Like all *muqaddamāt*, she headed women's religious circles in the shrines and guided women's rituals. Due to her strong religious personality, she appeared to be a woman with power and authority. How had she achieved that status?

In the field, I saw Fāṭima focused on the notion of good intention (*niyya*) as the primary condition of saint veneration. I heard her advising a woman to venerate ʾAzīza with good intention. She says: "*diri niyya temshi b-ḥajt-ek maqḍiyya*" (Maintain positive intention and your request will be accomplished). Here *niyya* was a standard of saint veneration and the achievement of a desired religious lifestyle and a strong spiritual personality. She encouraged women venerators to cultivate *niyya* in themselves while venerating their woman saint. In fact, *niyya* was more important than anything else in the construction of pious selfhood. That was why the women felt free to express their love to God in the way they wanted. They took liberties that could not be taken in mosques and that also met resistance from orthodox Muslims. Saint veneration is an important issue in the debate among Moroccan believers, men, and women alike, especially in the North. Many women venerators were fully aware of that. Despite, they adhered to their choice to participate in saint veneration. It was a practice that resonates with their inner feelings by allowing them to develop spirituality on a personal level. Caroline Humphrey (1994) called this process "ritual commitment". In this case, it means that women created for themselves a strategy to preserve their relationship with women saints and saint veneration.

Given the backgrounds of women saints, they also committed to their cultural heritage and to their ethnic identity. For example, all the rituals I observed in the South were performed in the Berber language. During the religious gathering in women saints' shrines, they chanted poetic *dhikr*-texts in the local *Tashlḥit*.[5] They also performed a number of old rituals like the tying of rugs to windows and trees, that still existed and that dated back to the pre-Islamic period. In the North of Morocco, women used their native Arabic dialect in the performance of their rituals. Women chanted poetic texts that they composed themselves or that they inherited from their Andalusian forefathers. Women in contemporary Morocco sought self-expression in rituals they saw as fit for

5 The gathering of women within the shrine to chant poetic text in Tashlḥit dialect is a ritual called "ʾagraw".

themselves. They defended their popular religion. This shows that although women's religious actions have been interpreted as passive and marginalized performances, women are active religious persons and are able to constitute their own religious voices. However, as I will discuss in what follows, the female venerators' opposition to Islamists and Islamism does not mean that they have a negative attitude towards orthodox Islamic education as such.

### 1.5 *Empowerment by Association with Saints*

Both in the North and the South of Morocco, pilgrims were keen to hold close personal relationships with their favorite women saints, but many liked to go one step further. They wanted their families to get involved, too. As I mentioned earlier, women bought small gifts from shops close the shrines to offer to the relatives left at home. Their goal was not only to transmit the saints' *baraka* to their family members but also to encourage them to establish independent relationships with their favorite women saints. In this way, their own bond with the sacred shrines grew even tighter, while the number of venerators of their women saints increased. Venerators, as I will discuss below, derived empowerment from saint veneration because it inspired them to actively change themselves and took their life into their own hands to become a servant to God and people.

Not surprisingly, these women devotees were eager to learn about the lives and deeds of their women saints. They were observed spending the whole day at shrines discussing their woman saint's life story. More importantly, the association with a widely respected female saint gained devoted women respect in their environment. Their overall status was enhanced by the perfection of their religious and social personalities. No one could deny the achievements of great women saints and the benefits pilgrims got from them. This was especially the case when these saints were also considered as the foremothers of their families or founders of their tribes.

In Morocco, saints were usually the founders of patrilineal and patrilocal societies. They passed on sainthood to their descendants. The extended saintly families came to have clans, which developed into tribes. The latter increasingly displayed their blood relationship to their saintly ancestor. There were even tribes that associated with a saint figure who was not really their biological forefather or ancestor. The continuous relationship with neighboring saintly clans made them followers of their saints. The saint here was the hub, the center of segmented tribalism.[6] Interestingly, in the field, foremothers of

6 On segmental tribalism in Morocco see Gellner (1969).

saintly families proved not to be uncommon with many women considered themselves their proud descendants.

Most of the saints' venerators acknowledged that both male and female saints could become founders of saintly families and that both had followed the same strategies to be the head of a lineage. Some venerators interpreted a woman saint as a foremother of their lineage in terms of the *baraka* that God bestowed on her. Khadīja, an illiterate female venerator, simply stated that *baraka* made people venerate saints (either women or men) and remained attached to them as the forefathers and foremothers of their tribes and saintly families.[7] Other venerators interpreted the way a woman became a founder of a saintly family in terms of her continuous struggles to have great piety and faith in God. These efforts resulted in her being admired by God and offered sainthood, and consequently, in becoming the foremother of tribes.

Bamou, a venerator, referred to *niyya* as a driving force for cultivating piety. According to her, Fāṭima had the intention to become a saint and stressed the role of piety in making a woman saint into the founder of tribes. This old woman contended:

> Our *tagurramt* used to be a great *tafqirt*.[8] She prayed to God day and night. I remember my grandmother telling me that Fāṭima was very patient. Her husband was very cruel to her. He brought a second wife into the house, and he did not give her a share of the housework. She did all the housework with her mouth shut. She never complained. In the night she threaded wool garments and her heart was reciting the names of God. It is her *ṣabr* which made her have all of these.[9]

She was saying this and referring to the cupola and the venerators. Here, *ṣabr* (patience) was not just a personal feature or characteristic but a technique that women saints actively used to face the hardships of life and to achieve a mystical life: *ṣabr* did not mean passiveness because it had an explicit and positive goal. Fāṭima embodied the practice of patience to become a saint. Her patience, as the old female venerator puts it, gained her a shrine where pilgrims have venerated her until today. It urged people to affiliate with her sacred lineage. More than thirty tribes claimed to be the descendants of Fāṭima.

7 Interviews, a venerator, Imintanout, 2010.

8 « *Tafqirt* » is a Berber word meaning a very pious woman. It is the equivalent of the Arabic word *faqīra*.

9 Interviews, a venerator, Imintanout, 2010.

This shows that gender is not taken into consideration in the veneration and affiliation with historical saints.

Holy women brought strength to families, clans, and tribes. Whole villages were named after them. It was not surprising that in the South of Morocco women saints like Fāṭima and ʿAzīza were called by the Berber word "*tamghart*", meaning female leader or greatest.[10] She was the greatest in spirituality and piety and all the people here were strongly attached to their "*tamghārt*", a woman venerator of Fāṭima explained.

## 1.6 *Women Saints as Empowering Role Models*

Most venerators in the North and the South of Morocco stressed that the women discussed in the preceding chapter are *qudwā* (example) in religion and piety. Whoever took these women saints as role models gain their strength and empowerment. Others added that they perceived them as such because they succeeded to reach a level of piety which was even stronger than that of male saints. With the achievement of a stronger *baraka* these exemplary women were able to impress both females and males.

The *shaykh* of *zāwiya* ṣiddīqiyya described ʿĀʾisha as his favorite woman saint.[11] She played such a big role in his spiritual growth that he considered her to be his spiritual mother.[12] Here the *shaykh* who usually performed weekly visits to his forefather Sīdīʾlbrāhīm whose tomb was close to ʿĀʾisha's decided to develop a strong relationship with her. ʿĀʾisha gave birth to his desire for spirituality and made him become more pious than before. The *shaykh* of the *zāwiya* ṣiddīqiyya strived to familiarize his disciples with ʿĀʾisha and other Moroccan women saints and Sufis. His aim was to teach them that women were able to become saints with miraculous deeds and to render themselves public religious figures. He propagated that they are worthy examples to be followed by everyone. Therefore, the venerators' visits to women saints' shrines did not have therapeutic purposes, they just aimed at improving themselves by creating moral personhood, in other words, an ethical self-formation.

And that was exactly why most of the venerators interpreted their relationship with women saints as a form of empowerment. The *fqīrāt* I met at the shrines of the women saints I studied regularly contended that their frequent visits to women saints empowered them to think of their piety and the way

10 By contrast, small domestic women saints who had not served their society in a similar way did not receive such honorific titles. This hierarchy of sainthood applies to men, too.

11 Interviews, *shaykh* of *zāwiya* ṣiddīqiyya, Qaṣr l-Kabīr city, 2010.

12 Interviews, shaykh *of zāwiya* ṣiddīqiyya, Qaṣr l-Kabīr city, 2010.

to improve their practice of religion and spirituality. Their aim was to achieve their women saints' perfect spiritual and social status.

More importantly, venerators did not only gain power from women saints, but they themselves also invested power in these holy women. Venerators sought help and empowerment from their saintly women to overcome their hardships and crises. For these venerators, these women's sacred blessing was a counterforce to gender injustice and discrimination. But these women venerators also empowered these historical women saints. This was evident from their continuous visits to their tombs, the rituals that they performed at shrines and the chanting of stories about their lives. One might notice here that venerators unconsciously revived the memory of these historical women saints and kept their legacy alive within their contemporary modern environment. They indirectly offered them a space to remain alive and present in their modern life. They gave them the status they felt the women saints deserved. They empowered them to empower them. Thus, one notices that there is mutual empowerment between women saints and their venerators. This conclusion is similar to that of Jansen, Hermkens, and Notermans (2009), who also acknowledge the relationship of empowerment existing between women saints and venerators.

## 2 *Murshidāt* and *Waʿiḍāt* as Religious Agents

At one moment during my fieldwork in the shrines, I heard the women venerators discussing a religious course that they attended in one of the mosques in the *medina* of Qaṣr l-Kabīr. My curiosity was raised so I asked them why they followed these courses. Khadīja had a primary level of education and decided to undertake an extra strategy to educate herself. She was not satisfied with the shrine and its traditional religious cults alone, so she also started frequenting the orthodox religious institution of the mosque Khadīja and other women venerators believed in saint veneration and in orthodox Islamic education at the same time. For them, visiting saints and visiting mosques were both important techniques that helped them to construct a stronger religious personality and to gain God's forgiveness. Khadīja admired ṣafiyya, her woman preacher in the mosque, and her way of teaching. She regularly attended her lessons. Her views on ṣafiyya prompted me to do further research on *murshidāt* and *waʿiḍāt* and highlight their active religious agency. The question that arises: what are the properties of Moroccan *murshidah* program? Before I discuss this question, I want to shed some light on Moroccan religious reform.

FIGURE 5 A *murshidah* preaching at a mosque in Rabat
PHOTOGRAPH BY AZIZA OUGUIR

Over the last decades, Morocco has undergone a radical transformation within the religious field. The growth of urbanity and education has prompted ruptures of traditional lifestyles and conduct rules Sadiqi (2008). In response, Morocco worked to combine the traditional and the modern in all walks of life including religion and gender.

The state has contributed enormously to changes in religious gender roles. Some of these changes were initiated and realized under the reign of the current king, Moḥammad VI. Moroccan women who had fought to achieve the highest level of education, succeeded in gaining approval for their employment in different fields of society (Ibid). Among these fields are politics and religion. The latter stopped to be an exclusively male domain on the official level due to Morocco's reform project to democratize the institution of religious authority. The main objectives of the reforms were first to modernize the religious sphere; second, to make the transmission of religious knowledge national, and, finally, to promote the state's new perspective on the management of religion.[13]

13 The bombing of Casablanca by radical extremists and terrorists in 2003 urged Moroccan state to introduce a change and a reform of the religious field. For more information see El-Katiri (2014).

One of the most remarkable moves introduced by King Muḥammad VI and the Moroccan authorities was to incorporate women's religious knowledge and authority in the public national network of religious affairs. Women became members in the High Council of *ʿulamāʾ* and set out delivering religious lectures during *ʾal-durūs ʾal-ḥassaniyya*[14] organized by the Ministry of Religious Endowments and Islamic Affairs during the month of *Ramaḍān*. In the following paragraphs, the Moroccan *murshidah* program will be discussed.

From 2005 onwards, the Ministry of Religious Endowments and Islamic Affairs has started an annual program in which fifty women are trained in religious matters. The graduates called *murshidāt* receive training that consists of Islamic courses in the *Qurʾān Hadīth*, *fiqh*, Muslim history, and courses in social sciences, humanities, law, technology, and foreign languages. The combination of Islamic and modern courses is important for them because their job is not only to transmit Islamic knowledge by preaching and education but also to serve women, offering them help to find solutions to their social and personal problems.

Some female preachers write articles on Islamic issues and publish them in monthly religious magazines, such as *ʾal-Tadhkira* and *ʾal-Tabshira* that are affiliated with the Ministry of Islamic Affairs, under whose auspices they work. Others present a daily religious program or weekly courses on the radio or on TV for the network *ʾal-Sādisa*. In addition women, preachers answer women's text messages or phone calls to give *fatwa*'s (legal advice). They may also make use of the internet and send their sermon texts by mail to their followers. Moreover, the ministry organizes trips for female religious guides outside Morocco to serve Moroccans living abroad and offer them religious knowledge.

Besides the *murshidāt*, other highly educated women appear in the official religious realm, albeit without being paid. These expert volunteers are called *wāʿiẓat*. They have varied backgrounds and educational experiences. They are not required to undertake the *murshidāt*'s long training program. Nevertheless, it is also expected from them to learn half of the *Qurʾān* and to present a lecture as parts of the evaluation process. As soon as they are admitted, they are offered spaces in mosques to preach to women and men about religious issues.

Moroccan women's participation in the religious public sphere has been viewed as constituting a radical change. However, women's public religious

---

14 *ʾal-durūs ʾal-ḥassaniyya* are religious lectures that Moroccan Ministry of Religious Endowments and Islamic Affairs organizes each year in *Ramadan*. They are also called the Hassanian lessons after the initiator the late king Hassan II. These lectures are presented in the presence of the king, the government, national and international *ʿulamāʾ*.

roles, particularly those played by *murshidāt* and *wāʿiẓat* are not new, as they are rooted in history, starting with women saints and Sufis who played public religious roles in early historical periods. What is new and what constitutes a radical change are the official and public aspects of the *murshidāt*'s and *wāʿiẓat*'s roles. These aspects include the fact that the Moroccan Ministry of Pious Endowments and Islamic Affairs established this official position for women, and the training program for it and the fact that *murshidāt* and *wāʿiẓat* perform their functions in official and public religious spaces such as mosques and other public spaces.

Due to the reforms, much has changed in the Moroccan religious sphere since 2005. The mosques, which used to assign a small space to women for worshipping God, have started to open more doors to women and to provide them with prayer rooms to exercise and learn religious knowledge. In my fieldwork, I observed *murshidāt* instructing women and men in the large, in the central space of the mosque and in other public institutions such as universities, hospitals, and schools. However, what is striking here is that it is the women religious guides who took the initiative to extend their religious activism to other audiences beyond mosque attendees. Nezha Nʿassi, a very active *murshidah*, consciously developed an independent lifestyle that is not dictated by traditions. As a *murshidah*, she not only considers her official training, she also uses her own personal development in her preaching. Female preachers and religious guides got permission to expand their religious activities to other institutions. Their strong desire of proliferating religious knowledge and to helping a large number of people impelled them to exert great energy and efforts. As I will demonstrate below, the success of their activism greatly exceeded that of their male preacher counterparts.

Consequently, *murshidāt* and *wāʿiẓat* enjoy more egalitarian educational and employment conditions than their female colleagues in Egypt. Their position could not be equated with that of the Egyptian women preachers in their mosque movement as described by Mahmood (2005), either. The latter just operate within the (largely traditional) women section of the mosque. Their opportunities to get public attention are minimal since they have no access to the media. Since they never preach to a mixed audience, their recognition by men is limited. In contrast, by entering spaces and practices previously closed for women, Moroccan female religious agents transgress the traditional limits imposed on women.

### 2.1 Murshidāt's *Activism and Education*

Nowadays, the institutions of *murshidāt* and *wāʿiẓāt* are well-known in Morocco. Finding several women religious guides proved to be rather easy, although not all of them wanted to talk to me.[15] I have already mentioned the *murshidah* N'assi. In the mosques of Rabat and Salé, I became acquainted with two other women preachers Na'īma Ghanām and 'Āmīna 'al-'Iraqī. Ghanām is married and has children. She worked as a university teacher. She taught Islamic studies for more than thirty years. When she retired, she dedicated herself to giving religious lectures in mosques.

In one of the mosques of the *medina* of Rabat, I found Ghanām sitting on the *minbar* (the *'imām*'s pulpit). She was preparing to deliver a lecture on the rules of qur'anic recitation. Both men and women were sitting on the carpet facing Ghanām, listening attentively to her *dars* (lesson). Through a loudspeaker, she opened her religion lesson by reminding the attendees of the last lesson. Then she started to explain other new rules of qur'anic recitation. "Today's course" Ghanām explains, "is on the way to pronounce the letter *'al-hamza* while reciting the *Qur'ān*." According to Ghanām, the pronunciation of *'al-hamza* depends on the context in which it occurs. She adds that the pronunciation of this letter is called *'iẓhār*, meaning "to make its pronunciation heard". Its non-pronunciation is called *'idghām*. Ghanām based her course on Nāfi` a Moroccan religious scholar 'al-Marghani (2007). Before she closed her session, she asked one of the male attendees and one of the female attendees to recite some *Qur'ān* verses applying the rules she had just explained. Her aim was to see to what extent her attendees had understood her *dars*. The next time I went to the mosque, I found Ghanām speaking about other rules of qur'anic recitation. There was also a cameraman filming her delivering her lesson. I was told that the Ministry of Religious Endowments and Islamic Affairs wanted to present Ghanām's lectures on the Moroccan religious TV channel *'al-Sādissa* so that the whole Moroccan public could watch her program and benefit from her religious courses.

It was in *masjid* Bader in Rabat that I met 'al-'Iraqī, who gave weekly lessons in this mosque. She is fifty years old, married and had two children. She works as a physician in a hospital. One Friday I found women sitting on the carpet in the room assigned to women in the mosque waiting for the arrival of 'al-'Iraqī. When 'al-'Iraqī arrived, she went directly to sit down on her armchair. Women were sitting shoulder-to-shoulder facing her. 'al-'Iraqī religious discourse in the mosque was different from that of Ghanām. In the course of four Fridays, 'al-'Iraqī gave lectures on good fasting during Ramaḍān. She instructed women on the importance of Ramaḍān for Muslims. She explained to women that the embrace of the virtues: patience, help, love, faithfulness, and others was very important to ensure God's acceptance of one's fasting. She also advised women

15 Up till now, however, the vast majority of women preachers have worked mainly in urban areas.

to pray to God and read the *Qur'ān* since the performance of these duties and good deeds during Ramaḍān was greatly rewarded *'ajr*. The *'ajr* in Ramaḍān, 'al-ʿIraqī explained, was doubled. She continued advising women to do their *ṣalat* on time, to feed the poor and fasting people, and to remember God. At another meeting, 'al-ʿIraqī continued her previous *dars* and explained its content to women. Her aim was to help women to understand Islamic instructions and to improve their worship of God.

Morocco's reforms did indeed enhance the position of female religious agents, but still, women needed qualifications in order to be admitted to these positions. How did the *murshidāt* and *wāʿiẓāt* get this far? An upbringing in a religious family proved not to be decisive. The women preachers I interviewed, including Ghanām and 'al-ʿIraqī, came from families with very divergent religious backgrounds. Some of them belong to families who were widely known for their piety and religion. Others came from ordinary religious families.

Ghanām, for example, belongs to a Sufi family. When she was still young, she spent her free time with her grandmother in her chamber reciting the *Qur'ān* and chanting of *dhikr*. In fact, Ghanām's grandmother had cultivated the seeds of piety in her.[16] In contrast, 'al-ʿIraqī belongs to a family with an ordinary religious background. According to her, her family is wealthy and involved in the business. Her family members, 'al-ʿIraqī contended, were not religious, meaning not totally devoted to religion. They led a modern life in which religion is not the main purpose. Her father, 'al-ʿIraqī said, was very modern and liberal. He did not want her to put on the veil and to preach in mosques. Nevertheless, she resisted him, and she became an active preacher. Her preaching gained her public recognition that empowered her to participate in *'al-durus 'al-ḥassaniyya* program and delivered a lecture in the presence of the king during Ramaḍān. Hence, these Moroccan women, either belonging to religious or non-religious families, succeeded in becoming active religious agents.

More importantly, 'al-ʿIraqī's and Ghanām's religiosity and piety emanated primarily from their own choices. These *wāʿiẓāt* had religious relatives, but neither of them was associated with a specific religious figure or was guided by a religious master, either male or female. 'al-ʿIraqī and Ghanām confirmed their own choice in becoming religious and practicing religion. These preachers engaged with religious education and got degrees in religious matters which empowered them to become actors in the official public religious institutions. They developed themselves into religious scholars who forged their own path, seeking different strategies to acquire religious knowledge and to participate in the women's preaching program.

16 Interviews, Ghanām, Rabat, 2010.

Importantly, acquiring religious and social knowledge made the *wāʿiẓāt* and *murshidāt* able to distinguish between what was Islamic and non-Islamic. According to women preachers and religious guides, it was the strong attachment to the bad local customs that hampered men and women from understanding the right Islamic instructions that guide their daily lives. Again Rachida, the *murshidah*, explained that it was this mixture of Islam and local customs that caused women's misunderstanding of the right Islamic instructions.

Women preachers' knowledge also impelled them to redefine women's status in Islam. Their continuous study of the *Qurʾān* and *Sunna* constituted an important strategy for the reconsideration of women's current oppressed position. Knowledgeable women preachers become able to state in front of their audiences in mosques and media that the *fiqh* is patriarchal and the primary cause of women's oppression and marginalization. Most of them condemn the patriarchal interpretation of Islam. Malika ʾal-Buʿnānī, a preacher and activist, stressed that women's situation got worse because of the *fiqh* which privileged man and discriminated against women. Thus, women's advanced religious education empowers them to criticize *fiqh* and to redefine women's roles.

## 3 *Murshidāt*'s and *Wāʿiẓāt*'s Reception of Women Saints

Although *murshidāt* and *wāʿiẓāt* appear to be a new phenomenon in Morocco, modern feminine preaching is rooted in history. *Murshidāt* and *wāʿiẓāt* have many common points with the historical women saints I discussed in the preceding chapter, such as several of their self-techniques. Unlike the women saints, they are not divinely ordained but their religious and social activities are similar.

Women saints and modern women religious guides and preachers all brought about change. They did not want to stick to conventional norms and gendered local values. They had a strong desire to have a vast religious knowledge in order to become powerful women. ʿAzīza, Muʿmina, and Maḥilla were all *faqīhāt*. They all studied the *Qurʾān Hadīth, fiqh* and other Islamic topics under the guidance of axial saints and jurists. Their religious knowledge was probably the most important factor in their self-presentation in their environments. They became more qualified to play social and religious roles that empowered them to gain respect and assert authority.[17]

17 Still, it is debated to what extent a woman's sermon, course or *fatwā* hold ground if compared to similar actions by a male colleague. Since meetings of the Religious Council are

Like the exemplary women saints, *murshidāt* and *wāʿiẓāt* used their Islamic knowledge to serve people by teaching, preaching and offering help and sustenance. Here, they were making their religious agency known to the public. Although historical women saints' societal roles were limited – they could not practice their religion in mosques, and they were not allowed to take part in institutionalized religious activities, and although they were not highlighted in written history, there were some exceptions of women saints who clearly marked history with their legacy, as I have discussed in the preceding chapter.

Most of the twenty contemporary voluntary women preachers I interviewed acknowledged the exemplary status of women saints. They told me for example that they admired the Berber woman saint ʿAzīza and fully aware of the challenges she had encountered in her family and her community in order to become who she wanted to be, a religious scholar, and a saint who performed miracles and who was a political leader for her tribe. The preachers admired her abilities to defend her Saksāwa tribe against enemies and secure its sovereignty. Most of them contended that all Moroccan women saints should be taken as role models.[18]

Given their extensive knowledge of women's rights in Islam and the examples of strong saintly women in the past of Morocco, women preachers and religious guides feel confident of cultivating feminist consciousness in their attendees' minds. As religious agents, they consciously work to plant the seeds of gender equality in men and women. Conventional ideologies that present women as passive individuals are challenged by all means.

On one occasion during my fieldwork, Nʿassi assigned a session to explain to women the *Qurʾān* verse that stresses gender equality. She explained to her attendees that God created men and women from the same soul and that gender injustice did not find its roots in the *Qurʾān* but in earlier cultural traditions, which privileged masculinity and discriminated against femininity. It was clear that Nʿassi was engaged in changing repressive ideologies inherent to the local patriarchal system. She wanted to correct her attendees' views, which marginalized women's social position. More importantly, she wanted women to understand that gender equality was divinely ordained. Nʿassi was striving to make women conscious of their rights within Islam and to create

---

not open to the public it is also difficult to judge whether or not the voices of *ʿālimāt* are marginalized in that official religious institution. Whatever the current situation, the female religious functionaries are surely backed up by the Moroccan authorities.

18 Instead, they have to live their religion and organize gatherings in private houses and *zāwiyas*.

new mentalities and a new generation with a new and non-dominant ideological perspective.

Munā, another woman preacher, was doing the same. She was always delivering stories on the role of women in the history of Islam. On Morocco's National Women's Day (the eight of October) she delivered a sermon entitled 'the status of women before and after Islam'. In her sermon, Munā did not only mention notorious women who lived in the Prophet's time[19], but also she made reference to a number of Moroccan women saints and Sufis such as Zaynab'al-Nafzāwiya and ʿAzīza ʿal-Saksāwiyya. For Munā gender equality and social justice were rooted in Islam, and history could not deny the examples of Muslim women who achieved powerful personalities which impacted their communities. The rarity of such exemplary women in today's Muslim world is, according to her, entirely due to Muslims' neglect of their religion and their lack of respect for God's instructions, particularly those related to women.

It was already stated that women preachers considered education crucial for their own development and the advancement of women's positions in general. According to them, illiteracy was women's main enemy in the Muslim world since they suffered the most from this backwardness. It resulted in conservatism, a denial of their rights and downright oppression since men and women did not understand the true messages of the *Qur'ān* and *Sunna*. That was why, Munā strongly encouraged women to educate themselves, to return to their cultural heritage and to understand for themselves that rights Islam gave to women. Education means empowerment. It makes women question the local patriarchal traditional system and social injustice. Many attendees agreed that the *murshidāt* and *wāʿiẓāt* already did this, and very successfully, too.

## 4 *Murshidāt*'s and *Wāʿiẓāt*'s Attendees

During my fieldwork in the mosques, I became friends with two women whom I will call 'Itto and Nūra. The former is fifty, the latter thirty-five years old. 'Itto has a secondary level of education, whereas Nūra has a B.A. in law. Both are unmarried and work as employees in the administration. They are eager to learn more about Islam, and they work hard to develop religious perfection. The main purpose of their endeavors is to ensure a happy hereafter. They want to do what is best for their own personal growth and welfare.

19 In many instances, women preachers also relate how the Prophet helped his women in the household and was looking after the children. For details see 'Abū Shuqqa 1999.

In their search for religious knowledge, both ʾItto and Nūra experienced a wide range of instructors: male Islamic authorities like *ʾimāms* and women professors who taught religion in schools and other religious institutions. Yet, they are actually loyal attendees of *murshidāt*. One of their favorites is ʾal-ʿIraqī. They are very outspoken about why they prefer her to the traditional teachers. Itto liked ʾal-ʿIrāqī's style of preaching. She found it relaxed, whereas, that of the *ʾimām* is frightening.

What is more, they were also particularly interested in the women preachers as persons, including their style of behavior and private life. Attendees even developed relations of friendship with their women preachers. Mobile phones and the internet greatly enhanced the strengthening of their mutual bonds. Women attendees told me that these bonds helped them to learn how women preachers achieved their careers.

Many of the followers of women preachers felt personally connected to them. Obviously, they had much in common. Not only did they all want to increase their religious knowledge, but they also wanted to improve the position of women. Many challenged the conventional norms by choosing an independent life of their own, much like my friends Itto and Nūra who preferred to remain celibate.

Nūra's and ʾItto's ages exceeded the standard age of marriage. Nonetheless, they talked about marriage, a common subject for women in Moroccan culture, without shame or hesitation. Both women were clearly not against marriage as such but refused to marry a man just for the sake of marriage. By reference to their friends, they were both too familiar with the outcomes of such opportune decisions. After marriage, many of them were no longer allowed to study or to work, and they were forced to stay at home. Some of them even endured physical abuse.

Nūra openly referred to a man who had asked her hand in marriage. He was sixty years old, already married and had children. Nūra was against polygamous marriages. She had felt no need to consult anyone and simply dismissed him. Indeed, many Moroccan women employees, doctors, and other highly educated women had chosen this path of freedom and individual life and they liked it. When I asked them about their celibacy, the first expression I heard repeatedly was: "*sɛlibatɛr ʾu-bikhīr*", I am celibate and happy.[20] In this way, women seemed to embody a cautious trend of highly educated Moroccan women who were starting to have a new lifestyle according to their personal choices. They used celibacy as a self-technique, choosing it over marriage, particularly in a space where marriage was highly desired. Most of them disapproved of the

20 Interviews, a mosque attendee, Rabat, 2010.

dominant social values that resided in the family. The personal lives of women mosque preachers clearly had an empowering impact on them as do the female saints whom they presented as role models in their talks.

In this chapter, I discussed four types of female religious agents in Morocco. There were the women venerators, who still preserved a strong relationship to women saints through the rituals they performed around their graves. Devotees regarded women saints as role models to be imitated to achieve religious authority and power. The female functionaries at the shrines surely embodied these goals in practice. *Murshidāt* and *wāʿiẓāt* achieved an orthodox religious education that empowered them to engage in religious and social activism. In fact, contemporary religious women and historical women saints had a relationship of active mutual empowerment. I conclude that, like the female saints, the women venerators created moral personhood, in other words, an ethical self-formation whose positive impacts are highly observed.

In order to gain more religious knowledge, some women venerators had also started to frequent the courses of *murshidāt* and *wāʿiẓāt* modern women preachers. These highly educated women had struggled and succeeded to achieve an active orthodox religious agency. Their knowledge also empowered them to question the status of women with reference to Islamic history. They were eager to point out to their audiences that equality between men and women was rooted in Islam itself. For them, literacy and education were required in understanding women's rights in the way they were meant by the *Qurʾān* and the *Sunna*. Women attendees in mosques considered female preachers and religious guides role models. In case these preachers had chosen a life of celibacy and learning they might gain even more respect. These highly educated women were happy with their own celibacy and independent lifestyles.

Moroccan women's religious agency thus seems to uncover another face of Muslim religious agency, which is different from that of Mahmood's respondents. Moroccan women within both the historical and the contemporary religious space display strong desires and commitments to not only perform religion but to shape themselves in a way that does not necessarily conform to the politics of the local culture. Their agency displays their desires to re-shape the religious sphere that was (once) reserved exclusively for males. Their agency also uncovers the cultural techniques that empowered them to make visible the progressive values hidden in their dominant cultural patterns.

In the next chapter, I will discuss the arena of secular and Islamist women movements in Morocco. What is the attitude of women activists in these movements towards the historical and contemporary women religious agents I came across thus far?

CHAPTER 5

# Moroccan Feminist Activists' Reception of Historical Women Saints

Do historical women saints arouse the interest of activists in Morocco's current women movements? This chapter discusses this question, and it consists of four sections. In the first section, I will give a brief historical review of Moroccan feminist movement, an organized women's movement expressing collective demands to reform the status of women, emphasizing its evolution in the pre-independence and post-independence periods. The second section will focus on current women organizations in Morocco, especially on three Islamist organizations: *ʾal-ʿAdl wa l-ʾIḥsān* (Justice and Charity) (JC), *ʾal-ʿAdāla wa Tanmiyya* (Justice and development Party) (PJD) and *Muntadā Zahrāʾ* (Zahra Forum) (ZF) and their different objectives, strategies, and activities. The third section will discuss the way the selected Moroccan Islamist associations draw on exemplary women in Islamic history to underpin their debate on women's rights. This section will also focus on Moroccan Islamist feminists' reception of historical women saints. Some secular feminists are interviewed as well, but mainly the Islamist activists' points of view come to the fore, because of their embedding in Islam. Here I will conclude that they receive historical women saints as a means of empowerment and as role models. In the final section, I will evaluate Moroccan Islamist feminism and examine whether or not the three Islamist associations belong to Moroccan feminism.

## 1 Moroccan Feminism[1]

Moroccan feminism today is a compilation of several elements; basically, it is the encounter of indigenous Moroccan culture and civilization with Western culture. It is linked to the nationalist movement, processes of modernization and development, as well as to Morocco's cultural heritage, thus involving tensions between secular and religious tendencies. The birth of the feminist movement dates back to the late fifties after independence. However, gender inequality had already been acknowledged by nationalist organizations during colonial times. My discussion of Moroccan feminism, therefore, entails a

1 For more details on Moroccan feminist discourse see Ennaji, Sadiqi and Vintges 2016.

 | DOI:10.1163/9789004429895_006

brief investigation of the historical context in which women organizations and feminist thought emerged and developed.

In Morocco, the origins of the women's movement were closely linked to the rise of nationalism. Since women participated in the nationalist movement against French imperialism, they soon moved beyond traditional gender roles. They attended schools with men and broke out of their seclusion to participate in associations and political parties. These female nationalists, like Mālika ʾal-Fāsī, resisted French colonialism and at the same time challenged the traditional values and ideas that oppressed women. The nationalists advocated the liberation of women in the name of Islam's triumph, not in the name of any genuine modern global ideology Mernissi (1987). They sought equality between the sexes and women's emancipation while simultaneously referring to their Arab Muslim identity.

Through contact with the West via colonization, as well as education and the pioneering discussions by Arab intellectuals on women's issues, Moroccan nationalists opposed the subordinated position of women in society. They were influenced by the Egyptians Rifāʿ Rāfiʿ ʾal-Tahtāwī, who claimed that women should have access to education in his *The Honest Guide for Education of Girls and Boys* (1873); Qāsim Amīn, who insisted on women's liberation in his famous work, *The Liberation of Women* (1992); and Hudā ʾal-Shaʿrāwī, author of *The Harem Years: The Memoirs of an Egyptian Feminist* (1987), who famously removed her veil, in 1923, upon her return from an international women's conference in Paris, and who fought for women's right to vote. Moroccan nationalists asked for the liberation of women and their participation in different domains. Moroccan Women's liberation was further emphasized during the 1940s with the emergence of three separate woman associations headed by nationalists. These three associations are: La Commission des Femmes (1940), L'Union des Femmes du Maroc (1944), and Sisters of Purity (1944). Whether liberal or conservative, they all based their ideology on social reform, directed against so-called superstition, including the non-orthodox cults surrounding holy men and women and other traditions.

The first demand of the nationalists was the education of girls. In the 1930s, ʿAllāl ʾal-Fāsī, the founder of the political party *ʾIstiqlāl* (The Party of Independence), and other nationalists had already stressed the necessity of educating girls, considering it an effective tool to fight ignorance within society.[2] They urged parents to send their girls to schools, but the majority refused out

2 ʿAllāl ʾal-Fāsī was a Moroccan (1906–1974) politician, writer, poet, and Islamic scholar. He was also a nationalist and the founder of the political party, *Hizb Istiqlāl*. He left behind a number of scholarly articles and books in diverse fields. One of his books was first published in 1948

of fear that their girls would be influenced by Western values. Consequently, girls' schools, which focused on Arabic, Islam, and nationalism, were created. Ibn Jallūn (1948, 165) shed light on the history of some women who were given the opportunity to study in the West, usually in France, in order to make them active members in their own society.

The intellectuals' efforts effectively contributed to the progress of female education during colonialism despite the barriers that limited it. It was not affected by the conservative claim that presented educated women as immoral Daoud (1999, 225). With Morocco's independence in 1956, many girls started to go to school Mouaid (2000, 181). Women also gained access to work. A few years later, they won the right to vote in the first parliamentary election in 1962. Some women's welfare organizations were led by nationalist women who had been active in the earlier women organizations Benadada (1999).

During the decades after the independence many women, who were members of associations created by men, increasingly felt marginalized. This experience made a number of these women become members of separate associations where the interest of women was taken up. Some of the associations that emerged in the 1980s were the Democratic Association of Moroccan Women (ADFM), the Union for Women's Action (UAF) and the Moroccan Association for Women's Rights (AMDF). These new women associations were representatives of secular feminism, a "modern trend, which seeks to improve the situation of women by adopting the Western style without discarding Moroccan religious culture." Sadiqi (2003, 195). Their major demands were the achievement of 'parity' (*munāṣafa*) in all the domains of society and the elimination of sexual harassment and violence against women.

Secular feminism in Morocco has a religious counterpart. Islamist women organizations emerged in the late 1990s. Although the Islamist women organizations likewise emphasized women's and girls' education, they put primary focus on the protection of the family, which is "society in miniature." Their aim was the improvement of women's conditions within the scope of Islamic principles. Like the secular feminists, they asked for changes in the *mudawwana*, the personal status code, as codified in 1957.

## 1.1 *Legal Reforms*

Just before Morocco's independence, the nationalist leader 'Allāl 'al-Fāsī had criticized the family law and proposed its reform in order to strengthen the

---

and was translated as *the Independence Movements in Arab North Africa* (1954). His most important book is *'al-Naqd 'al-Dātī* (self-critic) (1951).

position of women inside and outside the home. However, his reform suggestions were not taken into account in the 1957 codification of the *mudawwana*.

The *mudawwana*, based on Malikite rite, treated women throughout their lives as inferior entities. It obliged wives to unconditionally submit to and respect their husbands and their close relatives; it permitted polygamy, gave the right of divorce to men and implied that the sexes were complementary rather than equal. The *mudawwana*, instead of solving problems, inevitably contributed to the creation of conflicts and tensions. It described the personal status code as "a code that ... dutifully respects the seventh Century *sharīʿa*." Mernissi, however, asserts that the *mudawwana* is a transposition of *ʾal-Muwaṭṭaʾ* – a book about the law written by the founder of the Malikite law school Anas ibn Mālik – and the earlier Moroccan Code of Personal Status (Le Code du Statue Personnel) Mernissi (1987, 24).

After many years of debate to change this personal status code in favor of women, the late King Hassan II created a committee of religious scholars and judges, which was marked by the absence of women Sadiqi (2003, 28). In 1993, he announced new reforms, which included some changes for women. Feminist associations and activists were, however, unsatisfied since they argued that it still left women in subordinate positions. The 1993 *mudawwana* did not bring any essential changes concerning, for instance, polygamy and divorce.

By the ascent of Muḥammad VI to the throne in 1999, the demand for changing some articles of the *mudawwana* re-emerged. The National Plan of Action, a plan that was introduced by the Ministry of Social and Economic Affairs to enhance women's development, was launched in March 2000. It seemed to split Moroccan society between, on the one hand, adherers of international feminist views, and those of Islamic perspectives on the other hand. Secular feminists, including Said Saʿdi, Latifa Jbābdi and Amīna Lamrinī, supported the Plan of Action, to bring in line the *mudawwana* with international conventions. Islamist activists such as Aḥmad Raysūnī, Bāssima Ḥaqqāoui, and Jamīla Muṣallī refused the Plan of Action, arguing that it had no Islamic reference. Two years later, the King appointed a committee in which three women participated. Soon after, in 2004, the *mudawwana* was reformed on the basis of *sharīʿa* as well as on the universal human rights declarations.

The new reforms are briefly summarized in the following points. The two spouses are responsible for the household. They have similar rights and obligations. The minimal age of marriage is eighteen years old. A woman can marry herself with or without a tutor (legal guardian). Polygamy is restricted. The principle of divorce should be conducted by judicial supervision, and a woman has the right to ask for a divorce. Women also have the right to custody. The minimum age for children, both girls, and boys, to choose a custodian is the age of fifteen. A woman can transmit her citizenship to her children.[3]

Thanks to these reforms, Moroccan women are among the most emancipated women[4] in the Arab world in terms of their rights, second only to Tunisian women.[5] When Muḥammad VI became king, women's political situation was marked by several other changes. For decades after independence, women had never held key political positions. In June 1990 the minister of Islamic Affairs had declared on TV that women could not assume political responsibilities in Morocco, which provoked the rage of feminist associations and human rights organizations Daoud (1999, 320). In 2000, apart from instigating the Plan of Action, King Muḥammad VI appointed a female royal advisor; a woman as the head of the National Office of Oil Research and Exploitation; a female secretary of state and a woman as head of the National Office of Tourism. In the elections of September 2002, thirty women were elected as members of Parliament. Recently, the number of women as ministers in the PJD government decreased significantly, but the number of women at Parliament increased. There are more than fifty women members of Parliament as a result of the 'national list' of women candidates that was instigated by the government to ensure women's presence in Parliament.[6] In what follows I focus on Morocco's current women organizations.

## 2 Islamist Feminist Associations

Morocco's current women's organizations consist of two main strands: a secular and an Islamist. Secularism (*ʾal-ʿilmāniyya*) is broadly defined as the separation of politics and religion. One of its manifestations is that public activities and decisions, particularly political ones, should not be influenced by religious

3 For more details on the new reforms, see Harrak 2009; Ennaji (et al.) 2016.

4 For many Moroccan activists the *mudawwana* has not reached its perfect state though. The same applies to other codes of law. For example, Moroccan feminists have called for changes to criminal laws, including a statute that lets a rapist avoid punishment if he marries his victim, the so-called law article 475. At the end of 2017, the Ministry of Justice changed the law and introduced the new article 103–13.

5 In 1956, the Tunisian personal code of status has granted Tunisian women many rights including, the abolition of polygamy and repudiation, a minimum age of marriage, right in divorce and right in vote. These rights have stressed the secular freedom instituted by Habib Bourguiba who advocated other women's rights such as access to higher education and job activities. For more details see Charrad (2001).

6 In the last recent elections, more than 80 of Moroccan women were elected as members of Parliament.

beliefs and practices. Secular feminism is a discourse that advocates women's rights and empowerment on the basis of universal human rights instead of religious vocabularies.

By contrast, Islamism is a movement that uses Islam as a tool to achieve political goals and to gain power.[7] As the political strand of Islam, Islamism presumes that Islam should not only guide personal life but social and political life as well. It originally sought to legitimize patriarchal norms and values Dialmy (no date). As such, it targets illiterate, poor, and oppressed women as well as marginalized social classes where veiled and secluded women are commonly found. However, today's Moroccan Islamist feminists seek to reform patriarchal tradition. As such, they constitute a large part of Morocco's movement of Islamic feminism,[8] which is a movement that advocates women's rights and emancipation within the context of Islam.

According to Asma Lamrabet (2011), the Moroccan movement of Islamic feminism, largely consisting of Islamic women's organizations, emerged as an alternative discourse to resolve the conflictual relationship between rigid Islamist and Western secularist trends in Moroccan feminism Lamrabet (2011, 50–51). Islamic feminism seeks the reform and re-interpretation of Islamic original sources (*Qur'ān* and *Sunna*) to fight patriarchal approaches to Islamic jurisprudence that oppressed women for centuries in the name of Islam (Ibid., 51). Lamrabet stresses that the importance of Islamic feminism and the re-reading of the original texts lies in putting an end to patriarchy, which privileges men and discriminates against women. She also advocates a re-reading of the *Qur'ān* while taking social change into consideration. This process, in her opinion, deconstructs the misogyny that is involved in many different social phenomena, including forced marriages, violence, repudiation, and polygamy (Ibid., 53). Islamist women's organizations in Morocco call for the study of Islam to improve women's position. Their aims are gender equality and social justice grounded in an Islamic framework. For that purpose, they advocate a true understanding of the *Qur'ān* and *Hadīth* to free Islam from patriarchal ideologies and misunderstandings.

While the liberal feminist movement in Morocco calls for gender equality, social justice, and the elimination of unequal power relations between the sexes, it does so mostly in reference to universal human rights, which should be advanced by the state, political parties, and civil society. However, Moroccan

7 Moroccan Islamism has different faces, including conservative, moderate and radical. For more details see Sadiqi, Ennaji and Vintges 2016.

8 The term Islamic feminism is coined by the feminist Margot Badran (2007) and Ziba Mir Hussein (2004).

liberal feminism, as I will show below, also integrates elements from Islamic culture, as Mernissi (1977) did from the beginning.

In her book, Beyond Feminism and Islamism (2015), Doris H. Gray discussed whether or not women in North Africa and the Middle East were feminists. She also raised a number of questions, including whether being a Muslim is incompatible with feminism. Is there such a thing as Islamic feminism? If so, how does it promote women's rights? Through interviews with different Moroccan feminist activists, Gray addressed these questions. She analyzed the different views and agendas of the two Moroccan feminist movements, secularist and Islamist in character. Arguing to move beyond this binary, Gray proposed a third way for the Moroccan feminist movement. This third way is Islamic feminism. It is based on a re-interpretation of the *Qur'ān* and the *Sunna*, and the consideration of universal values. Gray explored the way Islamic feminist discourse attempted to bridge the gap between Islamism, a concept, which, as she puts it, refers to the revival of religious identity by those, who consider Islam as the main point of reference for their political discourse, and secularism. In this way, women's rights can be achieved without ignoring Islamic and universal values, including gender equality, democracy, and social justice. Gray discovered that the two strands of Moroccan feminism, secular and Islamist, reveal a kind of confluence because they share similar goals, including gender equality, democracy, and social justice. She concluded that Morocco is a country where gender equality and egalitarianism are not far from becoming a reality (Ibid., 17).

Osire Glacier (2013) discussed a number of Moroccan women in past and present who marked and impacted their contemporary political space. Her goal is to deconstruct the current popular belief that women's presence in political life is alien to Moroccan society. To highlight Moroccan women's active political role, Osire consulted the archives in search of Moroccan historical women's life stories. She discussed the fact that Moroccan women played in the past and continue to play today important political roles that highlight their leadership skills. Presenting a number of historical women who exercised power and marked history with their legacy, she demonstrated that Moroccan women's presence in political life did not emanate from modernity. Rather, it is rooted in history. Like Gray, she highlighted the point that Moroccan women's political power and leadership had to be revived in order to sensitize Moroccan men to women's presence in the realm of politics and to change the current patriarchal mentalities that consider political leadership solely a male specificity (Ibid).

According to Dialmy, Islamic feminists advocate women's rights within the context of Islam. It stresses the use of *'ijtihād* to achieve gender equality and the equal rights of men and women. Islamism, on the other hand, is a movement which stresses that men and women are not equal but different by nature: they use the notions of complementarity and equity instead of equality. The biological and natural differences between men and women make them play different roles and have different rights. Dialmy (2008) contends that Islamists do not reinterpret the *Qur'ān* from a modern social perspective. As I have discussed in chapter 2, the latter is exactly the aim of authors such as Aḥmad (1989), Wadūd (1992) and Barlas (2004), who argued that so as to do justice to the 'egalitarian ethical spirit' of the *Qur'ān* social change should be taken into consideration, which necessitates a revision of Islamic law.

The Islamists argued that the correct application of women's rights as specified in the Quranic text suffices for women to be respected and guarantees them just treatment, which corresponded with their interests. Dialmy (n.d.) sums up where the Islamists considered equal rights between women and men not applicable: namely where it concerns inheritance, polygamy, tutorship in marriage, as well as the right to marry a non-Muslim.

Dialmy also distinguished between three strands of Islamism in Morocco. The first is radical Islamism which emerged in the 1990s, and which has a "fierce hatred against the independent woman" and against women's participation in public life. The second is a "semi-integrated" Islamism, such as the association "Justice and Charity", with its women section (*qiṭāʿ 'al-nisā'ī*), which considers gender injustice due to people's distance from the sources of the Islam, the *Qur'ān* and *Sunna*. It calls for an equitable society, where men's and women's roles are complementary. "L'Islamisme intégré" constitutes the third aspect of Moroccan political Islam, such as represented by the PJD. According to Dialmy, however, all three strands are anti-feminist due to their emphasis on complementarity and equity instead of equality, which he characterizes as "l'anti-feminisme de l'Islamisme." Only an Islamic perspective that aspires to gender equality, based on *'ijtihād* and a reinterpretation of the *Qur'ān* from a modern social approach, can reconcile Islam and feminism. For this, Dialmy proposes that feminism must be the point of departure and arrival, the primary reference and ultimate objective.

Departing from the above presumptions and much to my surprise, my research on the different Islamist associations on their reception of female saints included other findings. From my fieldwork on three Islamist women associations in Morocco, I came to conclusions that are different from those of Dialmy's; namely, that Islamism in Morocco is a movement that contains modern voices, to the extent that the Islamist women organizations can be considered part of the feminist movement in Morocco. Danish researcher Julie

Pruzan-Jorgensen (2010, 18) supported my findings in her study of Moroccan Islamists feminist associations, albeit tentatively. Another researcher, Zakia Salime (2011, xxx), pointed in her study *Between Feminism and Islam: Human Rights and Sharia Law in Morocco* (2011) to "some arenas where the feminist and the Islamist women's movement are now overlapping". In what follows, these issues will come to the fore, through my discussion – based on my interviews with female Moroccan Islamists – of three Islamist women associations and their views on women in Islamic history in general and Moroccan women saints in particular.

The informants I have selected and interviewed are representatives of their Islamist organizations. Five out of these ten Islamist activists are the official spokespersons of their associations. The latter is Nadia Yāssīne, the leader of the women's section of the association *ʾal-ʿAdl wa lʾ-Ihsān*; Bāsima Ḥaqqāoui, head of the PJD women's organization as well as of ORWA (Organization of Renewal of Women's Awareness), and a member of the government as head of the Ministry of Family and Women's Issues; Jamila Muṣalī, the leader of *Wiʿām* association and a member of PJD and of *Muntadā Zahrāʾ*; Butayna Qarurī, the president of *Muntadā Zahrāʾ*; Khadīja Mufīd is the leader of Hiḍn association.

The other Islamist activists I interviewed are Aziza Baqqalī, a member of Parliament and a member of both *Muntadā Zahrāʾ* and ORWA; Raja Naji Mekkaoui, *ʿālima* and a representative of *Karama* association, Soumayya ben Khaldun, the ex-president of *Muntadā Zahrāʾ* and a member of PJD; Malika Bouʿnānī, a member of *Muntadā Zahrāʾ*; and finally Naʿīma Oughanīm, a representative of ʾal-*ʿAdl wa lʾIḥsān*. I have also chosen these activists because they are highly educated and active in academia as well as in politics. It took some time, and many phone calls, to actually interview these feminist scholars and Islamist activists. All the informants support the programs and written manifests of their organizations. I did not come across significant differences between their answers to the questions I posed them and the written documents and published papers on women's and family issues of their associations, as discussed below.

In the following section, I will have a look at the Islamist associations that constitute the mouthpiece of the Islamist movement in Morocco. These are *ʾal-ʿAdl wa l-ʾIḥsān, ʾal-ʿAdāla wa Tanmiyya*, which both have political orientations and the non-political Islamist association *Muntadā Zahrāʿ*. Most of the Islamist women affiliated with these Islamist associations enjoy, as I mentioned earlier, high levels of education, and most of them have a Ph.D.-degree in Islamic or non-Islamic sciences.

### 2.1 ʾal-ʿAdl wa l-ʾIḥsān

*ʾal-ʿAdl wa l-ʾIḥsān* (Justice and Spirituality) (JS) constitutes the largest Islamist *jamāʿa* in Morocco. Founded in 1983 by ʿAbdssalām Yāssīne, a charismatic leader and member of the Būdshishī Sufi order before his politicization, it is a Sufi-inspired organization.[9] *ʾal-ʾAdl wa l-ʾIḥsān* practices grassroots politics in a large network of charities and associations spread across Morocco and Europe as well as at the level of Morocco's civil society. The association also seeks to promote concrete social changes. It rejects the monarchy and strives towards a republican political system. Therefore, Moroccan authorities do not approve legally *ʾal-ʿAdl wa l-ʾIḥsān*, and it has not been allowed to transform itself into an official political party, nor partake part in Moroccan government.

*ʾal-ʿAdl wa l-ʾIḥsān*'s women's section constitutes an energetic force within the *jamāʿa* since its foundation. It has been headed by Nadia Yāssīne, holder of a university degree in political sciences and daughter of ʾAbdssalām Yāssīne. The number of women affiliated with *ʾal-ʿAdl wa l-ʾIḥsān* exceeds 30% of all activists affiliated with the three associations.[10]

Although the women's section is given priority on the agenda of *ʾal-ʿAdl wa ʾal-ʾIḥsān*, most of these women have played a symbolic role in its overall organization. In addition to their activism in the association, they hold regular employment positions. Among them are medical doctors, scientists, university teachers and government employees. Most of them are married, but some are single. Thus, many combine marriage and motherhood with participation in activism and in society as a whole.

*ʾAl-ʿAdl wa l-ʾIḥsān*'s women's section pursues several objectives. The education of women constitutes the major one. The Islamists teach illiterate women not only how to read and write, but they also teach them religion and Islamic studies and sensitize them about their rights. *ʾAl-ʿAdl wa l-ʾIḥsān* consider women as the core of familial and societal development. According to most of its activists, ignorant mothers produce ignorant children, and ignorant children become ignorant adults and citizens. In this way, society remains underdeveloped. The association also seeks the fulfillment of justice for women, be they victims of violence, the unemployed, economically underprivileged or the uneducated. In my interview with Nadia Yāssīne, she emphasized that most women have remained confined within poverty, ignorance and illiteracy, knowing nothing about the rights that Islam has given them. Male dominance,

---

9 Sufi influences are still felt in this orthodox Islamist movement, for example in the recitation of *wird*, religious poetic texts remembering God, thus resembling the mystical *dhikr*.

10 After the death of Yāssīne in 2012, *ʾal-ʿAdl wa l-ʾIḥsān*'s women's section, which has been led by Nadia Yāssīne, was dismantled.

Nādia Yāssīne continues, takes women's ignorance and illiteracy as a means to enhance women's oppression and discrimination.[11] For this reason, it is necessary to inform and educate women so that they can become conscious of their situation and of the rights that patriarchy has denied them.

The women's section undertook different strategies to reach the objectives stated above. A practical approach is helping women in crises, particularly illiterate and poor women, through education projects and financial support. Despite its poor budget, *ʾal-ʿAdl wa l-ʾIḥsān*, with the assistance of charitable members, financed women's micro-projects, such as wool production, baking and others. Another strategy of *ʿal-ʿAdl wa l-ʾIḥsān* is to criticize openly Moroccan women's daily problems, particularly those related to social injustice (such as sex segregation, women's illiteracy and unemployment). Their aim is to make women literate and with economic independence.

Most of the activists in *ʾal-ʿAdl wa l-ʿIḥsān* reject *Māliki fiqh*. They did not want to go back to it and refused to take it into consideration in their debates on women's rights. According to them, *Māliki fiqh* is the primary cause of Moroccan women's backwardness, marginalization and oppression. Nādia Yāssīne considered the *Māliki* law, on which the old family law code was based, a masculine law.[12] The rights that Islam gave to women are trampled due to the patriarchal interpretation of the foundational texts of Islam. Early marriage, which *Māliki fiqh* advocated, is a clear example of such a violation of Islamic and human rights. The activists of *ʾal-ʿAdl wa l-ʾIḥsān* also showed a negative reaction to polygamy and divorce that the old Personal Code of Status advocated; they stressed that polygamy and divorce of the old family law did not respect the Islamic instructions on polygamy and divorce. Thus, the women's section of *ʾal-ʿAdl wa l-ʾIḥsān* contended that *fiqh Mālikī* hinders Moroccan women's emancipation.

### 2.2 ʾAl-ʿAdāla wa Tanmīya (*PJD*)

The PJD was founded in the 1990s out of concern for Morocco's Islamic identity, which became increasingly criticized in the current global era. PJD women's section is composed of women with high levels of education. The Islamist activists of the PJD observed that Western styles of life, which to them are in many ways contradictory to Islam, had started to invade Moroccan families negatively affecting them. According to PJD activists, Morocco's own cultural heritage and identity were severely under pressure.

11 Interviews, Nadia Yāssīne, Salé, 2011.

12 Interviews, Nadia Yāssīne, Salé, 2011.

At the same time, PJD female members began to worry about the oppressive and discriminatory situation facing women. In their opinion, Moroccan women's contemporary situation was characterized by illiteracy, poverty and ignorance. As a consequence, the PJD women's association engaged in activism to protect Moroccan family institution, women's rights in a way that preserves their Islamic identity, while simultaneously being open to global discourses and development. For this reason, PJD's agenda deals with women and family issues. The *Qur'ān* and the *Sunna* constitute the major foundational sources in their debate on women's issues and the gender question. PJD Islamists rely on their own reading of the *Qur'ān* and *Hadīth*, using *'ijtihād* for the implementation of women's rights as described in these sources. Moreover, they explicitly acknowledge the importance of women's participation and input in *'ijtihād*. They appreciate *'al-majlis 'al-'Ilmī 'al-'a'lā* (the higher Scientific Council), which comes to include *'ālimāt* as participants in the process of *'ijtihād* and in the implementation of *Qur'ān* and *Sunna* on women's issues. Most of the PJD activists I interviewed also stressed universal declaration of human rights while dealing with the question of women. They are thus open to external sources besides the primary sources of *sharī'a*.[13]

The PJD participated in the foundation of the national Moroccan family committee, which opposed the Plan of Action, out of concern for the Moroccan family. It, however, also participated in different conferences and meetings both at the national and international level to promote women's rights, and in the debate over the old Code of Personal Status and the New Family Code, the *mudawwana*. The PJD is very interested in women's political roles. Female PJD members of Parliament founded a special women section for themselves, which primarily seeks to encourage and empower them to participate in politics. PJD members also empowered women economically. They taught them different kinds of crafts that could enable them to market their labor and achieve economic independence.

### 2.3 Muntadā Zahrā' li-l-mar'a 'al-Maghribiya

*Muntadā Zahrā'* is a network of Islamist women associations. It was founded in 2002 by a number of highly educated Islamist women. Some of them are members of Parliament. Others work as medical doctors, university teachers and administrative employees. *Muntadā Zahrā'* is made up of thirty-five associations, which are scattered in different Moroccan regions. There is the association 'al-Karāma in Tangier, Umm 'al-Banīn in Rashīdiyya, Khumaysa in

---

13 For more details on the relationship between Islamic law and human rights see Peters 1999.

Meknes and others. Moroccan urban and rural areas have established associations of the *Zahrāʾ* forum network to benefit from its agenda. The members I interviewed argued that their feminist agenda relies on the sources of Islam.

*Zahrāʾ* forum was founded for a variety of reasons. The members I interviewed express their concern about women being victims of oppression, discrimination and ignorance, and about the deterioration of the Moroccan family, which they see as the effect from changes inherent in modern life and the new global era. Ignorant, illiterate and poor mothers are unable to defend their own rights or those of their family members. They cannot guide their own lives or those of their children.[14]

For this reason, *Zahrāʾ* forum has engaged in different strategies to reach their purposes. Its activists have offered courses to women to combat illiteracy. They have also provided religious lessons to women to teach them about Islam and the rights Islam bestowed on them. *Zahrāʾ* forum members stress the importance of teaching women different crafts and professions such as embroidery and other marketable skills. It also offers financial assistance to women affiliated with their network to found economic projects and establish small businesses, or to look for work, with the goal of making them financially independent. *Muntadā Zahrāʾ* thus promotes women's social, religious and economic independence and empowerment.

In addition, *Zahrāʾ* forum plays the role of mediation to save women's conflectual relations. Zahraʾ Forum introduced the strategy of *ṣulḥ* (reconciliation) in order to support women's judicial cases. It mediates between married people in conflict to achieve reconciliation instead of divorce. According to interviewees, *Muntadā Zahrāʾ* receives a great number of couples contemplating divorce. Many oppressed women contact *Muntadā* forum for support and help. Reconciliation is also employed to rescue victims of domestic violence. *Muntadā* forum's preference for this strategy stems from the desire to perpetuate and proliferate healthy family lifestyles.

Another activity of *Muntadā* forum is youth and teenagers' education. The association continuously offers courses to male and female teens to instruct them on religion, and to give them a space where they can talk about private problems and crises. *Muntadā Zahrāʾ* thus functions as a therapeutic and educational center where youths can become informed adults, and women can master their lives more successfully.

---

14 Interviews, Islamist activist, Rabat, 2011.

## 2.4 *Similarities and Differences*

Today's Moroccan Islamists associations constitute a heterogeneous group, with different views. *da'wa wa 'al-tablīgh* (preaching and propagation) is a salafi movement that was founded in 1975 Tozi (2008, 277–98). It is more radical than *'Adl wa 'al-'Iḥsān* towards women's issues, in as far as this organization bases its preaching courses on the *Qur'ān, Sunna* and the book: *Riyāḍ ṣṣāliḥīn*[15] by the *'imām* Nawawī. It propagates the original qur'anic rules and religious instructions for men and women in urban and remote rural spaces. This movement has neither an official journal nor a published program, nor any manuscripts.

*Da'wa wa tablīgh* is a radical organization, whereas, the Islamists of PJD, ORWA, Hiḍn association and *Muntadā Zahrā'* are moderate. The Islamists of *da'wa wa Tablīgh* refuse the use of *'ijtihād,* meaning the exertion of conscientious and diligent effort in reinterpreting the primary sources of Islam. In contrast, *'al-'adl wa l-'Iḥsān*, PJD, ORWA, Hiḍn and *Muntada Zahrā'* do advocate the use of *'ijtihād* where it concerns women's and family rights. They consider the *Qur'ān* and *Sunna* as the primary sources on family and women's issues. However, they contend that the Islamic law that regulates women's and family's social status is to be constantly reinterpreted so that Islamic law adapts itself to new social developments. Apart from *da'wa wa tablīgh,* 'al-*'adl wa l-'Iḥsān*, PJD, ORWA, Hiḍn and *Muntadā Zahrā'* all Islamist organizations stress, on the one hand, the importance of preserving Islamic sources in dealing with women's issues, and on the other hand the necessity of using *'ijtihād.* On this basis, they share a number of guiding principles and programs. The principal cause of women's oppression to them is not Islam but the patriarchal interpretation of Islam. The PJD published an article entitled "*bayān ḥawla mashrū' khuṭṭa 'idmāj 'al-mar'a fī 'al-ttanmiyya*" (1999) (a report on a national plan for integrating women into development) in which its activists stress the importance of using *'ijtihād* in dealing with women's and family's situations. For, instance the issues of polygamy, repudiation and tutorship, in the views of the Islamists are to be reformed and are to be put under strict judicial control. The Islamists show satisfaction with these changes that are highly approved by the new *mudawwana* because they conform to Islamic law and preserve women's rights Mufīd (2005). Naji Mekkaoui, the first woman who presented a religious lecture in *'al-durūs 'al-ḥassaniyya* program, argues that the law regulating family issues has to be changed, while taking the sacredness of the family into consideration. Naji Mekkaoui (2005) also argues for a continuous change of family law, and for the necessity to adapt it to new social developments while at the same time preserving the Islamic heritage of Morocco. The

---

15 *Riyāḍ ṣṣāliḥīn* by Shafi'ī 'Abī Zakariyya Yaḥya Nawawī is a collection of *Hādīth*.

Islamists of ʾal-*ʿAdl wa l-ʾIḥsān* states that *fiqh* has to be changed too. In her article, "La Jurisprudence Musulmane est machiste," Nādia Yāssīne argues that it is necessary to re-interpret the *fiqh*, which entails a masculine and patriarchal interpretation of Islamic religion, through the process of *ʾijtihād*. She stresses the inclusion of women as participants in this process so that women enjoy equal rights as men. In another article entitled *ʾIshrāk ʾal-Marʾa fī ʾal-ʾijtihād sharṭ fī ʾal-ttaghyyīr wa ʾal-bināʾ* (2012) (Women's participation in *ʾijtihād* is a condition to change and build a new society), Yāssīne (2012) believes that there is no *ʾijtihād* without women's participation.

Aziza Baqqālī (2005, 129), an activist of ORWA and *Zahrāʾ* forum and a member of Parliament, argues in her article entitled *masʾūliyāt ʾal-ddawla fī ḥimāyat ḥuqūq ʾal-ṭṭifl*, (the responsibility of the state in the protection of child's rights) that the old *mudawwana* discriminated not only against women but against their children as well. She emphasizes that through *ʾijtihād* new amendments to the *mudawwana* should be implemented that preserve Moroccan's Islamic background and the importance of the family as a social institution and as a space where the rights of its members (father, mother and children) are guaranteed.

Mufīd (2005, 18–9) also stresses the importance of changing the family law through the use of collective *ʾijtihād* that includes the views of expert jurists, religious scholars, social scientists, activists and researcher. Major issues in this respect are violence against women, sexual violence and early marriages.

Apart from *Daʿwa wa Tablīgh*, all other Islamist organizations thus argue in favor of women's rights and full participation in society. In their programs, they emphasize that women should have a role in all domains, not only in the private sphere but also in public life.

Yāssīne argued that their *jamāʿa* encouraged women's participation in public political life. She added that they had women as members of her *majlis* (council) and as political decision makers. She also stressed the importance of women's education and participation in public life in fighting women's marginalization.[16] In *Tanwīr l-muʾmināt* (1996) her father, Abdssalām Yāssīne, discussed the necessity of women's religious and modern education and public participation. The book also presented procedures for women's education, and advices for women to emancipate themselves from the slavery that they lived for Centuries, so as to be able to work for God and society.

In *mushāraka ʾal-siyāsiyya lil marʾa bayna ʾal-wāqiʿ wa ʾal-maʾmūl* (Woman's political participation: between reality and expectation), Muṣalī (2011, 3–4) discussed the procedures that women should follow to become active participants

16 Interviews, Nadia Yāssīne, Salé, 2011.

in public and political life. Muṣalī (Ibid.) proposed several steps towards the integration of women into Moroccan society: first, the revision of social norms, second, the consolidation of democracy and the foundation of citizenship, and finally the strengthening of the legal system of the state in favor of women.

Besides addressing Islam, the Islamist activists I interviewed also attended the international norms and regulations on women's issues, in, particular the Convention on the Elimination of all forms of Discrimination against Women (CEDAW). Not all of the Islamist organizations I interviewed approved of the Universal Declaration of Human Rights in toto. *Daʿwa wa Tablīgh* and ʾal-*ʿAdl wa l-ʾIḥsān*, in particular, opposed the use of universal values. In contrast, the Islamist organizations PJD, ORWA, Hiḍn, association and *Zahrāʾ* forum stressed that it is possible to reconcile their Islamic approach with the international conventions.

As such Morocco and other Arab Muslim countries put forward certain reservations regarding CEDAW. Article Nine, which deals with the transmission of nationality to children, and article sixteen, which concerns the equality of men and women in the marital relationship, are considered to be in contradiction with Islamic religion. However, in 2003 on the sixtieth anniversary of the Universal Declaration of Human Rights Moroccan king Muḥammad the Sixth, however, announced that Morocco retracted its reservations of CEDAW. "Our reservations," the monarch said, "have become obsolete due to the advanced legislation that has been adopted by our country." The king's announcement had an impact in society, and stimulated the improvement of women's rights (Touahri 2008).

Activists of non-governmental organizations and women's organizations welcomed this progress. In contrast, all the Islamist associations mentioned above were worried about this elimination of reservations, particularly concerning article sixteen because, in their view, it contradicts Islamic religion. They argued that the total equality between men and women in terms of *tamātul* (symmetry) that was propagated by CEDAW was not approved by the *sharīʿa*. These Islamists advocated another kind of equality. Whereas they considered the roles of men and women similar in the public sphere, they conceived of their roles as complementary in the private sphere. Equity instead of equality is the norm here, meaning fairness and justice (Bourqiyya 2005). Naji Mekkaoui and Mufīd both stressed that women and men should live in harmony, cooperation and intimacy, and that no hierarchy or domination should exist in the family. Moroccan Islamists thus differed in their appreciation of the international conventions of human rights. The *ʿulamaʾ* likewise stressed that their attitude towards the reservations would not be changed (Touahri 2008).

## 3 Moroccan Feminist Activists' Reception of Women Saints

Another source the three Islamist associations rely on to underpin women's rights is the study of Islamic history to uncover the major roles women played in the past.

In the colonial era, it was the pioneers of the new Salafist movement – not to be equated with current fundamentalist Salafism – ʿAllāl ʿal-Fāsī (2008) and Hassan l-Wazzānī (1987), who appealed for the consideration of women who played outstanding roles in history to underpin women's rights. For example, they invited Moroccans, in general, to take the Prophet's wives as exemplary models. Likewise, ʾal-Fāsī referred to the Prophet's wife ʿĀʾisha as the greatest and most important example of a woman who played a crucial role in the history of the Muslim *ʾumma*. He also pointed to ʾUmm Dardāʿ, who was a *person* (a person who delivers formal legal opinions, *fatwa*) in the mosque, and to the fact that the Umayyad *sulṭān*, Sulaymān, regularly attended her religious lectures. ʾAl-Fāsī (2008, 254) also mentioned Nafīsa, the knowledgeable woman, whose knowledge impressed *ʾimām* ʾal-Shāfiʿī, the founder of Shāfiʿī school, and inspired him to continually attend her religious lectures and to become one of her faithful disciples.

As I mentioned earlier, *ʾakhawāt ṣafā* (sisters of purity) evoked Islamic history to underpin women's right to education and employment. The association explicitly referred to women who played important roles in the companionship of the Prophet.

Likewise, Islamist activists in the field of women's issues increasingly referred to historical Muslim women in history. They rely on Muslim scholars who wrote on these women, such as ʿAbdallāh Ḥalīm ʾAbū Shuqqa (1999), whose volume *taḥrīr ʾal-marʾa fī ʿaṣr ʾal-risāla* (Women's Emancipation in the Era of the Revelation) deals with social life in the Prophet's time and Prophet's female companions who played important social, economic and political roles. They are thus presented as exemplary models for women today. Clearly, the Islamist activist, Buʿnānī, glorifies the past where women played an important role. She contends:

> In the pre-Islamic era, female infants were buried alive and female adults were sold in the *nakhāsa* (slave trade market). They remained victims of slavery, male oppression and dominance for hundreds of years. Islam rescued women and moved them from a state of weakness to a state of power. Islam offered women a place next to men in every domain of life. Our Prophet offered a place to women next to him in the mosque (…). The mosque at that time was not only a space of *ʿibāda* (worship) but

> a kind of Parliament where the political and social affairs of the whole Muslim *ʾumma* were discussed and preserved. ʾUmm Salama, for example, was one of the Prophet's companions. She always participated in the Prophet's meetings, and she was always consulted on war matters. ʿĀʾisha, the Prophet's wife, was a *muftiya* and advisor for the entire affairs of Muslim *ʾumma*.[17]

The activists also highlighted the historical women and advocated the study advanced position of women in the Islamic past and contrast it with women's present situation. Most of them appeal for the necessity to return history to understand what is going on with women today.

*ʾal-ʿAdl wa l-ʾIḥsān* believed in historical women and advocated the study of historical references to understand how women became dominated by men and to argue that Islam does not give any justification for legal and social domination.

Islamist activists do not only refer to women's role in Arabic and Islamic history but in general, they also refer to Moroccan history. The later also constitutes another source Moroccan Islamists accounted on to uncover its feminist voices. Female saints hold a more ambiguous position. Although they are part of Moroccan religious history, there is the overall rejection of saint veneration by Islamists. The question then that arises: how Islamist feminists receive Moroccan women saints?

### 3.1 *A Source of Empowerment*

For reasons explained above, this section mainly concerns the Islamists' reception of Moroccan women saints. I will only occasionally refer to some of my interviews with secular feminists.

Although the Islamist interviewees disapproved of saint veneration because it is not permissible in orthodox Islam, from my interviews it turned out that they approved of the use of Moroccan history and women saints as original sources to inform their debate on women's rights. Ḥaqqāouī acknowledged that women saints who attained spiritual and political leadership are « *marjiʿiyya* » (reference), that emanates from Islamic and Moroccan ethnic backgrounds. The Islamists acknowledged the importance of understanding the historical roles of women saints. In their opinion, modern women should employ this understanding to face the future and to build strong personalities. Otherwise, the status of women will remain underdeveloped.

17 Interviews, Buʿnānī, Rabat, 2011.

However, the relationship between the Islamist activists and women saints is in no way created by pilgrimages since Islamist activists refuse to visit saints' shrines. Some of them said that they did frequent visits to saints' sacred tombs in their childhood. They would go with their mothers and grandmothers to spend the day in the vicinity of their favorite women saints. It is their orthodox religious education that made them discover that saint veneration is not permissible in Islam and stopped them from following the example of their female family members.

The Islamists' understanding of *baraka*, thus, is different from that of the saint venerators we met in the previous Chapter. The Islamists, however, did not believe in women saints as holders of *baraka* in the sense of blessing power. They rejected the pilgrims' understanding of *baraka*, which defined it as a force for curing the ill, sheltering the homeless, facilitating girls' marriages and other therapeutic services. The Islamists offered another understanding of *baraka*. They interpreted it in terms of the knowledge (*maʿrifa*) and wisdom (*ḥikma*) that women saints succeeded in acquiring. In their opinion, the *baraka* of a woman saint also encompassed her ability to acquire knowledge that enabled her to attain decision making positions. Ḥaqqāouī argues:

> *Baraka* not in terms of a divine force that fulfills a particular wish, but rather in terms of the abilities and capacities that a woman saint develops to reach fame, power, and authority. *Baraka*, in the sense that pilgrims attribute to it, cannot help a saint (male or female) attain power. The proof is that there are many saints with so-called strong *baraka* but fail to reach decision-making positions.[18]

Thus, Ḥaqqāouī acknowledged that *Baraka* is the ability to acquire knowledge and wisdom that enabled its holder to impact the public order. Therefore, *baraka* as knowledge and wisdom is highly appreciated in the Islamist feminists' discourses.

The Islamist activists respected the saintly female personalities themselves. Most of the activists argued that a feeling of admiration and even of love towards women saints started to rise inside of them when they learned of the stories about their lives and about the heroic role these women played in the past. Although the activists did not visit the saints' shrines to bond directly with them, they felt an emotional bond with them from a distance. *ʾAl-ʿadl wa l-Iḥsān* activists refer in their discourses to women saints in history as their sisters. They establish a relation of sisterhood with the women saints because

18 Interviews, Ḥaqqāouī, Rabat, 2011.

they shared religious doctrinal ties with them and because they believed that they would encounter them in the hereafter. Most of the Islamist interviewees confirmed that they received historical women saints as a source of great inspiration and empowerment. This empowerment is characterized by a taking up of several different self-techniques of the female saints, or elements of their examples, which the interviewees integrate into their self-techniques and ethical self-formation. Most of the Islamists I interviewed employed a number of terms to designate women saints as role models. These terms are: *fakhr* (honor), *qudwā* (model), *mathal* (example) and the Berber word *tamghārt*. The activists used this terminology in their discourses to express their pride, respect, and admiration vis-à-vis these historical women saints and their achievement of saintly personalities.

### 3.2 *Ethnic Identities*

Islamist activists valued Moroccan local cultural heritage with the exception of the ritual of saint veneration. *Zahrā'* forum Berber Islamists even named their associations after the Berber women saints who belong to their Berber tribes and regions, such as *Lalla* Zaynab. Likewise, Arab Islamist activists chose names of Arab women saints who were buried in the urban and rural locations of Morocco, for their associations, schools, youth houses and other institutions, such as Khumaysa, Umm 'al-Banīn. The life stories of female saints inspired activists to revive the cultural heritage as an element of their ethical values, albeit without disregarding modernity. Interestingly, the appreciation of local cultures did not create tensions in the Moroccan Islamist activists' discourses on women saints as a constituent of their ethnic identity. Although their ethnicity was recognized by them, most of the Islamists treated women saints from different ethnicities in a similar manner. According to them, women saints, whether Berber or Arab, are all Muslims and are to be appreciated regardless of their different origins. What is essential to them is the way these historical women achieved sainthood and ethical personalities that marked history. Thus, the Islamists acknowledge that women saints bridged cultural boundaries and ethnic specificities, and, as such, can empower Islamist feminists today. According to the interviewees, women saints have indeed taught them to appreciate their cultural and Islamic background in building their ethical personalities, or ethical self-formation.

### 3.3 *Spirituality and Knowledge*

The activists were interested in some of the spiritual aspects of historical women's sainthood. They value women saints' abilities to achieve piety and the spirituality that enabled them to reach God's closeness. Attaining divine proximity was not an easy task, Ḥaqqāouī asserted. She called the women saints teachers of piety and religion.[19] Women saints were spiritual masters who taught Sufis how to reach the divine and to become models of women engaged in mysticism to achieve pious personalities.

The feminist activists did, however, appreciate women saints' style of achieving great social and knowledgeable personalities more than their strictly pious efforts. Their self-techniques of attaining greatness through education were the most important reasons why activists considered women saints role models. Some of the activists asserted that these women saints' knowledge empowered them to become more interested in education and knowledge. They were conscious of the phenomenon of illiteracy, which is still high particularly among Moroccan women.[20] For this reason, feminist activists kept stressing in their discourses the high educational level historical women achieved. They even discussed how many women in history postponed or even challenged traditional early marriages for the sake of the achievement of educated and knowledgeable personalities. In this way, Buʿnānī said that she succeeded to convince illiterate mothers of the importance of education in woman's life. This made women attend regularly her courses. She taught them how to read and write and also how to educate their children and orient their lives. Another activist also explained to illiterate women how their education could help them cultivate the seeds of education and knowledge in themselves and in their children's mind.

Being conscious of the importance of women saints' education, the activists became persuaded by their studies of women in history that more examples of historical women had to be researched and presented in educational centers. The revival of historical women's biographies and life stories is one of these strategies. Farīda Zumurrud, an activist and *ʿālima* in the high *ʿulama'* council in Rabat, founded the cultural center *ʿiḥyā' 'al-turāth wa-l-mar'a* (Revival of the Heritage and the Woman) in 2010 in Rabat for research on Moroccan women in history.[21] According to Zumurrud, the activist researchers, volunteers, and students, in the center are engaged in collecting biographies and life stories mentioned in written history. Another way the Islamist activists had chosen to keep historical women saints present in the activists' daily lives was the propagation of their biographies on the Internet.

19 Interviews, Ḥaqqāouī, 2011.

20 40% of illiterate Moroccan women in urban spaces and around 60% in rural areas are illiterate. See Sadiqi 2008, 13.

21 Interviews, Zumurrud, Rabat, 2011.

The Islamist feminists also spread information on female saints and other important women in Islamic history via national and international conferences. Actually, the activists I interviewed continually organized round table meetings to which they invite specialists in the field to discuss the meaning of women in religious and social history. Seminar titles like *'ishraqāt khālida* (eternal lightness) and *nisā' khālidāt* (eternal women) often highlighted the historical women as exemplars. The Justice and Spirituality association founded a school named *'Akhawāt 'al-'Akhira* (Sisters of the Hereafter) where women were regularly discussing women saints' life stories. *'Al-'Adl wa l-'Iḥsān* organized monthly meetings in which they discussed life stories of women known for their sainthood and piety. The aim of their discussions was, as Nādiya Yāssīne puts it, to understand the way these historical women created saintly personalities and lived in a context that enabled them to attain sainthood. The example of educated historical women saints also encouraged women to carry on their education, as was supported by the *'Akhawāt 'al-'Akhira School.* This school trained female students and guided their higher studies. It has produced until now one hundred *'ālimāt.*[22]

### 3.4 *Transgressing Patriarchal Limits*

Islamist activists contended that it was exactly women saints' self-transformation into knowledgeable and spiritual leaders that empowered them to challenge the conventional roles that oppressed women. From my interviews, the Islamists appreciated historical women saints because they created personalities that yielded positive impacts that empowered them to transgress the dominant social norms. PJD member 'al-'Uthmānī, (1998, 13) who took an interest in Morocco's female cultural heritage, stressed in his writings that the Islamic perception of women, which is based on the *Qur'ān* and the *Sunna*, derived from three important principles: equality, emancipation and participation. These principles, in the opinion of 'al-'Uthmānī, were distinctly displayed by historical Moroccan women. Muṣalī, a present day PJD Islamist activist, explicitly appreciated both Arab and Moroccan researchers' writings on women in history, and their desire to understand the significance of women's historical roles to underpin women's rights.[23] All the historical women concerned refused to be confined to their private spaces, freed themselves from the chains of the dominant system and succeeded in creating public personalities. More importantly, the Islamists explained that the local communities approved these historical women's transgression of conventional

22 Interviews, Nadia Yāssīne, Salé, 2011.

23 Interviews, Muṣalī, Salé, 2011.

values. This was also the case for secular feminists I interviewed. Khadīja, another liberal activist of the ADFM, added that education empowered women to make their voices heard and to change the dominant rules and the gender division of labor. In their opinion, these historical women used Sufism as a technique to live their conventional religious norms but their construction of sainthood resisted their local patriarchal ideologies. Thus, Islamists and secular feminists take Morocco's cultural heritage to uncover its feminist voices.

Most of the Islamist activists also said that they wanted to propagate women saints' historical role because it constituted a challenge to the dominant system not only of their time but of any other historical era. They admired the way Moroccan female saints were able to play a role in the private as well as in the public sphere serving as spiritual, social and sometimes even political leaders.

Historical Muslim women displayed that women and men should equally participated in all domains of life. The Islamist activists turned out to experience a sense of continuity in relation to them, particularly where it concerned these social and political roles. Ben Khaldūn, an activist in PJD, asserted that modern activists could be viewed as successors to the women saints in that they were continuing their social and political activities. In fact, all activists stressed that activism and voluntary work had their roots in history. Muṣalī explained that it started with the *zāwiya, dar l-fəqīrāt, dār l-maʿāləma,* and *dār ðəmāna.*[24] These names cover different traditional houses where women gathered to perform charitable and other religious rituals and social roles. The Islamist activists considered these religious and social houses as forms of civil society and voluntary associations of equals in which the participants (women saints, Sufi, and other women) were united by common goals, namely, teaching the *Qur'ān* education of the *murīd*, feeding the poor and sheltering the refugees and the homeless. These women saints and Sufis, in the opinion of Ben Khaldūn, could be considered as the pioneers of social activism.

One can conclude that the activists were inspired by women saints especially the self-techniques involved in their development into socially and politically active women. The Islamist activists emphasize women saints' social role in the public sphere as a strategy to impact other women to be participants in voluntary associations and social activism.

But how does this relate to their views on gender equity and complementarity as normative ideals, instead of as equality? During my interviews I explicitly asked for their opinion on these issues. As it is mentioned previously, the Islamists' ideas about complementary roles for the sexes are based on the conviction that men and women are different by nature. They argue that

24 Interviews, Muṣalī, Rabat, 2011.

women's hormonal constitution and bodily roles as mothers predispose them to certain emotions and, therefore, to certain preferences in terms of types of work. These are connected to a natural tendency to be passive and need the protection of men, who, as a result of their own hormonal constitution, tend to be physically stronger and more aggressive and inclined to take on the role of protecting women.

But from my interviews, I found that most of them approved gender equality in the public sphere and limit complementarity to the private sphere. Ḥaqqāouī explained that she believes in gender complementarity in the private sphere, but in the public sphere she believes in strict gender equality and parity.[25] The Islamists argue that, in spite of their natural constitution and dispositions, women are able to realize what they need and want in various situations. They can work toward, insist on, and even fight for the right to fulfill these needs and wants. Some of them see no contradiction between women's natural dispositions and the desire to pursue higher education and employment in a variety of areas and at multiple levels. Some believe that holding high-level positions is not incompatible with their natural constitution and dispositions provided they are also able to incorporate their roles as wives and mothers into the lives and lifestyles that such positions demand them to lead.

The Islamists do not see a contradiction or incompatibility between being passive and protected in the private sphere and being assertive and strong in the public sphere at the same time. Sāmiya, an Islamist who works as a medical doctor, argued that she was proud of taking care of her husband, children, and the whole family, and she was also proud of her duties in the hospital. Being assertive and strong has an impact on the way Islamists think and act in general, and enables them to live according to a gendered division in the home, and simultaneously stand up for their rights in the public sphere. One respondent argued that the perspective of complementarity entailed that it was up to women themselves to decide if they wanted to remain in the private sphere. Women should have the choice to go out and enter the public sphere. Their responsibilities at home sometimes demanded sacrifices, but it was the other way around as well.

In some cases, some of the men are taking on new responsibilities in the private sphere. They are doing things that they were not doing before. Some of the efforts of the Islamist activists thus are leading to changes in the attitudes and actions of the men in their lives. Sāmiya, argued that when she came back home, she found her children and her husband had done at least half of

25 Interviews, Ḥaqqāouī, Rabat, 2011.

the housework.[26] This shows that the Islamists see themselves as promoting change in both the private and public sphere, even though they would reject the principal elimination of gender-based rules and practices. It is therefore difficult to speak in terms of a strict complementarity between the sexes. The Islamist women I talked to are seeking change in the private and the public sphere, and aimed to gain access to the latter through education, activism, and employment, so as to eliminate oppression and attain equality. In other words, they are seeking to have more say, more control and more power over the conditions of their lives, making them, in that sense, similar to secular feminists.

## 4 Islamist Feminism

In this section I will evaluate from my interviews with members of the three Islamist women associations – which were basically about the role of female saints – whether the Islamists activists do or do not belong to Moroccan feminism. In what follows I will sum up what I have found as the main characteristics of their outlooks. The first principle stressed by the Islamists I talked to is gender equality. It is seen as inherent to Islam, as is clear from the *Qur'ān* verse that articulates that man and woman are created from the same soul, and from the Prophet's *Hadīth* which states that *'al-nisā' shaqā'iq 'al-rijāl* (women are siblings of men). Both references support the idea that men and women's equality is *'al-'aṣl* (the origin or basis) of Islamic law. Islamists believe that gender equality is inherent in Islam. Islamists define equality between man and woman in terms of having similar rights and similar opportunities in all domains of life. A second principle the Islamists stress is emancipation. According to the PJD, women should be emancipated, and emancipation means that women are free in their choices, not dependent. Complementarity constitutes the third principle of their discourses, i.e., the idea that a man compliments a woman and a woman compliments a man. Islamist activists are keenly aware that the idea that men and women need to complement each other in order to create harmony and cooperation within the family arouses doubt among secularists. That is why many of them assert that the idea simply refers to the biological and emotional differences between the sexes, and accordingly, a possible preference of women for motherhood and certain types of work. They stress that it does not refer to diverging gender roles outside the home that may limit women's choices for education, work and activism. In short: a woman should be able to choose what she wants. In that sense Islamists are definitely demanding

26 Interviews, Islamist activist, Rabat, 2011.

changes, outside and inside the home. The fourth principle that the Islamists are greatly concerned with is the family. The latter, in the Islamists' opinion, constitutes the primary basis around which women's issues revolve. Family dynamics get emphasis on Islamist agenda, because the family is seen as a society in miniature. Most of the Islamists advocate the cultivation of gender equality in the education of children, the future generation. This necessitates, in the opinion of the Islamists, the re-education of mothers and the advancement of their roles. For them, the prioritization of mothers logically follows from their non-existent or poor education, which is not beneficial to the upbringing of children in which they nevertheless play a major role. This does not mean that fathers should not play a larger role in their offspring's education. On the contrary, Islamists believe they should. The fifth point of interest for Islamists is the relationship between *ʾijtihād*, modernity, and modernization. They define modernity in terms of the quest for progress, development, and renewal in all areas of life, with *ʾijtihād* being the key element in the transition to a new phase; one, in which human beings can fulfill their aspirations, and justice and equality can prevail. The Islamists' reinterpretations concerning gender relations take social change into consideration. To them, *ʾijtihād* can facilitate a revolution in tradition and conservative thinking, which has so far negatively impacted the understanding of religion vis-à-vis women's rights. The last principle emphasized by the Islamists' discourses is women's participation in politics and public life. They believe that both men and women have to be present in public life. They believe that the feminization of the public religious sphere is rooted in history. The Islamists all assert that the public religious sphere, which is often conceived of as a masculine space, has come to be increasingly marked by a feminine presence. An important aspect of Islamist feminists' struggle is the public recognition of women's right to full participation in this sphere.

From my interviews the Islamist activists are impressed by the women saints' strong and ethical personalities, and by their abilities to challenge male domination. They consider historical women saints as role models and are determined to follow historical women's footsteps by carrying on their religious, social and political activities, which they take up in the context of their own ethical self-formation. They ensure the continuing presence of these historical women saints in modern life by accumulating accounts of their lives. The revival of women saints' stories supports their agenda as they empower women to educate themselves. They also remind Moroccans that women are not obliged to submit to the customary system that seeks to disempower them and render them inactive.

The interviewed activists use historical women saints in different ways to show how pious women of history are inspiring to them. Most of the Islamists activists include the study of women saints and Sufis in their programs. As I mentioned earlier, Yāssīne organized monthly lectures on women saints.[27] The PJD and *Zahrā'* forum also organized seminars and meetings under the motto of a particular woman saint and invited scholars and researchers to present papers on women in history. In her thesis, Muṣalī referred to *'Akhawāt Ṣafā* (sisters of purity) as the first feminist association in Morocco. This association, in her opinion, was founded by Sufi women who were considered as the pioneers of the feminist movement in Morocco Muṣalī (2010); Mufīd (2009). Muqri' 'al-Idrissī abū Zīd, a PJD researcher and a religious scholar, presented a paper in one of the meetings organized by Hiḍn association about the Sufi woman Zaynab 'al-Nafzāwiya's life, services and roles during the Almoravīd dynasty ('al-'Idrissī 2011). Qarūrī (2011) also headed seminars organized for the revival of women in history and other exemplary women to correct the stereotypes around women today. In one of her papers, she explained that women saints and Sufis constituted a role model that modern women should be proud of and should take up.

Like these Islamist women organizations, the liberal feminist movement as well accounts on historical women and history as important references to underpin their fight against patriarchy and for women's rights. Thus, both Moroccan Islamist and secularist activists consider historical women saints as a source of empowerment from which they gain power and in which they invest power. What struck me from my research, was that, whereas Islamist women's organizations are often described as traditional and conservative with regard to women's issues, I more or less found the opposite to be the case. Moroccan Islamist associations' discourses and practices seek the political, social and economic empowerment of women to such a degree that they, in my view, can be called Islamist feminist organizations. As such, they belong to Moroccan women's ethical freedom practices, which underpin women's rights in a critique of women's oppression.

Islamist activists base their struggle for the improvement of women's positions on different sources. They count on the primary sources of Islam, the *Qur'ān* and *Sunna* and on their own interpretation of these sources. They strongly believe that *Mālikī* jurisprudence's definition of women's status is a patriarchal interpretation of Islam and the primary cause of Moroccan women's oppression and discrimination. More importantly, Islamist associations

27 Interviews, Nadia Yāssīne, Salé, 2011.

also make reference to Islamic history and to Moroccan local cultural heritage in their debate on women's issues. Finally, the Universal Declaration of Human Rights constitutes another source that Moroccan Islamist feminists count on for their discourses on women's issues. They strongly believe that humanism advocated by human right discourses is part of Islam. This additional adoption of universal human rights may be considered remarkable. However, Sadiqi (2016, 70–71) states that what Morocco is witnessing at the present is the secularization of Islamist feminism and the Islamization of liberal feminism. Moroccan Islamist feminism and secular feminism have similar objectives: to fight patriarchy at all levels of society and personal life. Islamist feminism is thus part of Moroccan feminism, which is, as such, a polyvocal one.

# Conclusion

The results of my research challenge the conventional image of passive Moroccan Muslim women and the depiction of women as victims of patriarchal religious ideologies. Instead, my book draws an alternative discourse that presents women, whether in the past or in the present, as active religious agents whose religious agency displays their active engagement in creating, redefining, re-interpreting and transforming their religious roles both in private and public spheres.

Shrines of female saints still stand throughout the Maghreb, especially Morocco. Little is known about these female saints. Practically the only sources on them are hagiographies and oral stories. From these sources, my book discusses these women's construction of sainthood through inventorying the self-techniques they used in this context. My research thus approaches them as agents, discussing the way they actively sought sainthood, and at the same time did transgress or failed to transgress the social limits that were imposed on them. It does so in the context of current discourses on Moroccan women and feminism, specifically by researching how the narratives of these female saints are received by Moroccan venerators and by feminist activists today. My book questions whether there is continuity in Moroccan female spiritual agency throughout history, which can inspire Muslim women today and others in defying the negative images of them sketched above.

Chapter 1 gives a first indication of my hagiographic sources and describes my fieldwork throughout several regions in Morocco. It discusses the scholarly research on Moroccan female saints thus far and indicates the researches on which I build. Some important concepts of my book are discussed in this chapter; one of them being Sufism especially in its popular version. It explores the basic principles of Sufism as formulated by 'al-Ghazalī, which form the basis of orthodox as well as of popular Sufism, with the latter being additionally characterized by the practice of saint veneration. The *ribāt* is discussed as space where this veneration of saints and other religious rituals take place. The concept of *baraka* is also discussed and defined. Thirdly, my understanding of rituals in this book comes to the fore, namely as performative acts. Following this, I discuss a few theoretical approaches related to the concepts of the agency. Embodiment refers to the fact that the body is modified by social categories and thus lives – embodies – its social and spiritual environment. Theoretical debates about the agency, such as they currently take place among anthropologists, often refer to the works of Foucault (1997b),

 | DOI:10.1163/9789004429895_007

Butler (1990) and – recently – Mahmood (2005). Like Mahmood's study, this book builds on the final Foucault's ethics and the conceptual tools it presents, such as ethical self-formation and ethical self-techniques, both of which refer to embodied ethical ways of life. But unlike Mahmood's work, this book also employs Foucault's ethical concept of "freedom practices." Freedom practices are ethical self-practices that involve ethical self-formation, and which create new ethical ways of life in opposition to existing forms of domination. Finally, the chapter introduces the concepts "effects of equality," and "effects of egalitarianism" as developed in the work of the Dutch historian Siep Stuurman. Discourses and texts – and I add: ways of life and life stories – can express notions and thoughts of equality and egalitarianism, without any explicit reference to these terms.

In chapter 2, Moroccan Sufism is discussed in more depth, especially in relation to gender. Here, I briefly discuss Moroccan history in the context of its Islamization, in which proliferation of Sufism has been crucial. Moroccan Sufism is then discussed, as different from the Middle Eastern versions, in that it focuses more on social reality, dealing with people's social matters and crises. The Moroccan Sufi saints engaged in society: saints in Morocco played spiritual, religious, social and political roles. The approaches of Moroccan Sufism from some important anthropological studies are discussed in several respects. Contrary to these studies it is argued that there is some continuity instead of a sharp distinction between Moroccan orthodox and popular Sufism, given that in many instances since the latter also involves an acceptance of the foundational texts, beliefs, and practices of orthodox Islam. In this chapter, the relationship of Sufism and gender is also discussed primarily in relation to the works of some Sufi scholars of the past, which make it explicit that women are included in Sufism, in as far as they can reach the highest ranks of spirituality and sainthood just like men do. The relationship of Sufism and gender is further discussed by approaching Sufism as a strand of spirituality that finds its basis in the *Qur'ān*. Several contemporary Muslim authors argue that the spiritual side of Islam which is found in the *Qur'ān* is egalitarian in character. These works thus argue for intrinsic gender equality at the heart of Islam. I finally discuss some examples of female Sufi mystics, such as Rabīʿa ʿal-ʿAdawiyya, and Fāṭima of Cordova, who, from the narratives, come forward as living their lives on equal footing with their male counterparts.

The chapter also discusses Islamic and Moroccan hagiography. It follows up on chapter 1's first discussion of hagiography in that it focuses on its main characteristics amidst other laudatory genres. Moroccan hagiography is then discussed as being basically similar to Islamic hagiography, though with an additional emphasis by way of lengthy narratives on the saints' miracles, personality, and piety. Many types of saints come to the fore in Moroccan hagiography, as is clear from their inclusion of women saints. The authentic character of these hagiographies is a topic of debate among scholars. The hagiographers remained true to the saints' cultural space and time, and reveal how people understood sainthood. The chapter ends with a brief survey of the Moroccan hagiographies that were consulted for the inventorying of Moroccan female saints in history.

Chapter 3 focuses on Moroccan women's construction of sainthood. It discusses the stories of female and male saints belonging to Morocco so as to explore the ways these saints achieved friendship with God, which turned out to be most similar in character. Only some examples of non-Moroccan female saints are included, where they elucidate that female saints' positions and strategies were not different from those of their male counterparts. Life stories found both in the archives and oral literature show that these saints employed self-techniques that empowered them to become saints. Some of the main self-techniques used by male and female Sufi are the practicing of piety, acquiring learnedness, the performing of miracles, practicing *jadhb*, the taking up of social and political roles or the practicing of private sainthood in the context of the family.

The self-techniques of searching for knowledge were seen as crucial to reaching God's closeness. Women like men developed themselves into knowledgeable personalities. Moroccan history includes exemplary women who achieved orthodox religious education and reached high decision-making positions. Life stories show how women and men saints are able to perform miracles to publicly display their sainthood. *Jadhb* was another self-technique used by men and women to become friends of God. Both women and men found themselves attracted to the divine and endowed with divine grace. Taking up social and political goals, or choosing for ordinary sainthood instead, were self-techniques of female and male saints alike. The stories studied thus show that the self-techniques that men and women employed for their ethical self-formation, namely to achieve sainthood, are mostly similar. However, in their description of the similar self-techniques of male and female saints, the narratives convey the effects of equality and effects of egalitarianism. In the context of the dominant patterns the women saints lived in their self-practices – i.e., their ethical self-formation through applying certain ethical self-techniques – come forward as ethical freedom practices: they created new ethical ways of life for women that were in opposition to forms of domination. Their transgression of dominant patterns is furthermore illustrated by a discussion of the lives of three interesting and notable women saints: ʿAzīza, ʿĀʾisha and Fāṭima. These exemplary women saints cultivated personalities in a way that gained them power and authority. They impacted their communities with their personalities and marked history with their legacy.

Chapter 4 discusses the way historical women saints are received by Moroccan women today. I document the impact historical women saints have on a variety of contemporary women, including the venerators of women saints, women attending mosque lessons and *murshidāt*. The chapter shows how these contemporary religious women transform themselves to become religious agents, like their holy predecessors. Women visit shrines and mosques to live their piety and spirituality. In the shrines, women perform freely different rituals to express their piety and their strong veneration to their women saints besides the celebration of mainstream religious feasts. There are also functionaries of the shrines who play important active roles. These women display women's leadership in the shrines in their centrality in leading rituals and in their overall religious agency.

Women venerators use women saints' shrines as a self-technique to develop their spirituality and construct a pious personality. Both Northern and Southern Moroccan women found in their women saints a source of empowerment for a new ethical self-formation. They defined women saints as their role models and moral exemplars. Some of them started to search for religious knowledge by attending mosque lessons headed by *murshidāt* and *waʿiẓāt*. As such, Moroccan women show an interest in seeking orthodox education so as to become active religious agents.

Both the *murshidāt* and *waʿiẓāt* women attendees integrate women saints in their discourses as empowering role models so as to change themselves into religious agents. *Murshidāt*'s and *waʿiẓāt*'s religious knowledge empowers them to engage in activism and to question women's status in contemporary society. They refer to the rights that Islam gave women, and they question cases where these rights are violated. The conclusions of Mahmood (2005) on the Egyptian mosque women movement do not apply to the Moroccan context. Moroccan women venerators, women attendees, and *murshidāt* and *waʿiẓāt*, by using various self-techniques in which women saints of the past to play a certain role create religious personalities, in ways that involve a transgression of patriarchal patterns, thus making their self-practices count as ethical freedom practices.

The fifth chapter of the book deals with the way activists in current Moroccan women's movement receive women saints in their discourses. It focuses on Islamist activists' attitude towards historically exemplary women and their legacy. Both Islamist and secular strands of Moroccan women's organizations show a positive attitude towards women saints. They consider women saints as role models who – among other exemplary women in Islamic history – occupy an important place in their agendas and discourses. From my interviews with Islamist activists, it turns out that the Islamist associations, *ʾal-ʿAdl wa l-ʾIḥsān*, *ʾal-ʿAdāla wa Tanmiya*, and *Muntadā Zahrāʾ*, have similar strategies, objectives, and activities. In contrast to some researchers' writings that describe Islamist women activists as being conservative and traditional towards women issues – my interviews show that these activists, like their secular counterparts, seek political, social and economic empowerment of women and equality with men. Islamist feminism's discourse on men and women's equity, instead of equality, involves the private sphere only, and even there they are also after egalitarianism. This egalitarianism is clear from the strategies Islamist associations employ to underpin women's empowerment and women's rights. They base their struggle for women's crises on different sources. They account on the primary sources of Islam, the *Qurʾān* and *Sunna* and on their own interpretation of these sources. They strongly believe that the Maliki jurisprudence definition of women's status is a patriarchal interpretation of Islam and the primary cause of Moroccan women's oppression and discrimination. More importantly, Islamist associations also refer in their debate on women's issues to Islamic history and to Moroccan local cultural heritage. The Universal Declaration of Human Rights constitutes another source that Moroccan Islamist activists account on to fight patriarchy as secular feminists do.

From the material studied and explored in the chapters above, the overall conclusion can be that in spite of the obvious contextual differences, there is continuity in the presence of female religious agency in Moroccan history. Moroccan women saints of the past – in the context of Sufism – applied a set of self-techniques to define construct and create a saintly personality that at the same time challenged male domination. Likewise, contemporary Moroccan women's religious agency displays a continuity as well, in as far as the women saints of the past continue to exert agency through the women who venerate them. The main continuity that I found, however, is that we find ethical freedom practices among Moroccan women of the past and the present: new ethical ways of life for women, in opposition to domination. Moroccan women throughout history, have created new practices or revised or transformed existing ones, in order to achieve a wide range of goals, many of which have been directly or indirectly linked to a felt need to make a difference, to achieve a new ethical self-formation, to express their views, to have a voice in their communities, to become leaders, teachers, scholars, and activists, to counteract and attempt to change the conditions of their own lives, of their communities, and of the society at large.

The results of my research also show that historical women who were excluded from the practice of religious orthodoxy created for themselves space where they lived their piety and spirituality and achieved saintly personalities. Sufism opened its gates so as to let the marginalized to live his/her piety and spirituality. Mysticism did not exclude women from the practice of religion. Rather, it offered them a space to practice their religion. Sufism did not take gender into consideration where it concerned the achievement of sainthood, but rather was and continue to be gender neutral in this respect. Sufism here needs to be more explored because it reflects clearly the egalitarian spirit of Islam.

Contemporary female religious agents draw on historical women saints as saintly personalities to support their struggle against women's discrimination and male dominance. Thus, history as such turns out to be a crucial source for women in their defense of women's rights. Historical Moroccan women's religious agency thus has positive effects on modern Moroccan society. Moroccan women today have come to believe that it is very important to reconsider the past in dealing with women's issues and women's religious rights today. The importance of culture and history for the revising of contemporary women's roles and positions necessitates more research. The study of Moroccan historical women does not attract the interest of Moroccan scholars though there is a body of rich evidence and materials particularly in oral history on historical women saints. An abundance of research still has to be done particularly on the archive and oral historical that await editing and analysis. More study also needs to be done on the contexts that enabled these historical women to become saints with miraculous abilities and active religious and social agency. The objective of my book is to be part of a new scholarship on historical women saints and to uncover the silenced histories of women's power in Morocco.

What also emerges from my study of women saints and their reception by women today is that gender equality and egalitarianism are highly stressed as fundamental Islamic principles. It turns out that Moroccan women, like men, desire to realize the ultimate goals of religion and thus engage in a struggle to achieve God's closeness. The women also express that God disregards gender differences and favors equality and that equality and egalitarianism reside at the heart of Islamic religion.

Theoretically, I have based my research on Mahmood (2005) whose concept of agency – analogous to Foucault's work on ethics – emphasizes women's self-techniques in the construction of religious personalities in terms of an ethical self-formation. From my research, I can conclude that Moroccan women, both as historical and as contemporary religious agents, similarly developed their religious personalities. However, contrary to Mahmood's findings, which found that her respondents want to do religion and remain within the limits of the conventional patterns they live in, my research demonstrates another face of Muslim women's agency. It shows that Moroccan women's religious agency, whether in the past or in the present reveals their individual choices and their own voices. These women either in the past or the present engage with Islamic sources, to demonstrate that Moroccan women have another way of challenging patriarchy. They engage with the system, local culture and dominant social norms to uncover its techniques that empower them to create strong piety and intellectual ownership and socio-political leadership. These achievements as such receive great approval from the part of their cultural norms. Each of these women sought in her own way to impact their societies and to leave their legacies and intellectual luggage to future Moroccan generation.

These historical religious women took up the concept of freedom practices of Foucault that explains how Muslim women in collective settings and communities have been able to push boundaries and challenge dominant norms. Freedom practices as collective vocabularies subvert and show existing norms, and offer people tools for developing an agency that as well challenges existing norms and that as such involves ethical self-creation or ethical self-invention. The concept of freedom practices surpasses notions of freedom as individual autonomy, in that it points to the enabling sides of collective settings and vocabularies. At stake in the concept are collectivities and vocabularies that subvert and indicate norms, and that as such offer the tools for a personal ethical self-creation and self-invention. The Moroccan female saints in my study practiced an ethical self-creation in the context of a community/vocabulary of Sufism and uncover its techniques to create sainthood. Their creation of sainthood as such is approved by social norms. This means that dominant social values include progressive values.

In the course of my study of Moroccan women's religious agency, I have come to recognize that although Moroccan women saints and Sufis respect the local norms in the process of self-formation, they succeeded to have a saintly powerful personality. Their power anthem authority (as I discussed it in chapter 3) are clear from the great impacts these historical women saints had on the people of their time and people of Morocco today. As I have mentioned earlier, their agencies involve freedom practices that made them have access to political leadership. This means that progressive values are part of dominant social relations. It shows that a supposedly conservative and conventional Muslim culture has another side, which encompasses relatively independent voices and messages, and which harbors the content of feminism.

Moroccan women's roles in history also entail gender equality and parity that the 2011 Moroccan constitution appeals for. Moroccan feminists today either in activism or in academia engage with the study of historical records and the archives to highlight women's roles and promote women's contemporary presence in the public political sphere which has been radically ignored in the recent time. The current Moroccan government, which is governed by Islamists, marginalize women and refuse to give them a chance to have access to political decision making positions. The Moroccan emancipated women, in the opinion of traditional Islamists, constitute a danger for Moroccan ethics and religious culture. They still oppose feminists' efforts to improve women's status. This negative perception of the Islamists and traditionalists has found refuge, particularly among Moroccan citizens who misunderstand Islam and are not well informed about its history that encompasses feminist voices.

Gender equality and egalitarianism that reside both in the heart of Islam and local culture need to reach the different Moroccan social classes, particularly the rural areas where poverty, illiteracy, and ignorance are in place. Moroccan feminists still have problems to propagate their feminist agenda among rural and Berber Moroccans and to sensitize them to their cultural heritage and its feminist voices. Moroccan women's religious agency in the past and present counters the current radical Islamist belief that women's emancipation is something alien to Moroccan culture and Islamic religion. It also demonstrates to the West and non-Islamic cultures in general that women's agency that stresses their public leadership and power is an integral part of Moroccan religious and cultural heritage. More importantly, an awareness of Muslim women's roles in the past may contribute to the changing of mentalities concerning feminine leadership and gender dynamics in the current Muslim world. My study in this respect appeals for a fundamental shift in the social order, in customs and traditions. Moghadam rightly appeals for the improvement of women's status and the fulfillment of women rights not only from within the context of Islam but also within other systems Moghadam (2013, 23).

Moroccan feminists appeal for a meta-cultural approach to local culture. An assessment of the foundations and nature of the culture is very urgent. It helps us to strengthen and draw on the more adaptive elements and avoid the harmful ones. The positive side of the local culture helps in fighting conservative thinkings and change patriarchal mentalities. Spreading knowledge of the legacy of historical Muslim women may help in filling gaps not only between Berber and Arab cultures, but also between the West and Islam, and may contribute to mutual respect and peaceful existence of different religions and cultures. To highlight Muslim feminist voices, one need to unpack the different cultures existing in the Arab and Muslim world, explore their history and their constitutive elements and study their meanings and impacts. This procedure certainly will help us to understand that conservative cultures also encompass freedom practices, practices of Muslim women's ethical self-formation that transgress patriarchy, within the context of specific cultural communities. The prominent role of Muslim women in Moroccan history clearly uncovers the universality of the values of both Islam and feminism and the possibility of reconciling Islam and gender equality. My study of Moroccan women's religious agency shows that the values on which feminism rests are an endemic part of Moroccan culture. Therefore, feminism could be covered from within and not only from outside a dominant local culture.

This reconciliation between Islam and the feminist universal values could be highly achieved if only the process of *ʾijtihād* and the consideration of the social change are stressed. *ʾIjtihād* is the reinterpretation of the sacred text. The prophets' companions approved the use of *ʾijtihād* and reinterpreted the *Qurʾān* and changed the laws. The *Qurʾān* has not one reading. In contrast, the *Qurʾān* could be read differently taking into account the new modern life circumstances that Muslim people come to live. I mean here that all what concerned the quranic laws related to traditional social life are to be changed because Muslims today come to live a new life different from that of the past. If the acts of worship remain unchangeable, the acts of social interactions and laws are to be renewed and even changed. The *ʾijtihād* here does not contradict religion which stresses the acts of worship and the spiritual side that protects religion. Rather, *ʾijtihād* allows Muslims to change the laws once the context is changed. It is a crucial means to fight the patriarchal interpretation of the sacred text. It is a way to bridge the gups between secularism and Islamism. Moroccan Arab Spring movement, feminist activism, and civil society believe in *ʾijtihād* to meet women's rights and socio-political current crises and reconcile Moroccan local culture with global feminism. Their demands for a revision of the constitution involve the importance of gender equality, social justice and democracy. Fighting patriarchy and propagating democracy in Morocco are intertwined, which encourages Moroccan women to feel optimistic about their future.

# Bibliography


ʾal-ʿAbbādī, Ḥassan. 2004. *ʾal-Ṣāliḥāt ʾal-Mutabarak bi-hinna fī Sūs*. Rabat: Wizārat ʾal-Awqāf.

ʾabū ʿAzīz, Yūsuf. 2008. *Rijāl wa Nisāʾ Ḥawla ʾal-Rasūl*. Casablanca: Dār al-Maʿrifa.

ʾabū Barīk, Raḥāl. 2010. *Barakat ʾal-Nisāʾ ʾal-Dīn bi Ṣīghat ʾal-Muʿanat*. Casablanca: ʾIfrīqiyya ʾal- Sharq ʾal-Maghrib.

ʾabū Shuqqa, ʿAbd ʾal-Ḥalīm. 1999. *Taḥrīr ʾal-Marʾa fī ʿAṣr ʾal-Risāla*. Beirut: Dār ʾal-Qalam li ʾal- Nashr wa ʾal-Tawzīʿ.

ʾabū Zīd ʾal-Muqriʾ, ʾal-Idrissī. 2011. "Zaynab ʾal-Nafzāwiya." *ʿAshghāl ʾal-Multaqā ʾal-Waṭanī ʾal-ʾAwwal lil ʾal-ʾusra dawrat Zaynab ʾal-Nafzāwiya*. Silsilat nadawāt wa muḥāḍarāt nuḍimat bi Murrākush ʾayām 1, 2, 3 May 2009. Casablanca: Jamʿiyya ʾal-Waṭaniyya ʾal-Hiḍn, 19–28.

ʾal-ʾAṣfahānī, ʾAbū Nuʿaym. 1932. *Ḥilyat ʾal-Awliyāʾ*. Maḥmūd Fakhūrī, (ed.). 10 vols. Beirut: Dār ʾal-Maʿrifa.

ʿAṭṭār, Farīd ʾal-Dīn. 1905. *Tadhkirat ʾal-ʾAwliyāʾ*. Manāl ʿAbd ʾal-ʿAzīz (ed.). Cairo: ʾal-hayʾah ʾal- Miṣrīyah ʾal-ʿĀmmah lil-Kitāb.

ʾal-Bādisī, ʿAbd ʾal-Ḥaq ʿIsmāʿīl. 1982. *ʾal-Maqṣad Sharīf wa ʾal-Munziʿ ʾal-Laṭīf bi Ṣulaḥāʾ ʾal-Rīf*. Saʿīd Aʿrāb, (ed.). Rabat: ʾal-Maṭbaʿa ʾal-Malakiyya.

ʾal-Banī Muḥammad, Nāṣir ʾal-Dīn. 1988. *Ṣaḥīḥ Sunan bin Māja bi ʾIkhtiṣār ʾal-Sanad*. Maktab ʾal-Tabiya ʾal-ʿArabī li Duwān ʾal-Khalīj ʾal-Riyyāḍ: Ṭabʿa ʾal-Thālitha.

Baqālī, ʿAzīza. 2005. "Masʾūliyyat ʾal-Dawla fī ḥimāyat ḥuqūq ʾal-Ṭifl ʾInṭilāqan min ʾal-Taʿʏdīlāt ʾal-Wārida fī Mudawanat ʾal-ʾUsra." *Min Mudawanat ʾal-ʾAḥwāl ʾal-Shakhṣiyya ʾIlā Mudawanat ʾal-ʾUṣra: ʾAyyu Jadīd?*. Casablanca: Jamʾiyya ʾal-Waṭaniyya ʾal-Hiḍn, ʾal-ʿadad 1, 129–139.

Benḥsīn, Fatima ʾal-Zahra. 2011. "ʾal-Baḥt ʾal-Maydānī lil ʾal-Mandūbiyya ʾal-Sāmiyya li-Takhṭīṭ ḥawla ḍāhirat ʾal-ʿunf: Qirāʾa Naqdiyya." *Ṣawt ʾal-Muntada*. ʿAdad, 2 wa 3.

Ben Mansour, Muḥammad. 2006. *ʾal-Mahgreb Qublu ʾul-ʾIstiʿmār: ʾal Mujtamaʿ wa ʾal-Dawla wa ʾal-Dīn* 1792–1822. Trans, Muḥammad Hubayda. Casablanca: Markaz ʾal-Taqāfī ʾal- ʿArabī.

Burqiyya, Raḥma. 2005. "Mudawanat ʾal-Aḥwāl ʾal-Shakhṣiya: min ʾal-Taʾsīs ilā ʾal-Taghyīr?." *Min Mudawanat ʾal-ʾAḥwāl ʾal-Shakhṣiyya ʾIlā Mudawant ʾal-ʾUṣra: ʾAyyu Jadīd?* Jamʾiyya ʾal-Waṭaniyya ʾal-ḥiḍn. Casablanca: Maṭbaʾa ʾal-Najāḥ ʾal-Jadīda, 59–69.

ʾal-Bukharī wa Muslim. 2007. *Ṣaḥīḥ ʾal-Bukhārī*. Casablanca: Dār ʾal-Ṣubḥ. Vol. 5. Kitāb ʾal-Nikāḥ, Bāb ʾal-Targhīb fī ʾal-Nikāḥ. Vol. 8. Kitāb Faḍāʾil ʾal-Ṣaḥāba, Bāb Manāqib Qurābat Rasūl Allāh wa Manqabat Fāṭima ʿalayha ʾal-Salām bint Rasūl Allah.

ʾal-Būṭī, Muḥammad Saʿīd. 1993. *Fiqh ʾal-Sīra*. Beirut: Dār ʾal-Nashr.

Corbin, Henri. 2006. *ʾal-Khayāl ʾal-Khallāq fī ʾal-Taṣawwuf li ʾIbn ʿArabī*. Farīd ʾal-Zāhī, (ed.) and trans. Rabat: Maṭbaʿat Būraqrāq.

Dāwūd, Muḥammad. 1959. *Tārīkh Tiṭwān*. Tetouan: ʾal-Markaz Jāmiʿī lil-Baḥth ʾal-ʿIlmī.

ʾal-Fāsī, ʿAllāl. 2008. *ʾAl-Naqd ʾal-Dāthī*. Rabat: Muʾassasat ʿAllāl ʾal-Fāsī.

ʾal-Ghazālī, Abū Ḥāmid. (no date). *ʾIḥyāʾ ʿUlūm ʾal-Dīn*. Beirut: Dār ʾal-Kitāb ʾal-ʾArabī.

Ḥajjī, Muḥammad. 2008. *Maʿlamat ʾal-Maghrib*. Rabat: Jamʿiyyat Taʾlīf wa ʾal-Nashr.

ʾal-Ḥakim, Suʿād. 2000. ʾal-Marʾa Walī wa ʾUnthā: Qirāʾa fī Naṣ ʾibn ʿArabī'. *ʾAl-Turāth ʾal-ʿArabī*, 36–45.

Hamam, Muḥammad. 1998. ʾal-Nisāʾ fī ʾal-Ṣalāḥ wa ʾal-Wilāya bi ʾal-Maghrib Khilāl ʾal-Niṣf ʾal-Thānī min ʾal-Qarn ʾal-Thāmin ʾal-Hijrī ʾal-Rābiʿ ʿAshar li ʾal-Mīlādī: Namūdhaj Muʾmina ʾal- Tilimsāniyya wa ʿAzīza Saksāwiyya. In *Fikr wa Tārīkh*, 97–115. Rabat: Manshūrāt Kulliyyat ʾal-ʾAdāb wa ʾal-ʿUlūm ʾal-ʾInsāniyya bi Ribat: Silsilat wa Buḥūth wa Dirasāt, Raqm 23.

ʾal-Ḥawāt Abū Rabīʿ, Sulaymān. 1994. *ʾal-Rawḍa ʾal-Maqṣūda wa ʾal-ḥilal ʾal-Mamdūda fī Maʾāthir Banī Sūda*, Abd ʾal-ʿAzīz ʾal-Tilānī. Fez: Maktabat Aḥmad bin Yaḥya.

ʾal-Ḥuḍaykī, Muḥammad. 2006. *Tabaqāt ʾal-Huḍaykī: li ʾal-ʿAllāma Muḥammad bin Aḥmad ʾal- Huḍaykī*. Boumzguou Muḥammad, (ed.). Casablanca: ʾal-Maṭbaʿa Jadīda.

Ibn ʿAbd Allāh, ʿAbd ʾal-ʿAzīz. 2001. *Maʿlamāt ʾal-Taṣawwuf ʾal-ʾIslāmī*. Rabat: Dār ʾal-Nashr ʾal- Maʿrifa.

Ibn ʿArabī, Muḥyī ʾal-Dīn. 1985. *ʾAl-Futūḥāt ʾal-Makkiyya*, vols. 2. 3. Beirut: Dār ʾal-Ṣādir.

Ibn ʿAskar, ʾal-Ḥusaynī Shafshāwunī Muḥammad. 2003. *Dawḥat ʾal-Nāshir li-Maḥāsin man Kān bi ʾal-Maghrib min Mashāyikh ʾal-Qarn ʾal-ʿĀshir*. Casablanca: Manshūrāt Markaz ʾal-Turāth ʾal- Thaqāfī ʾal-Maghribī.

Ibn Jallūn, Leila. 1948. "Dawʊr ʾal-Marʾa fī ʾal-Nahḍa ʾal-Maghribiyya". *ʾAmal*. Qurtuba Edition. Issue 1, 164–167.

Ibn Jawzī, Abū ʾal-Faraj. 1985. *Ṣifāt al-Ṣafwa*. Maḥmūd Fakhuri, (ed.). 4 vols. Beirut: Dār ʾal-Maʿrifa.

Ibn Khaldūn, Abū Zayd ʿAbd Raḥmān. 1960. *ʾal-Muqaddimah*. ʿAbd ʿal-Wāḥid Wāfī, (ed.). Cairo: Dār Shaʿab.

Ibn Khaldūn ʾal-ʿAmranī, Muḥammad ʾal-Salḥi. 2009. *Sabʿ Sayyidāt Marrakʊshiyyāt bi ʾIstiḥqāq*. Marrakech: Jarīdat ʾal-ʾAfaq ʾal-Maghribiya.

Ibn Manṣūr, Muḥammad. 2006. *ʾal-Maghrib Qabla ʾal-ʾIstiʿmār: ʾal-Mujtamaʿ wa ʾal-Dawla wa ʾal-dīn 1792–1822*. Muḥammad Hubayda, trans. Casablanca: Markaz ʾal-Taqāfī ʾal-ʿArabī.

Ibn Manẓūr, ʾAbū ʾal-Faḍl ʾal-Dīn Muḥammad ibn Muhammad. (No date). *Lisān ʾal-ʿArab*. Beirut: Dār ṣādir.

Ibn Qunfudh ʾal-Qusṭanṭinī, ʾAbū l-ʿAbbās Aḥmad ʾal-Khaṭīb. 1965. *ʾUns ʾal-Faqīr wa ʿizz ʾal-ḥaqīr*. M. Fasi wa A. Faure, (eds.). Rabat: Manshurāt ʾal-Markaz ʾal-Jāmiʿī li ʾal-baḥth ʾal-ʿiIlmī.

ʾIbn Zaydān, ʿAbd ʾal-Raḥmān. 1990. *ʾItḥāf Aʿlām Nās bi Jamāl ʾAkhbār Ḥāḍrat Maknās.* Casablanca: Maṭābiʾ Idyāl.

Jalāb, Ḥassan. 1995. *Buḥūth fī ʾal-Taṣawwuf ʾal-Maghribī.* Marrakech: Maṭbaʿa wa Warāqa ʿal- Waṭaniyya.

Janbūbi, Muḥammad. 2008. *ʾal-ʾAwliyāʾ fī ʾal-Maghrib.* Casablanca: Maṭbaʿat Dār ʾal-Qarawiyyīn.

ʾal-Jirārī, Abdallāh. 1994. *Waraqa fī ʾAwliyaʾ ʾal-Ribaṭ wa Masājidih wa Zawayāh.* Casablanca: Maṭbaʿat ʾal-Jadīda.

Kaḥḥāla ʿUmar, Riḍā. 1982. *ʾAʿlām ʾal-Nisāʾ.* Beirut: Muʾassasat Risāla.

Kanūnī, ʿAbdallāh. 1961. *ʾal-Nubūgh fī ʾal-ʾAdab ʾal-ʿArabī.* Beirut: Dār Kitāb. Vol. 3.

ʾal-Kattānī, Muḥammadʾibn Jaʿfar b. Idrīs. 1900. *Salwat ʾal-ʾAnfās wa Muḥādathāt ʾal-Akyās bi- man ʾUqbira min ʾal-ʿUlamāʾ wa Ṣulaḥāʾ bi-Fās.* Casablanca: Maṭbaʿat ʾal-Jadīda. Vol. 2 wa 3.

Lamrinī, ʿAbd ʾal-Haq. 1993. *Dalīl ʾal-Marʾa ʾal-Maghribiyya.* Rabat: Dār Nashr ʾal-Mʿrifa. Ṭabʿa ʾal-ʾūlā.

Mahmah, Mustafā ʿAbdassalām. 1978. *ʾal-Marʾa ʾal-Maghribiyya wa ʾal-Taṣawwuf fi ʾal-Qarn ʾal-ḥādī ʿAshar ʾal-Hijri.* Casablanca: Matbaʿat ʾal-Dār ʾal-Bayḍāʾ.

ʾal-Manūnī, Mohamed. 1979. *Waraqāt ʿan ʾal-ḥaḍāra ʾal-Maghribiyya fī ʿAṣr Banī Marīn.* Rabat: Manshūrāt Kuliyyat ʾal-ʾĀdāb wa ʾal-ʿulūm ʾal-ʾInsāniyya bi Ribāṭ.

ʾal-Marghani, Ibrāhīm. 2007. *Nujūm ʾal-Tawāli ʿalā Darari ʾal-Lawāmiʿ fī Aṣli Maqari ʾal-ʾImām Nāfiʿ.* Casablanca: Dār ʾal-Rashād ʾal-Ḥadīth.

ʾal-Marrākushī, ʿAbd ʾal-Mālik. 1965. *ðhayl wa ʾal-Takmila.* Muḥammad bin Sharīfa, (ed.). Beirut: Dār ʾal-Taqāfa wa Nashr wa Tawzīʿ.

ʾal-Marrākushī, ʾal-ʿAbbās bin ʾIbrāhīm. 1983. *ʾal-Iʿlām bi man ḥalla bi Marrākush wa ʾAghmāt min ʾal-ʾAʿlām.* ʿAbd ʾal-Wahhāb bin Manṣūr, (ed.). Rabat: ʾal-Maṭbaʿa ʾal-Malakiyya.

Miftāḥ, Muḥammad. 1981. *ʾal-Tiyār ʾal-Ṣūfī wa ʾal-Mujtamaʿ fī ʾal-ʾAndalus wa ʾal-Maghrib ʾatnāʾa ʾal-Qarn Thāmin ʾal-Hijrī ʾal-Rābiʿ ʿAshar ʾal-Milādī.* Rabat: Jāmiʿat Muḥammad ʾal-Khāmis.

Mūndīb, ʿAbd ʾal-Ghanī. 2006. *ʾal-Dīn wa ʾal-Mujtamaʿ Dirāsa Susyulūjiyya lil ʾal-Tadayyun bi ʾal-Maghrib.* Casablanca: Ifrīqiya Sharq.

Muntadā Zahrāʾ ʾal-Maghribiyya. 2011. "Dawr ʾal-Marʾa ʾal-ʿArabiyya fī ʾal-Tanmiya ʾal-Mustadāma". *Silsila Zahra.* ʾal-ʿAdad ʾal-Rābiʿ, Ṭabʿa ʾal- ʾūlā.

Muṣali, Jamīla. 2011. *ʾal-Ḥaraka Nisāʾiyya biʾal-Maghribʾal-Muʿāṣir: ʾIttijāhāt wa Qaḍayā.* Rabat: ʾal-Markaz ʾal-Maghribī li-Dirasāt waʾal-ʾAbḥāthʾal-Muʿāṣira.

Naji, Rajaa Mekkaoui. 2005. "Munṭalaqāt ʾal-Taḥdīt wa ʾal-Tajdīd fī ʾal-Shaʾn ʾal-ʾusarī. *Min Mudawanat ʾal-ʾAḥwāl ʾal-Shakhṣiyya ʾIlā Mudawanat ʾal-ʾuṣra: ʾAyyu Jadīd?*". Jamʿiyya ʾal-Waṭaniyya ʾal-Hiḍn. Casablanca: Maṭbaʿa Najāḥ Jadīda, 47–57.

ʾal-Naṣirī, Aḥmad ben Khalid. 1954. *ʾAl-Istiqṣāʾ li-ʾAkhbār ḥawla ʾal-Maghrib ʾal-ʾAqṣā.* Casablanca: Ṭabʿat Dār Baydaʾ. Vol. 3.

Ouʿachi, Muṣṭapha. 2004. ʾal-Kāhina. *Maʿlamat ʾal-Maghrib*. Salé: Jamʿiyya ʾal-Maghribiyya li- Taʾlīf wa ʾal-Nashr. Vol. 20, 6731–6732.

Oughanīm, Ḥabība. 2007. *Maghribiyāt ḥāfiẓāt lil Qurʾān*. Rabat: Maṭbaʿat Ribaṭ.

ʾal-Qādirī, Muḥammad Ṭayyib. 1977. *Nashr ʾal-Matānī li ʾahl ʾal-Qarn ʾal-ḥādī ʾAshar wa ʾal-Tānī*. Muḥammad Hajji and Aḥmad Tawfiq, (eds.). Rabat: Dār ʾal-Maghrib li Taʾlīf wa ʾal-Tarjama wa ʾal- Nashr Silsila Tarājim.

ʾal-Qarūrī, Butayna. 2011. "Shabakat ʾal-Muntadā Taʿrif-u Taḥassun nawʿiyy-an wa Kamiyyan". *Ṣawtʾal-Muntada*. Muntada Zahraʿ, ʿadad 2, Māris.

Qaṭṭān, Rashīd. 1998. "ʾal-marʾa ʾal-Maghribiyya fī ʾadabʾal-Manāqib: ʾal-Tashawwuf ilā Rijāl̂al- ʾTaṣawwuf Namūdhajān". *MajallatʾAmal* 13, no. 1:129–138.

ʾal-Shādhilī, ʿAbdʾal-Laṭīf. 1989. *ʾal-Taṣawwuf waʾal-Mujtamaʿ: Namādhij min al-Qarnʾal-ʿĀshiř al-Hijrī*. Casablanca: ʾAl-Najāḥ.

ʾal-Ṣahrawardī, Shihāb ʾal-Dīn. 1999. *ʿAwārif wa-l-Maʿārif*. Baghdad: Dār Maʿārif.

Shrīṭ, ʿAbdallāh. 1975. *Fikr ʾal-ʾAkhlāqī ʿinda ʿibn Khaldūn*. Beirut: ʾal-Sharika ʾal-Waṭaniyya li ʾal- Nashr wa ʾal-Tawzīʿ.

ʾal-Sulāmī, ʿAbd ʾal-Raḥmān. 1993. *ʾal-Niswa ʾal-Mutaʿabbidāt ʾal-Ṣūfiyyāt*. Mahmūd ʾal-Ṭanjī, (ed.). Cairo: Maktabat ʾal-Khanjī.

ʾal-Sūsī, Mukhtār. 1960. *ʾal-Maʿsūl*. Vols. 2, 4, 12, 13, 14, 15. Casablanca: ʾal-Najāḥ.

ʾal-Sūsī, Mukhtār. 1963. *ʾAfwāh ʾal-Rijāl*. Tetouan: Maṭbaʿat ʾal-Mahdiya, vol. 2. 56–59.

ʾal-Sūsī, Mukhtār. 1986. ʾal-Muʾassasāt ʾal-Taʿlīmiyya ʾal-ʾūlā bi Sūs. *Majallat Manāhil*, 34.

ʾal-Ṣuyūṭī, Jalāl ʾal-Dīn ʿAbdʾal-Rahmān et al. 1979. *Tafsīr ʾal-Jalālayn*. Beirut: Dār ʾal-Fikr.

ʾal-Tādilī, Abū Yaʿqūb Yūsufi bin Yayḥa. 1997. *ʾAl-Tashawwuf ʾilā Rijāl ʾal-Taṣawwuf wa ʾAkhbār ʾAbī ʾal-ʿAbbās ʾal-Sabtī*. Aḥmad Toufīq, (ed.). Casablanca: ʾal-Najāḥ.

ʾal-Tajdīd. 1999. "ʾal-Jamʿiyya ʾal-Maghribiyya li ʾal-ttarbiyya wa Riʿāyat ʿal-ʾuṣra: Bayān ḥawla Mashrūʾ Khuṭṭat idmāj ʾal-Marʾa fī ʾal-Tanmiyya." ʿadad 32, 1.

ʾal-Tajdīd. 2000. ʾal-Bayān ʾal-Ṣādir ʿan ʾal-Masīra ʾal-Waṭaniyya ʾal-Shaʾbiyya li-Taḍāmun Maʿa Jarīdat ʾal-Tajdīd. ʿAdad 60, 3.

ʾal-Tāzī, ʿAbd ʿal-Hādī. 1992. *ʿAl-Marʿa fī Tārīkh ʾal-Gharb ʾal-Islāmī*. Casablanca: Nashr Finik.

ʾal-ʿUthmānī, Saʾδd ʾal-Dīn. 1998. *Qaḍiyyat ʾal-Marʾa wa Nafsiyyat ʾal-Istibdād*. Casablanca: Manshūrāt ʾal-Furqān.

ʾal-Wazzānī, Muḥammad bin Laḥsan. 1987. *ʾal-Islām wa ʾal-Mujtamaʿ wa ʾal-Madīna*. Fez: Muʾassasa bin Laḥsan ʾal-Wazzānī. Silsila dirasāt wa Taʾammulāt, 195–222.

Yāssīne, Abdssalām. 1996. *Tanwīr ʾal-Muʾmināt*. Beirut: Dār Lubnān.

Yāssīne, Nadia. 2012. ʾIshrāk ʾal-Marʾa fī ʾal-ʾijtihād Sharṭ fī ʾal-Taghyyīr wa ʾal-Bināʾ. Available at the website: https://www.youtube.com/watch?v=8ftMdKC4Yuw.

Zarrūq, Aḥmad. 1992. *Qawāʿid ʾal-Taṣawwuf*. M. Z. ʾal-Najjar wa A. M. Farghalī, (eds.). Beirut: Dār ʾal-Jīl.

## French and English Sources

Abu-Lughod, Lila. 2002. “Do Muslim Women Really Need Saving?” *American Anthropologist*, 3, 783–90.

Ahmed, Leila. 1989. “Feminism and Cross-Cultural Inquiry: The Terms of the Discourse in Islam.” In: E. Weed (ed.), *Coming to Terms*. New York and London: Routledge, 143–151.

Ahmed, Leila. 1992. *Women and Gender in Islam: Historical Roots of a Modern Debate*. New Haven: Yale University Press.

Ahmed, Sumayya. 2016. “Learned women: three generations of female Scholarships in Morocco.” *Journal of North Africa Studies*, vol. 21, no. 3, 470–484.

Akhmiss, Mustapha. 1984. *Rites et secrets des marabouts a Casablanca*. Casablanca: Editions S.E.D.I.M.

Amri, Nelly. 1999. « Femmes, sainteté et discours hagiographique au maghreb médieval: Naissance à l'histoire: le cas d'une sainte de Tunis, Āyisha Al-Manūbiya, 665–1267. » In: M. Monkachi, *Histoire des femmes au Maghreb: Réponses à l'exclusion*. Faculté des Lettres et Sciences Humaines, Kenitra, Série Colloques et séminaires, n°5, 253–274.

Amri, Nelly. 2000. « Les *sâlihât* du V^e^ au IX^e^/XI^e^XV^e^ siècle dans la mémoire Maghrébine de la sainteté à travers quatre documents hagiographiques. » *Al-Qantara*, XXI, fasc. 2, Madrid, 481–509.

Andezian, Sossie. 1995. « Femmes et religion en Islam: un couple maudit. » *Histoire, Femmes et Sociétés*, vol. 2, 181–199. Available at the website: http://clio.revues.org/493.

Andezian, Sossie. 1997. “The Role of Sufism in Algerian Pilgrimage Ritual.” In: E. Evers and D. Westerlund (eds.), *African Islam and Islam in Africa: Encounters between Sufis and Islamists*. London: Hurst and Company, 193–215.

Badran, Margot. 2001. “Understanding Islam, Islamism, and Islamic Feminism.” *Journal of Women's History*, vol. 13, 47–52.

Badran, Margot. 2007. *Feminism beyond East and West: New Gender Talk and Practice in Global Islam*. New Delhi: Global Media Publications.

Badran, Margot. 2002. “Feminism and the Qur'an.” In: J. Dammen McAuliffe (ed.), *Encyclopedia of the Qur'ān*, vol. 2, 199–203.

Barlas, Asma. 2002. *Believing Women In Islam: Unreading Patriarchal Interpretations of the Qur'ān*. Austin: University of Texas Press.

Barlas, Asma. 2004. *The sexual equality and feminism*. A paper presented at the University of Toronto. January 12, 2004. Available at the website: http://www.asmabarlas.com/TALKS/20040112_UToronto.pdf.

Bartels, Edien. 1993. *Eén dochter is beter dan duizend zonen* (One daughter is better than a thousand sons). Utrecht: Van Arkel.

Beauvoir, Simone de. 1976. *Le deuxième sexe*. Paris: Gallimard.

Beck, Lois. 1980. "The Religious Lives of Muslim Women." In: J. L. Smith (ed.), *Women in contemporary Muslim Societies*. London: UK Associated University Press, 27–60.

Beek, Mariette van. 2002. "Images of Lalla ʿAwish, a Holy Woman from Marrakech." In: M. Marin and R. Deguilhem (eds.), *Writing the Feminine: Women in Arab Sources*. London: IB Tauris, 199–219.

Bel, Alfred. 1938. *La religion musulmane en Berbérie*. Paris: Paris Librairie Orientaliste Paul Geuthner.

Benadada, Assia. 1999. « Les femmes dans le mouvement nationaliste Marocain. » *Histoire, Femmes et Sociétés*, vol. 9, 67–73. Available at the website: http://clio.revues.org/1523.

Benhabib, Seyla. 2002. *The Claims of Culture: Equality and Diversity in the Global Era*. Princeton: Princeton University Press.

Ben Rochd, Rachid. 2007. *Douze Siècles de Soufisme au Maroc*. Casablanca: Imprimerie Najah al-Jadida.

Bosworth, Clifford Edmund, et al. 1991. *Encyclopedie de l'Islam*. Leiden: Brill.

Buffault, Anne Vincent. 1986. *Histoire des larmes XVIIIe–XIXe Siecles*. Marseille: le Rivage.

Buitelaar, Marjo. 1993. *Fasting and Feasting in Morocco: an Ethnographic Study of the Month of Ramadan*. [Academisch proefschrift]. Nijmegen: Katholieke Universiteit Nijmegen.

Butler, Judith. 1990. *Gender Trouble*. New York: Routledge.

Chādilī, Abdelatif. 1989. *Le soufisme et la societé*. Casablanca: Publication de l'Université Ḥasan II.

Charrad, Mounira. 2001. *States and Women's Rights*. California: University of California Press.

Chikhaoui, Naima. 1997. « La sainteté féminine face a l'occultation des femmes, quels sens? » *Histoire des femmes au maghreb: Réponse à l'exclusion*. Série colloques et Seminaires, n°5. Kenitra: Publications de la faculté des lettres et des sciences humanes de Kenitra, 19–37.

Chodkiewicz, Michel. 1993. « *La sainteté féminine dans l'hagiographie Islamique*. » In: D. Aigle (ed.), *Saints orientaux*. Paris: De Boccard, 99–115.

Coon, Linda. 1986. *Sacred Fictions: Holy Women and Hagiography in Late Antiquity*. Philadelphia: University of Pennsylvania Press.

Cornell, Vincent. 1983. "The Logic of Analogy and the Role of the Sufi Shaykh in Post-Marinid Morocco". *International Journal of Middle East Studies*, vol. 15, 67–93.

Cornell, Vincent. 1998. *Realm of the Saint: Power and Authority in Moroccan Sufism*. Austin: University of Texas Press.

Cornell, Rkia. 2007. '"Soul of a Woman was Created Below": Woman as the Lower Soul (*Nafs*) in Islam.' In: H. M. Vroom (ed.), *World Religions and Evil: Religious and Philosophical Perspectives*. New York: Rodopi Press, 257–280.

Crapanzano, Vincent. 1981. *The Hamadsha: a Study in Moroccan Ethnopsychiatry*. Berkeley / London: The University of California Press.

Daoud, Zakiya. 1999. *Féminisme et Politique au Maghreb*. Casablanca: Eddif.

Dennerlein, Bettina. 2002. "Asserting Religious Authority in Late 19th / Early 20th Century Morocco: Muḥammad B. Jaʿfar ʾal-Kattānī (D. 1927) and His Kitāb Salwat ʾal-ʾAnfās." In: G. Krämer and S. Schmidtke (eds.), *Speaking for Islam. Religious Authorities in Muslim Societies*. Leiden: Brill, 128–52.

Dialmy, Abdessamad. 1997. *Feminisme, islamisme et soufisme*. Paris: Edition Publisud.

Dialmy, Abdessamad. 2002. « Un fqih marocain et les droits de la femme au XVIe Siècle. » *Prologues*, no. 2, 71–83.

Dialmy, Abdessamad. 2008. *Le féminisme au Maroc*. Casablanca: Toubkal Editions.

Dialmy, Abdessamad. (no date). « Féminisme Islamique et Antiféminisme Islamiste au Maroc ». Available at: www.ru.nl/publish/pages/633339/prof_dr_1.doc.

Douglas, Mary. 1970. *Natural Symbols: Explorations in Cosmology*. London: Routledge.

Dubel, Ireen and Karen Vintges (eds.). 2007. *Women, Feminism and Fundamentalism*. Amsterdam: SWP Publishers.

Durkheim, Emile. 1995. *Les formes elémentaires de la vie religieuse*. Paris: Presses Universitaire de France.

Dwyer, Daisy Hilse. 1978. "Women, Sufism and Decision Making in Moroccan Islam." In: L. Beck and N. Keddie (eds.), *Women in the Muslim World*. Cambridge: Harvard University Press, 585–598.

Eickelman, Dale. 1981. *Moroccan Islam: Tradition and Society in a Pilgrimage Centre*. Austin: University of Texas Press.

Ennaji, Moḥa. 2007. « La langue Amazighe, une Composante Fondamentale de la Culture Marocaine. » In: M. Ennaji (ed.), *La culture populaire et les défis de la mondialisation: une perspective maghrébine*. Rabat: Al-Maʿārif al Jadida, 47–50.

Ferguson, Kathy. 1989. "Patriarchy." In: H. Tierney (ed.), *Women's Studies Encyclopedia Project*. Westbury, CT: Greenwood Press, 265–267.

Ferḥat, Halima and Hamid Triki. 1986. « Hagiographie et Religion au Maroc Médiéval. » In: *Hespérés*, 24, 17–51.

Ferḥat, Halima. 1995. « Une source pour l'histoire des femmes: Les corpus hagiographiques. » In: *Pour une Histoire des Femmes au Maroc*. Kenitra: Publication de La Faculté des Lettres et des Sciences Humains, Kenitra n°4, 77–83.

Ferḥat, Halima. 2000. « Le saint et son corps: une lutte constante. » *Al-Qantara*, vol. 21, Fasc. 2, 457–470.

Ferḥat, Halima. 2003. *Le Soufisme et les Zāwiyas au Maghréb: Mérite Individuel et Patrimoine Sacré*. Casablanca: Edition Toubkal.

Foucault, Michel. 1977. *Discipline and Punish: The Birth of the Prison*. New York: Vintage.

Foucault, Michel. 1986. *The History of Sexuality, Volume III: The Care of the Self.* New York: Pantheon.

Foucault, Michel. 1997a "On the Genealogy of Ethics: An Overview of Work in Progress." In: P. Rabinow (ed.), *Ethics, Subjectivity and Truth: The Essential Works of Michel Foucault 1954–1984*, vol. I. New York: The New Press, 253–280.

Foucault, Michel. 1997b. "The Ethics of the Concern for Self as a Practice of Freedom." In: P. Rabinow (ed.), *Ethics, Subjectivity and Truth: The Essential Works of Michel Foucault 1954–1984*, vol. I. New York: The New Press, 281–301.

Foucault, Michel. 2007. "Ethics Subjectivity and Truth." In: S. Lotringer (ed.), *The Politics of Truth*, Los Angeles: Semiotext(e).

Geertz, Clifford. 1968. *Islam Observed: Religious Development in Morocco and Indonesia*. Chicago: The University of Chicago Press.

Gellner, Earnest. 1969. *Saints of the Atlas*. Chicago: The University of Chicago Press.

Geoffroy, Eric. 2010. *Une voie soufie dans le monde: La shâdhiliyya*. Paris: *Maisonneuve & Larose*.

Ghali, Muḥammad Mahmoud. 2009. *Towards Understanding the Ever-Glorious Qur'ān*. Cairo: *Dar* 'al-*Nashr* for Universities.

Gibb, H. A. R., and J. H. Kramers. 1960. *Encyclopedia of Islam*. Leiden: Brill.

Gibb, Camilla. 1997. *Religion, Politics, and Gender in Harar*. Oxford: Oxford University Press.

Glacier, Osire. 2013. *Femmes politiques au Maroc d'hier à aujourd'hui: la Résistance et le Pouvoire au Féminin*. Casablanca: Tarik Editions.

Gross, Rita M. 1993. *Buddhism After Patriarchy*. Albany: Suny Press.

Hammoudi, Abdallah. 1974. « Segmentarité, stratification sociale, pouvoir politique et saintété: Reflexions sur les thèses de Gellner. » *Hesperis* 15, 147–180.

Hammoudi, Abdallah. 1997. *Master and Disciple: The Cultural Foundations of Moroccan Authoritarianism*. Chicago: University of Chicago Press.

Harrak, Fatima. 2009. "The History and Significance of the New Moroccan Family Law." *Institute for the study of Islamic Thought in Africa.* (*ISITA*) 9-002. Available at the website: http//:www.cicsnorthwestern.edu/documents/workingpapers/ISITA_09-002_Harrak.pdf.

Heffernan, Thomas J. 1988. *Sacred Biography: Saints and their Biographers in the Middle Ages*. Oxford: Oxford University Press.

Helminski, Camille Adams. 2003. *Women of Sufism: A Hidden Treasure: Writings and Stories of Mystics, Poets, Scholars & Saints*. Boston and London: Shambhala.

Hoffman, Valerie. 1995. *Sufism, Mystics, and Saints in Modern Egypt*. Columbia, SC: University of South Carolina Press.

Hoffman, Bernard G. 1967. *The Structure of Traditional Moroccan Rural Society*. La Haye – Paris: Mouton.

Hopkins, Nicholas S. 1976. "The Hamadsha: A Study in Moroccan Ethnopsychiatry by Vincent Crapanzano." *International Journal of Middle East Studies*, vol. 7, 141–43.

Humphrey, Caroline et al. 1994. *The Archetypal Actions of Ritual: A Theory of Ritual Illustrated By The Jain Rite of Worship*. Oxford: Clarendon Press.

Jansen, Willy, Anna-Karina Hermkens, and Catrien Notermans. 2009. *Moved by Mary: The Power of Pilgrimage in the Modern World*. Farnham and Burlington: Ashgate.

Jansen, Willy. 1987. *Women Without Men: Gender and Marginality in an Algerian Town*. Leiden: Brill.

John, Renard. 1944. *Friends of God: Islamic Images of Piety, Commitment, and Servanthood*. Berkeley: University of California Press.

Kabeer, Naila. 1999. "Resources, Agency, Achievements: Reflections on the Measurement of Women's Empowerment." *Development and Change*, vol. 30, 435–464.

El-Katiri, Mohammed. 2013. "The institutionalization of religious affairs: religious reform in Morocco." *The Journal of North African Studies*, 18: 1, 53–69.

Khushaim, ʿAlī Fahmi. 1976. *Zarrūq, the Sufi*. Libyan Arab Republic: General Company for Publication.

Kugle, Scott. 2007. *Sufis and Bodies: Mysticism, Corporeality, and Sacred Power in Islam*. Chapel Hill: The University of North Carolina Press.

Kugle, Scott. 2005. "Uṣūlī Sufis: Ahmad Zarrūq and his South-Asian Followers." In: E. Geoffroy (ed.), <u>*Une voie soufie dans le monde: la Shādiliyya*</u>. Paris: Maison neuve and Larose, 181–201.

Kugle, Scott. 2006. *Between Spirit and Law: Ahmad Zarrūq, sainthood, and authority in Islam*. Bloomington: Indiana University Press.

Lamrabet, Asma. 2011. *Femmes Islam Occident Chemins vers l'universel*. Casablanca: la Coisée des Chemins.

Laroui, Abdallāh. 1997. *Les origines sociales et culturelles du nationalisme Marocain* (1830–1912). Paris: F. Maspero.

Mahmood, Saba. 2001. "Feminist Theory, Embodiment, and the Docile Agent: Some Reflections on the Egyptian Islamic Revival." *Cultural Anthropology*, vol. 16, 2, 202–236.

Mahmood, Saba. 2005. *Politics of Piety: The Islamic Revival and the Feminist Subject*. Princeton and Oxford: Princeton University Press.

Massignon, Louis. 1968. *Essai sur Les Origines du Lexique Technique de la Mystique Musulmane*. Nouvelle édition revue et considérablement augmentée. Paris: J. Vrin.

Mauss, Marcel. 1979. 'Les techniques du corps'. *Journal de Psychologie* 32, 3–4.

Mazumdar, Shampa and Sanjoy Mazumdar. 2002. 'In Mosques and Shrines: Women's Agency in Public Sacred Space'. *Journal of Ritual Studies*, vol. 16, 2, 165–78.

Mernissi, Fatima. 1977. “Women, Saints and Sanctuaries.” *Signs* 3, 1, 101–112.

Mernissi, Fatima. 1987. *Beyond the Veil: Male-Female Dynamics in Modern Muslim Society*. Bloomington: Indiana University Press.

Michaux-Bellaire, Edmond. 1921. « Essai sur l’histoire des confréries Marocaines. » *Hespéris* I, 141–159.

Mir-Hosseini, Ziba. 2003. “The Construction of Gender in Islamic Legal Thought: Strategies for Reform.” *Hawwa*, vol. 1, 1, 1–28.

Mir-Hosseini, Ziba. 2004. “The Quest for Gender Justice: Emerging Feminist Voices in Islam.” *Islam*, vol. 21, 36, 1–7.

Mir-Hosseini, Ziba. 2005. “Islam and Gender Justice.” In: V. J. Cornell (ed.), *Voices of Islam: Voices of Change*. Princeton: Princeton University Press, 85–114.

Moghadam, Valentine. 2002. “Islamic Feminism and Its Discontents: Toward a Resolution of the Debate.” *Signs*, vol. 27, 4, 1135–71.

Moors, Annelies. 2004. *‘Muslim Cultural Politics’: What’s Islam Got to Do With It?* Amsterdam: Vossius Press.

Mouaid, Fāṭima. 2000. “Moroccan Females’ Perceptions of Women’s Liberation.” In: F. Sadiqi (ed.), *Feminist Movements: Origins and Orientations*. Fes: Publications de l’Université Sidi Muhammad Ben Abdellah.

Munson, Henry Jr. 1993. *Religion and Power in Morocco*. New Haven, CT: Yale University Press.

Munson, Henry Jr. 1993. “Rethinking Gellner’s Segmentary Analysis of Morocco’s Ayt Atta.” *Man*, vol. 28, 2, 267–280.

Pateman, Carole. 1988. *The Sexual Construct*. Stanford: Stanford University Press.

Pemberton, Kelly. 2010. *Women Mystics and Sufi Shrines in India*. Colombia, SC: The University of South Carolina Press.

Peters, Ruud. 1999. “Islamic Law and Human Rights: a contribution to an ongoing debate.” *Islamic and Christian-Muslim Relations*, vol. 10, 1, 5–14.

Pruzan-Jorgensen, Julie. 2010. “New Female Voices within the Islamist Movement in Morocco.” *IPRIS Maghreb Review* 6, 15–18.

Qāsim, Amīn. 1992. *The Liberation of Women and the New Woman*. Cairo: The American University Press.

Rausch, Margaret. 2004. “Ishlhin Women’s Rituals in Southwestern Morocco: Celebrating Religio-Cultural and Ethno-Linguistic Identity.” In: *Minority Matters: Society, Theory, Literature*. Oujda: Publications de le Faculté des Lettres. Série: Colloques et Séminaires, 32, 199–224.

Rausch, Margaret. 2011. “Women Mosque Preachers and Spiritual Guides: Publicizing and Negotiating Women’s Religious Authority in Morocco.” In: M. Bano and H. Kalmbach (eds.), *Women, Leadership, and Mosques: Changes in Contemporary Islamic Authority*. Leiden: Brill, 59–84.

Reysoo, Fenneke. 1991. *Pèlerinage au Maroc: Fête, politique et échange dans l'islam populaire*. Neuchâtel: Institut d'ethnologie, Paris: Ed. de la Maison des Sciences de l'homme.

Rddad, Sadik. 2016. « Qadiriya Brotherhood in Morocco. » Moroccan Cultural Studies Journal, no. 4, 43–74.

Sabour, Muḥammad. 1993. « La baraka: Capital et Pouvoir Symbolique. » In: R. Bourqia and M. Al Harras. *Westermarck et la Société Marocaine*. Rabat: Faculté des Lettres et des Sciences Humaines, Université Muhammad V, 125–129.

Sadiqi, Fāṭima. 2001. « La dynamique du berbère au Maroc: situation actuelle et perspectives d'avenir. » *Languages and Linguistics*, vol. 8, 21–41.

Sadiqi, Fāṭima. 2003. *Women, Gender and Language in Morocco*. Leiden: Brill.

Sadiqi, Fāṭima. 2006. "The Impact of Islamization on Moroccan Feminisms." *Signs*, vol. 32, 1, 32–40.

Sadiqi, Fāṭima. 2008. "Facing Challenges and Pioneering Feminist and Gender Studies: Postcolonial and today's Maghrib." *African and Asian Studies*, Vol. 7, 4, 447–470.

Sadiqi, Fāṭima. 2008. "The Central Role of the Family Law in the Moroccan Feminist Movement." *British Journal of Middle Eastern Studies* 35, 3, 325–337.

Sadiqi, Fāṭima. 2014. *Moroccan feminist Discourse. Feminist Studies Series*. Palgrave Macmillan.

Sadiqi, Fāṭima. 2016. "An Assessment of Today's Moroccan Feminist Movement (946–2014)." In M. Ennaji (et al.) *Moroccan Feminisms New Perspectives*. New Jersey: Africa World Press.

Salime, Zakiya. 2011. *Between Feminism and Islam: Human Rights and Shari'a Law in Morocco*. Minneapolis: University of Minnesota Press.

Schimmel, Annemarie. 1975. *Mystical Dimensions of Islam*. Chapel Hill: The University of North Carolina Press.

Schimmel, Annemarie. 1982. "Women in Mystical Islam." *Women's Studies International Forum*, V, 145–152.

Schimmel, Annemarie. 2003. *My Soul is a Woman: The Feminine in Islam*. New York: The Continuum International Publishing Group Inc.

Sells, Michael. 1996. *Early Islamic Mysticism: Sufi, Qur'an, Mi'rāj, Poetic and Theological Writings*. New Jersey: Paulist Press.

Shaikh, Sa'diya. 2009. "In Search of Al-Insān: Sufism, Islamic Law, and Gender." *Journal of the American Academy of Religion*, vol. 77, 4, 781–822.

Skali, Faouzi. 2007. *Saints et sanctuaires de Fes*. Rabat: Editions Marsam.

Smith, Margaret. 1984. *Rabīʿa the Mystic and her Fellow-Saints in Islam*. Cambridge: Cambridge University Press (1928).

Strathern, Andrew. 1996. *Body Thoughts*. Ann Arbor: University of Michigan Press.

Stuurman, Siep. 2004a. "How to Write a History of Equality?." *Leidschrift* 19, 3, 40–62.

Stuurman, Siep. 2004b. "The Voice of Thersites: Reflections on the Origins of the Idea of Equality." *Journal of the History of Ideas*, vol. 65, 2, 171–189.

Tapper, Nancy. 1978. "The Women's Sub-Society among the Shahsevan Nomads of Iran." In: L. Beck and N. Keddie (eds.), *Women in the Muslim World*. Cambridge MA: Harvard University Press, 374–398.

Tapper, Nancy. 1983. "Gender and Religion in a Turkish Town: A Comparison of Two Types of Formal Women's Gatherings." In: P. Holden (ed.), *Women's Religious Experience: Cross-cultural Perspectives*. London: Croom Helm, 71–88.

Tapper, Nancy. 1990. "Ziyaret: Gender, Movement and Exchange in a Turkish Community." In: D. F. Eickelman and J. Piscatori (eds.), *Muslim Travellers: Pilgrimage, Migration, and the Religious Imagination*. Berkeley: University of California Press, 236–255.

Tapper, Nancy and Richard Tapper. 1987. "The Birth of the Prophet: Ritual and Gender in Turkish Islam." *Man*, vol. 22, 1, 69–92.

Terrasse, Henri. 1949. *Histoire du Maroc*. Casablanca: Edition Atlantides.

Tickner, *Ann J.* 2001. "Patriarchy." In: R. J. Barry Jones (ed.), *Routledge Encyclopedia of International Political Economy*. London & New York: Routledge (Taylor & Francis Group), 1179–1189.

Torab, Azam. 2007. "Performing Islam: Gender and Ritual in Iran." M. Badran and V. Moghadam (eds.), *Women and Gender: The Middle East And The Islamic World*, vol. 4), Leiden: Brill.

Touahri, Sara. 2008. "Morocco Retracts CEDAW Reservations." *Magharebia*, December 17. Available at the website: http://magharebia.com/en_GB/articles/awi/features/2008/12/17/feature-02.

Tozy, Muḥamed, et al. 2007. *L'Islam au Quotidien: Enquête Sur les Valeurs et les Pratiques Religieuses au Maroc*. Casablanca: Editions Prologues.

Tozy, Muḥamed. 2008. *Monarchie et Islam Politique au Maroc*. Paris: Presses de sciences Po.

Turner, Bryan. 1984. *The Body and Society*. Oxford: Basil Blackwell.

Vikor, Knut. 2000. "Sufi Brotherhoods in Africa." In: N. Levtzion and R. L. Pouwels (eds.), *The History of Islam in Africa*. Athens: Ohio University Press, 441–476.

Vincent-Buffault, Anne. 1986. *Histoire des larmes: XVIIIe–XIX siècles*. Marseille: Rivages.

Vintges, Karen. 2004. "Endorsing Practices of Freedom: Feminism in a Global Perspective." D. Taylor and K. Vintges (eds.), *Feminism and the Final Foucault*. Urbana and Chicago: University of Illinois Press, 275–299.

Vintges, Karen. 2007. "The Life of Rabia al-ʿAdawiyya: Reflections on Feminism and Fundamentalism." In: I. Dubel and K. Vintges (eds.), *Women, Feminism and Fundamentalism*. Amsterdam: SWP Publishers, 53–60.

Vintges, Karen. 2012. "Muslim Women in the Western Media: Foucault, Agency, Governmentality and Ethics." *European Journal of Women's Studies*, vol. 19, 3, 283–298.

Wadud, Amīna. 1992. *Qur'an and Woman: Re-reading the Sacred Text from a Woman's Perspective*. New York: Oxford University Press.

Weber, Max. 1964. *The Theory of Social and Economic Organization*. A. M. Henderson and T. Parsons (eds.). New York: Free Press.

Westermarck, Edward. 1926. *Rituals and Beliefs in Morocco*. 2 vols. New York: University Books.

Yāssīne, 'Abdsalām. 2013. "The Believing Women and Men are Equal." Available at the website: http://yassine.net/en/document/5015.shtml.

Yāssīne, Nadia. 2003. « La Jurisprudence Musulmane est Machiste. » October 10, 2003. Oumma. Com. Available at the website: http://www.nadiayassine.net/fr/thema/11.htm.

Yāssīne, Nadia. 2008. « Le Feminisme Islamique : Combats et Resistances. » Available at: http://www.nadiayassine.net/fr/thema.11.htm.

Zeggaf, Abdelmajīd. 1991. « L'écriture Hagiographique dans l'Islam Maghrébin. » *Bulletin De Littérature Ecclésiastique*, vol. 92, 83–92.

Zouanat, Zakia. 2009. *Le Royaume des Saints*. Graz: éd. ADEVA.

# Index

Note: Arabic and Berber terms are listed when different words are used for the same term. To specify gender difference, feminine (fem) and masculine (masc) forms are also given.

Printed in the United States
By Bookmasters